THE PRIMITIVE CHRISTIAN CALENDAR

A STUDY IN THE MAKING OF
THE MARCAN GOSPEL

VOLUME I
INTRODUCTION & TEXT

BY

PHILIP CARRINGTON
Archbishop of Quebec

CAMBRIDGE
AT THE UNIVERSITY PRESS
1952

CAMBRIDGE
UNIVERSITY PRESS

University Printing House, Cambridge CB2 8BS, United Kingdom

Cambridge University Press is part of the University of Cambridge.

It furthers the University's mission by disseminating knowledge in the pursuit of education, learning and research at the highest international levels of excellence.

www.cambridge.org
Information on this title: www.cambridge.org/9781316603772

© Cambridge University Press 1952

First published 1952
First paperback edition 2016

A catalogue record for this publication is available from the British Library

ISBN 978-1-316-60377-2 Paperback

THE PRIMITIVE CHRISTIAN CALENDAR

To
MY BROTHER
CHARLES EDMUND CARRINGTON
FROM WHOSE PATIENCE AND WISDOM I HAVE
PROFITED GREATLY IN THIS ENTERPRISE

CONTENTS

vii

THE GOSPEL ACCORDING TO ST MARK

LIST OF ILLUSTRATIONS

FOREWORD

The steps by which the liturgical theory of St Mark's Gospel came to be formulated will be found in the Introduction, together with the literary, critical, and mathematical proofs by which it was established. It can be very simply enunciated. The Gospel consists of a series of lections for use in the Christian ecclesia on the successive Sundays of the year, and of a longer continuous lection which was used on the annual solemnity of the Pascha (Passover) at which the Passion was commemorated. The series of lections for the year are numbered from 1 to 48 (or 49) in Codex Vaticanus (B), and the remaining lections (49–62) constitute the Passion lection. The chapter-enumerations of Vaticanus are used because they are the oldest, in our opinion, that are preserved; it is not contended that they preserve the original divisions of St Mark with complete accuracy, but they form a better guide to study than any enumeration which we might make for ourselves.

The 48 or 49 lections for the Calendar Year are found to fit the Hebrew agricultural and ritual year without difficulty. This would be the actual calendar by which the first Christians regulated their lives.

The first stage of the research had no connexion with the calendar or the liturgy. It had to do with the meaning of the Seed Parable, to which the composer of the gospel attributes an importance which some critics have regarded as excessive. He regards it as possessing an inner significance to which most of its hearers were blind and deaf. In order to understand the gospel, it was necessary to solve the mystery of what this significance was.

Literary research established a connexion between the Seed Parables, the Feeding of the Five Thousand, the Feeding of the Four Thousand, and the Confession at Caesaraea Philippi, which was followed by the Transfiguration. Neglecting the Four Thousand for the moment as a doublet of the Five Thousand, we found we had a sequence of three events, each connected with a convocation or withdrawal from the world to a mountain. The mystery announced in parables shortly after the First Mountain was enacted in a sacramental act at the Second Mountain, and 'openly' declared shortly before the Third Mountain. It was the death and resurrection of the Son of Man.

It was not for some time that the thought occurred that these events might be points in the agricultural and ritual year. As soon as this thought arose, it was naturally brought into connexion with the conviction of the Gnostic heretics that the preaching of Jesus lasted twelve months from the Baptism to the Passion.

At this stage I was asked to read a paper to the New Testament Club of the Union Theological Seminary, New York. I was ill-prepared for such a venture, but thought there would be no harm in assembling these ideas, and laying them before so learned a gathering. If I was on the wrong track, it could be pointed out to me. Without in the least making that learned body responsible for any of my opinions, I would like to thank them for their forbearance and even encouragement.

It was, however, no more than a literary hypothesis; and such hypotheses are extremely fragile. My friend Dr F. C. Grant suggested to me that it might be tested by an examination of the chapter-numbers which exist in almost all the old manuscripts.

Before doing this, however, I resolved to try it out on a basis of literary judgement. I found that the gospel could easily be divided into the requisite number of lections, and that the Five Thousand could be placed at Passover, the Four Thousand at Pentecost, the Transfiguration at the Midsummer Festival, and the teaching at Jerusalem at the Feast of Tabernacles; the first part of Mark (without the Passion narrative) would thus fill the Hebrew liturgical year, beginning at the autumn solstice.

I was particularly pleased about the Feeding of the Five Thousand and the Feeding of the Four Thousand, as a reason was supplied for what appears to be a duplication. In writing a history, one does not duplicate chapters. In composing a lectionary, there is no objection to including two versions of the same lection. It is commonly done.

I spent the summer of 1947 in England, and received many

suggestions and helpful advice from friends who were interested in the New Testament. I now took the chapter-numbers of the ancient manuscripts, which are to be found in the margin of Nestle's edition, and soon found that the chapter-enumeration in *B* fitted the liturgical theory far better than any I had designed for myself. I found here an external mathematical confirmation of the theory. I abandoned my previous work, and from henceforth used the lection-system of *B*, though I do not think that it is in all respects identical with the original system. It has undergone a few changes. Later on, a close examination of the photographic reproduction of *B* revealed major divisions in that manuscript which corresponded almost exactly with the major divisions which I had made on the basis of literary judgement.

It was still not clear, however, whether the chapter-enumeration in *B* could be proved to be much older than the manuscript itself, which is usually assigned to the first half of the fourth century. Two forms of research convinced me that it was old. In the first place the manuscripts other than *B* have a lection-system in Matthew which is clearly identical with that which *B* has for Mark, though it has six more lections. On studying these, I was led to believe that Matthew must have been composed in order to fit in with the Marcan system; the liturgical system which I had deduced from literary analysis, and confirmed from manuscript evidence, was prior in date to the actual writing of Matthew.

This was confirmed by a second line of argument. The manuscripts other than *B* have a shorter condensed system of chapter-enumeration for Mark, which I did not doubt was later in date than the longer system found in *B*. This shorter secondary arrangement of Mark was followed by Tatian in the composition of his gospel harmony, the *Diatessaron*, before A.D. 170. The whole process, therefore, of the development of these lection-systems was complete by the middle of the second century.

A further consideration leaves little doubt on this point. The process we have been studying was only possible in the period when each church made use of a single gospel for its liturgical purposes, and this may be considered to have closed in the first quarter of the second century.

A further line of research, which proved most interesting, was that which linked up these processes with the earliest features of the Christian calendars, and even with customs which endure to this day; it tells us why, for instance, we have the Feast of the Epiphany in the first week of January, and why, in the Anglican Church, we read the 'Palm Sunday' Gospel in Advent.

It appeared, too, that the theory shed light on some of the early statements with regard to the gospels, and particularly on the dictum of the 'Elder John', head of the Christian school in Asia Minor about A.D. 85–95. It gave a new turn to the discussion about the *logia* of St Matthew, and the 'order' of St Mark, to which Papias refers in reporting this famous opinion of St John.

Nor did the theory seem to run counter to the general drift of present-day criticism of the New Testament. The gospel-lections of Mark would seem to be identical not only with the '*logia* of the Lord' mentioned by Papias, but also with the gospel-units which are handled by what is called 'form-criticism'; indeed our theory seems to rescue that study from the rather nebulous conditions in which it exists. It would also seem to be in line with the researches of the *Myth and Ritual* school, which have met with such success in regard to the Old Testament, and to indicate a pathway by which their researches can be continued into the New Testament.

The 'Liturgical Theory of St Mark' has been presented in the Introduction, which is followed by certain notes and tables of figures which are necessary to it. What follows then is the Text of Mark arranged in accordance with the Liturgical Theory with full information as to the various relevant systems of chapter-division, introductions which supply information with regard to the Hebrew Calendar, and notes from these points of view. The text used is that of the Revised Version of 1881.

The 'Commentary' which will form vol. II of this publication is necessary in order to relate the calendrical order of the gospel to its general background in thought and history, and to establish its significance in relation to the Christian movement. The results of the school of thought represented by *Myth and Ritual* and *The Labyrinth* are rather taken for granted in this Commentary.

I am aware that old-fashioned students may find the methods used in this study rather too free and critical, and that students brought up in the latest schools of criticism may find the general outlook rather conservative and old-fashioned. There are circles to-day in which the statement is made that the first Christians had no interest in establishing historical facts about Jesus, and indeed no certain information about him; the gospel-units were built up in the ecclesia for purposes of edification only. It is necessary to record the conviction that statements of this kind are not scientific in character, and cannot be sustained by the evidence, or by common-sense inferences from the evidence.

When the reader finds the name 'Mark', or even 'St Mark', used for the author of the gospel under consideration, he can, if he likes, regard this as a mere symbol for an unknown author. It will not in any way affect the validity of our theory or of the reasoning by which it is established. In the same way, the use of the names 'Matthew', 'Q', 'Luke', and 'John', by no means implies the acceptance or rejection of current theories. The expression 'Elder John' or 'St John' is used, quite without prejudice, for the disciple of Jesus who was the master in the Asiatic school at the period *circa* A.D. 90.

The author is under obligation to numerous persons and institutions, without whose assistance the project would never have come to fruition; first he would place the name of the Rev. Canon Naylor, Rector of Trinity Memorial Church, Montreal, 'amicus, necessarius, necnon philosophus'; then the Rev. F. C. Grant of the Union Theological Seminary, New York, a 'master in Israel', who has borne patiently with the author, and supplied from time to time suggestions which have involved further labours, though he is not of course responsible for any errors or omissions which may appear on these pages; during a visit to England in 1947 the author had the privilege of discussing his theory with a number of friends, and would like to thank the Dean of Winchester and Father L. S. Thornton for their encouragement, without in any way involving them in responsibility for the opinions which he has expressed; he is also grateful for library facilities extended at Chichester Theological College, at the Union Seminary, New

York, at Laval University, Quebec, and at Knox College, Toronto, as well as for the courtesy of Mr T. C. Skeat, Keeper of the Manuscripts in the British Museum, in allowing him to examine the New Testament manuscripts, and for his kind advice on many points.

He must also thank the officers of the Cambridge University Press for their patience and courtesy in what has proved a complicated and protracted enterprise. The book owes much to their skilled services and suggestions, though it must still exhibit numerous faults, for which of course the author must take the responsibility.

I should further add that the liturgical theory was anticipated by A. Wright, President of Queens' College, Cambridge, in his 'Synopsis of the Gospels in Greek': Introduction, Chapter XV, and pp. lxix to lxxi.

PHILIP QUEBEC

BISHOPTHORPE, QUEBEC, QUE.
25 April, Feast of St Mark, 1948

INTRODUCTION

INTRODUCTION

THE LITURGICAL THEORY OF ST MARK

This Introduction is the record of the various stages in the researches which led to the establishment of a relationship between the old Jewish Calendar, the composition of St Mark, the primitive Christian Calendar, and the chapter-enumerations in the oldest manuscripts. It began with the attempt to discover the principal lines of thought connecting one part of St Mark with another. The present writer never at any time cherished the notion that St Mark was a biography in the modern manner, intended to satisfy a purely historical interest; nor can he proceed to the opposite extreme, sometimes advocated to-day, that the first Christians had no historical curiosity, and were supremely indifferent to the historical facts about Jesus. The following propositions, perhaps, might be accepted as a guide to modern research:

(a) The purpose of the writer was evangelistic; his supreme aim was to present Jesus as Son of Man and Son of God.
(b) Much of the material which he used was current in the Church and well known to his readers, or hearers.
(c) The book was designed to be used in church, and was therefore related to current ecclesiastical custom.

Such aims and objects do not exclude the historical; indeed they require the historical. Historicity was the essential quality of the evangelistic message; but not historicity or historical methods as we conceive them; historicity and historical methods as they conceived them.

1. THE MYSTERY OF THE SEED PARABLES

The point at which the present investigation began was the mystery of the Seed Parables, with regard to which many scholars confess that they are baffled. Their problem arises from the fact that St Mark insists with all the emphasis at his command that these parables have a meaning to which 'those outside' are completely blind. There is quite a battalion of Protestant scholars who cannot accept this view. Following A. Jülicher, they maintain that the parables are simple, and even obvious, sermon illustrations, and that St Mark is guilty of what I have heard described as 'gratuitous mystery-mongering'. The doctrine of spiritual blindness is supposed to be taken over from the anti-Jewish propaganda of the Gentile churches, according to which the Jews who crucified Jesus had been spiritually blinded, and their hearts hardened, in accordance with a mysterious divine decree which had been announced beforehand in the writings of the ancient prophets.

It is important to recognize that this 'anti-Semitic' doctrine actually existed. It was contained in the *Book of Testimonies*, and was widely spread among Christians from earliest times. It was well known in Rome before the Marcan gospel was composed; for Paul discussed it in his Epistle to the Romans. He would only accept it, however, in a much modified form; he did not agree that God had rejected 'his people whom he foreknew', but he conceded that 'a hardening in part has fallen on Israel' (xi. 2 and 25).

The *Book of Testimonies* is the name given by Dr Rendel Harris to a collection of passages from the Law and the Prophets drawn up in the earliest period of the Church to illustrate and prove certain propositions with regard to the new faith, especially of course the propositions which were regarded by the Jews as an 'offence'; that the Messiah died for our sins, and was buried, and rose again on the third day. In connexion with this it was not possible to overlook the supreme over-all mystery, that the Messiah had been rejected by his own people, who had been educated by the Law and the Prophets to accept him, and had been accepted by the Gentiles, who had been left without this education. This non-recognition by the Jews must have been part of the divine plan, Christians thought, and therefore must have been predicted by the Prophets. There was indeed no escape for them from this further proposition.

4

The Hebrew Scriptures provide an abundance of texts which condemn the unreceptivity of the chosen people; 'Israel doth not know, my people doth not consider' (Isa. i. 3); but the cardinal testimony of this kind occurs in the great sixth chapter of Isaiah in which the prophet describes a vision of God in the Jerusalem Temple and of the divine glory which fills heaven and earth. The prophet sees the 'King in his beauty', and hears the song of the seraphim; but Israel as a whole is blind. This 'Testimony' is constantly quoted by Christian writers, and it is closely associated in Mark with the Seed Parable, and with the use of parables by Jesus.

> Unto you is given the mystery of the kingdom of God:
> But unto them that are without, all things are done in parables:
> That seeing they may see, and not perceive;
> And hearing they may hear, and not understand;
> Lest haply they should turn again, and it should be forgiven them.
> (Mark iv. 11–12; Isa. vi. 9–10)

The significance is clear. In the days of Isaiah Israel had been blind to the glory of God in the temple worship and indeed in the whole panorama of creation. It was blind now to the glory of God in the gospel of Jesus. The paradoxical turn of the language, which is so shocking to the literal and logical mind, was not the invention of Mark or even of Jesus, but comes straight from Isaiah himself; and it is characteristic of the old Hebrew theology which never shrank from attributing to the divine purpose those results which follow from a chain of consequences. It is a hard saying. Mark does not say, however, that Jesus adopted the method of teaching in parables so as to conceal his meaning. What he says is that there are certain minds to which *everything* comes in riddles —for that is what the word parable means—;[1] they understand nothing.

Mark repeats from page to page the language about eyes that see not, and ears that hear not, and hearts that are hardened and understand not. The school of critics who follow Jülicher believe that Mark has misunderstood Jesus, and that there is no great

---

[1] 'Parable', 'proverb', 'riddle', are words of similar use and meaning.

mystery about these parables. We can afford to waive this question at this point so far as their original purpose is concerned; but we cannot waive it so far as Mark is concerned. For Mark, at any rate, there was a deeper meaning which does not lie on the surface (not even in the interpretation appended to the first parable). We are not likely to understand the aim and purpose of the evangelist until we have grasped what that meaning is. Anyone who claims to interpret or criticize this gospel must bring forward some explanation of it.

2. EXAMINATION OF THE EVIDENCE

The passages which refer to this deeper meaning may be grouped under three heads, which we may allude to as the Three Mountains.

1. *The First Mountain.* The episode of the First Mountain follows the council held by the Pharisees and Herodians to 'destroy' Jesus. Widespread popular support is demonstrated by the crowds who come to hear him preaching by the seaside. He goes up into 'the Mountain' where he chooses Twelve Disciples (iii. 13).

The Parable of the Sower is then delivered from a boat on the Lake of Galilee (iv. 3). No explanation is offered; for the explanations, such as they are, take place when he is alone with his disciples. Four miniature parables follow these explanations (the Lamp, the Hidden Thing, the Measure, and He who Hath). Then come two more Seed Parables, making a total of seven parables in all.

The Parable of the Sower is *in situ*; it is related to its context, but the explanations and additional parables were appended because of their topical interest. They form one of those collections of sayings which, we think, were put together by teachers or evangelists for practical use in their work. It would be natural for a teacher to make such a collection on the necessity of insight and understanding in the pupil.

2. *The Second Mountain.* The beginning of this episode echoes the opening passages of the First Mountain. The Twelve who were

chosen have now been sent out to preach. Herod, whose party was then mentioned, has now heard of Jesus. The Passion of John the Baptist is narrated; and this is followed by the Feeding of the Five Thousand and the Walking on the Water. This event ends with the strange remark, 'They were sore amazed in themselves; for they understood not concerning the loaves; but their heart was hardened' (vi. 51–2); the latter phrase being taken directly from the Testimony from Isaiah which was quoted in connexion with the Sower.

It is generally recognized that the Feeding of the Four Thousand is a duplicate of the Feeding of the Five Thousand, and for our present purposes we may treat it as a second account of the same event. It is followed by the Demand for a Sign (which John connects with the Five Thousand) and the caution about the Leaven of the Pharisees and of Herod. Then comes a whole battery of mystery-sayings,

> Do ye not yet perceive neither understand?
> Have ye your heart hardened?
> Having eyes, see ye not? And having ears, hear ye not?
> And do ye not remember? (viii. 17–18)

and, after recounting the statistics of both miracles, he adds, 'Do ye not yet understand?' Understand what? How often have I attempted to find a meaning for this question!

3. *The Third Mountain.* The Third Mountain is that of the Transfiguration. It is preceded by echoes of those words of Herod which open the episode of the Second Mountain. (It will be shown later on how Mark's Gospel is built on a series of threefold repetitions linked by various subtle connexions.) It also echoes the reference to John the Baptist. It then goes on to Peter's salutation of Jesus as the Messiah, which Jesus commands his disciples to keep secret. He then unfolds the teaching that 'the Son of Man must suffer many things...and be killed, and after three days rise again'; to which Mark adds this extraordinary comment, 'And he spake the saying openly' (viii. 31–2).

What is meant by speaking the word 'openly'? Nothing at all, unless we take it in connexion with the mystery-sayings of the

Sower and of the Feeding of the Five (Four) Thousand. But if we link it up with those, its meaning becomes luminously clear. There is no riddle or enigma now: here is the plain truth which underlies the riddles and enigmas. *The Son of Man must die and rise again.*

The word 'plainly' is found in the same sense in John xvi. 29: 'His disciples say, Lo, now speakest thou plainly, and speakest no proverb' (the word in both cases is *parrēsiā*). This understanding of the words gives meaning to all the mystery-sayings from beginning to end. And it reveals the structure of the Marcan gospel.

The view which forces itself on the mind is that the death and resurrection of the Son of Man is announced in parables after the events of the First Mountain, enacted sacramentally at the Second Mountain, and revealed 'openly' at the Third Mountain. The sowing of the seed opens the process which finds a natural climax in the breaking of bread. We are studying a sequence of thoughts which our author assures us has a logical and consistent, but mystical and secret meaning; and we have stumbled on an idea which seems to be the key to that meaning.

3. Seed-time and Harvest

The death-and-resurrection theme is one that was naturally associated with seed-time and harvest. This association is fairly well known to modern readers through the writings of Sir James Frazer, Mr A. M. Hocart, and others, on the ritual of the divine king or the dying god. The series of ideas was very much at home in Syria. We must guard ourselves carefully, however, against any suggestion that Jesus was a Jewish corn-spirit. The preposterous idea that the gospel is merely another form of the kind of ritual we get in the cult of Attis and Adonis is not in line with the facts of history. Jesus died at the spring festival in Jerusalem on Nisan 14; Julius Caesar died at the same season of the year, on a corresponding day in the Roman calendar called by them the 'Ides of March'. Both were deified by their followers. Both are fully historical figures.

No myth or ritual has been borrowed from pagan sources and incorporated into the gospel; but pagan and Christian and Hebrew thinking on such points were all coloured by the spirit of the age. There was a mystical and symbolical way of thought which was natural to men at that time, and found expression in art and poetry and ritual and drama and religion. In the springtime life returns from the underworld in leaves and grasses and flowers; when the harvest comes, it is cut down in the shape of fruit and grain; it dies, but it will come again. Such is the destiny of man himself. Old Nature, who is the mother of mankind, reflects in her many-coloured drama the destiny of her divine son. Such is the truth which underlies the old way of thought.

But we must return to our gospel passages, and examine them again; and first we must note the threefold pattern which ramifies through the whole gospel. There are Three Mountains which mark the three points of highest dramatic interest in the Galilean story. There are Three Seed Parables which follow the episode of the First Mountain. There are Three Announcements of the Passion which begin at the Third Mountain; and each of these serves to introduce a collection of sayings of Jesus on what we might call the philosophy of the Cross and Passion.

The continual reference to the 'triads' of Mark may at first prove rather irritating; the index on pp. 94–5 shows that they are a simple fact. A recognition of the triads is equivalent to a recognition of the structure of the gospel.

The minor triads (which are confined to a single section) have no bearing on our study at this point; but the major triads are of great importance. A major triad consists in the repetition of some striking or important phrase three times at different points of the gospel. All critics have observed the threefold repetition of the Passion-announcement; and the threefold announcement of the seeing of the Son of Man (or Kingdom). Analytical study soon finds many more, such as the 'beloved son', or the breaking of the bread. A dramatic and convincing one is the reference to the right hand and the left; or the still more subtle one of the right hand without reference to the left.

It is to be feared that many moderns will regard this exquisite

9

literary technique as 'artificial'. It is no more artificial than the hexameter of Homer, the *terza-rima* of Dante, or the blank verse of Milton. It serves to distinguish passages that have some connexion in thought, and to link them together by verbal associations. Further detail will be found in the note on the Triadic Structure (p. 90).

The first Seed Parable is the Parable of the Sower (Mark iv. 3–9). We may distinguish, first of all, its literal meaning which is superficial and pictorial. We may pass secondly to its ostensible meaning which is given in the explanatory passage (iv. 14–20); I owe this word 'ostensible' to a Hindu scholar, Dr Ananda Coomaraswamy, who made it clear to me that, in ancient thought, a saying of the order of a parable might have an intellectual or moral interpretation which would be complete and satisfying as far as it went in its own dimension, and yet was incomplete and unsatisfactory from a point of view which included depth and mystical reality.

The 'ostensible' meaning of the Sower Parable has to do with the proclamation of the Word of God or Gospel, as Jesus began it in Galilee. As the explanation rightly says, 'The sower soweth the word'. But it is obvious from the further cautions of Mark that this explanation is not regarded as revealing the mystery. An analogy is established between 'word' and 'seed', or 'word' and 'light'; but why is it assumed that the 'word' has in it something corresponding to fertility or luminosity? On what basis does the analogy repose? For the idea seems to be that mere contemplation of the germinating seed should of itself suggest or reveal mysteries to the seeing eye.

The second Seed Parable (Mark iv. 26–9) is usually called 'the Seed Growing Secretly'. It is hard to see that it has any special ostensible meaning of its own. Sometimes it is interpreted to mean that the development of the gospel, or growth of the Kingdom, comes slowly and by natural stages. Sometimes the 'suddenness' of the harvest is emphasized. We might leave it for the moment with the observation that it seems to do no more than provide a complete picture of the whole drama of seed-time and harvest. Matthew and Luke omit it; and yet it must have served some important purpose in Mark's design.

The third Seed Parable (Mark iv. 30–2) is that of the Mustard Seed. The ostensible meaning is obvious. It is the extension of the Kingdom, as a result of the proclamation of the Word, into a world-empire or church. The tree in whose shadow the birds of the air may build their nests is taken from Dan. iv. 10 and 20, where it is a figure for the world-empire.

We must now ask what is the unity of movement which links the three parables; for there is some purpose in the threefold repetition, and in the threefold variety of form; unless, of course, we take the view that Mark has simply collected the three parables, each of which happens to mention a seed, and thrown them together without any regard to their relations to one another or to his main theme. But this theory of unintelligent topicality is contradicted not only by his insistence on a special significance in the parables, but also by the care and genius with which the gospel as a whole is articulated.

In considering the parables as a triad we may ask first what is the particular force of the second parable in its present position. What is it that intervenes, or must intervene, between the proclamation of the Word in Galilee and its extension throughout the world as a Church? Secondly we may ask what expressions are common to the three parables. What is it that is actually repeated three times so as to receive the highest degree of emphasis?

The first point common to all three is the reference to the land. 'And others fell into the good ground' (iv. 8); 'as if a man should cast seed upon the earth' (iv. 26); 'a grain of mustard seed...sown upon the earth' (iv. 31). The part played by the good earth is particularly emphasized in the second parable; in fact a good name for this parable might be the Parable of the Good Earth. The connexion between the Sowing of the Seed and the Earth-mother is one we need not enter into, though it seems to have profoundly affected Gnostic, and even official, Christian theology.

The second point common to the three parables is not expressed in quite identical language. It is the rising up of the seed: 'growing up and increasing' (iv. 8); 'spring up and grow' (iv. 27); 'groweth up, and becometh greater than all the herbs' (iv. 32).

Having been put in the earth, it rises again; that is the point; and it coincides fairly closely with the earliest known outline of the Word or Gospel: 'that Christ died...was buried...hath been raised' (I Cor. xv. 3–4).

This idea may be the special point of the second parable; for we are told the Kingdom is to be compared to a man who would (*a*) 'cast Seed upon the Earth', and (*b*) 'Sleep and Rise Night and Day'. The analogy of Sleep with Death and Night is too common in all ancient thought to need further comment. One example will suffice. In the *Book of Testimonies*, as quoted by St Justin Martyr and others, the words 'I laid me down to sleep and rose again' were taken quite naturally as a reference to the death and resurrection of Christ. This theme is not forgotten in Mark.

This examination shows that if there is a mystical meaning in the Three Parables, there is no objection to identifying it with the theme of death and resurrection. We now turn to the Second Mountain.

The episode of the Second Mountain begins with the Passion, and even the possible resurrection, of St John the Baptist. The Passion story is placed here with perfect skill. It closes the first half of the gospel just as the Passion of Jesus closes the second half. The idea of the resurrection of John is only a piece of popular fancy like the return of Nero; but it serves to continue the thought and shows that it was not a strange one at the time.

The references to the Baptist in this gospel are frequent and important. According to Matt. xiv. 12, it is the disciples of John who now come to Jesus, not the apostles as in Mark. The sense of bereavement felt by the people is dramatically expressed by Jesus who 'had compassion on them, because they were as sheep not having a Shepherd' (vi. 34). What actually happened on the Second Mountain was no doubt the assumption by Jesus of that spiritual leadership which John had exercised; for his words are plainly taken from Num. xxvii. 16–17, 'Let the Lord, the God of the spirits of all flesh, appoint a Man over the congregation, which may go out before them...that the congregation of the Lord be not as sheep which have no Shepherd'.

The Breaking of the Bread occurs three times in Mark, and on the third occasion (at the Last Supper) it is associated with a second Shepherd-saying (xiv. 27), which is openly connected with death and resurrection. The words 'go before' are also repeated three times (x. 32, xiv. 28, xvi. 7), and have the same connexion. This reminds us of the Shepherd in John x. 4; and indeed the symbol of the Shepherd everywhere has this connotation. Tammuz, Adonis, and Attis were all shepherds. So were Moses and David.

We come lastly to the Third Mountain and the dialogue which precedes it, in which Jesus announces openly the doctrine that the Son of Man must die and rise again, not of course in any ritual or mythological sense, but actually and historically at Jerusalem after rejection by the chief priests and scribes. This is followed by the vision of his glory called the Transfiguration.

This sequence of events and sayings (iii. 7–x. 45), connected with the Three Mountains, is obviously the core or main substance of the Petrine or Galilean gospel; and it is preserved without much change in the other gospels. The Lucan form is shorter; for it omits all the Marcan material which intervenes between the Five Thousand and the Confession of Peter. Matthew retains most of this material, only omitting two acts of healing. He emphasizes its connexion with the Sower by placing his chapter of parables immediately before the passion of John the Baptist. John follows it too, in his own characteristic manner, from the Five Thousand as far as the Confession of Peter. All retain the same series of events as the central episodes of the Galilean tradition, or Galilean gospel as we shall call Mark i–x.

John has a passage corresponding to the Transfiguration in his twelfth chapter. In xii. 25 we have 'He that loveth his life', etc., which is followed by the voice from heaven, xii. 28; just as 'Whosoever would save his life', etc., in Mark viii. 35, is followed by the voice from heaven in the Transfiguration. But in John these passages are appended to a miniature version of the Seed Parable: 'Except a grain of wheat fall into the earth and die, it abideth by itself alone', etc. The train of thought which we have attributed to Mark is here found expressed openly and without mystery in John.

The same train of thought is found, of course, in I Cor. xv. We find here the idea of the Son of Man (or 'Second Adam' as St Paul's usage is) whose death and resurrection is the pattern of the death and resurrection of Christians. In explaining this, St Paul goes straight to the Seed Parable in a form very close to that of John: 'Thou foolish one, that which thou thyself sowest is not quickened, except it die', etc.

St Clement, too, writing about the year A.D. 96, enlarges upon the Seed Parable in a similar way: 'The sower went forth to sow [Mark iv. 3] and cast upon the earth each of his seeds, which, falling upon the earth bare and dry, are dissolved; then out of the dissolution the majesty of the forethought of the Lord raises them up', etc. (I Clem. xxiv. 5). The evidence of Clement is particularly interesting; for not only was he a descendant of the apostolic school, but he held office in the Roman Church, and was writing officially in its name, only thirty years after Mark's gospel was composed there. He and his colleagues would remember the composition of the gospel, and no better authority than theirs could be quoted as to its meaning.

We need not therefore apologize for our theory which seems to derive support from various quarters. It seems quite fair to adopt it provisionally and see how it works out; the test of any theory being that it not only solves the problem which led to its formulation, but is found to shed light on other problems which were not under consideration at the time.

One of these is the structure of the gospel. With regard to the structure of the gospel, we may begin with these observations.

1. No one fails to observe that this gospel falls into exactly two halves, one beginning with the Baptism of Jesus, and the other with the Transfiguration. The divisional point is not easy to define, but perhaps it comes most naturally between ix. 1 and 2; but the two parts are interlaced.

2. It is equally clear that the Passion Narrative can be separated from the rest of the gospel, and regarded as a separate document. It is usually thought of as beginning at xiv. 1, 'Now after two days was the feast of the Passover'.

3. Our own researches reveal a picture rather like this:

STRUCTURE OF MARK: FIRST SUGGESTION

(*a*) Prologue. The Baptism of Jesus, etc. (i. 1–13).
(*b*) Preaching and Teaching in Galilee (i. 14–iii. 6).
(*c*) Seed-Time and Harvest (iii. 7–x. 45).
    i. The Three Mountains.
    ii. The Three Passion Announcements.
(*d*) Jerusalem material: we are left here with the Entry into Jerusalem, the Teaching in the Temple, and the Discourse on the Mount of Olives (xi. 1–xiii. 37).
(*e*) The Passion Narrative (xiv. 1–xvi. 8).

We shall see that this is not far wrong; but we shall change our views with regard to (*d*) and (*e*). The Passion narrative begins at xiii. 1, and includes the Discourse on the Mount of Olives.

4. THE LITURGICAL YEAR

It was not for some time that the rather natural hypothesis occurred to me that the Galilean gospel was based on the Hebrew Liturgical Year; and when it did so, it came in this form. According to John vi. 4, the Five Thousand occurred when the Passover was near, and this is confirmed by indications in Mark. The Transfiguration has an appearance of Tabernacles about it, an identification which I have since abandoned, though it has been supported with a great wealth of learning by Riesenfeld in *Jésus Transfiguré*. Did the other main features of the Galilean gospel have liturgical connexions? P. Levertoff (in Gore's *Commentary*) argued for a connexion between the Preaching of the Baptist in Q and the Jewish New Year. Was there a festival at the season of Sowing to which the parables could be assigned? What was the Four Thousand?

We have assumed that the Four Thousand is an alternative account of the Five Thousand. If this is correct we must ask why Mark included a duplicate account of this event. Not merely in error; he knew what he was doing. His gospel is beautifully constructed, delicately balanced, and intricately woven together.

His inclusion of duplicates was deliberate. Now if you are writing a history, you cannot very well repeat a chapter; but if you are constructing a calendar there is no objection to repeating a lection. In the Anglican Prayer Book we read the Five Thousand on two Sundays in the year, even though the Four Thousand has a place as well.

The thought then occurred that if the Five Thousand was a Passover lection, the Four Thousand might be a Pentecost lection. Officially Pentecost was little more than the completion of Passover. Pentecost was simply a word meaning 'fiftieth' (like Quinquagesima). The Four Thousand might be a very good lection to close these fifty days, thus recalling the lection with which they began.

Of course the notion of a liturgical year in the Christian Church at so early a date may seem a novelty, but we have been anticipated in this thought by A. Loisy and E. Lohmeyer and other scholars. It should not be lightly assumed, as it is in certain quarters, that the Christianity of the first generation was formless and unorganized, merely because the surviving contemporary evidence is small in quantity. If the character of this evidence requires us to assume the existence of a certain degree of organization in early years, no presuppositions, however widely held, should prevent us making this assumption and trying out a theory; and there are many facts which combine to render the idea of a formless unreflective *Urchristentum* exceedingly unlikely, or even impossible.

The course of evangelization from east to west, culminating in the Roman martyrdoms of A.D. 64, in which an 'enormous number' (*ingens multitudo*, says Tacitus) gave their lives for Christ, is a *prima facie* argument for a strong missionary organization. The existing documents bear witness to such an organization under the leadership of authoritative persons called Apostles. Patient research has demonstrated the existence of a copious early literature much of which has survived by incorporation into the New Testament or into New Testament books: the catechisms, the Testimonies, the apocalypses, the epistles, the evangelistic announcements, and the collections of words and acts of Jesus.

These imply in their turn a system of readers, teachers, evangelists and so forth, who exercised their functions on various liturgical and didactic occasions. In this period we can also trace the rudiments of a Liturgical Year; for we have, at the very least, the weekly observation of the Lord's Day and the annual observation of Christian Passover, in connexion with which the Passion Narrative must have been in use.

It has also become abundantly clear that the vigorous organization of the Christian ecclesia was not a new creation which evolved slowly out of nothing, but simply the normal organization of the old Jewish synagogue transformed by the injection into it of the Christian gospel and apostolate with its faith in Jesus and its possession of the Holy Spirit. Up to the 60's the leading church was that of Jerusalem which was the first centre of evangelization, even for Paul (see Rom. xv. 19), and up to the 50's a majority of Christians were Jews, who certainly observed all the festivals of the Jewish liturgical year. It follows that the literature and procedures which grew up in those circles would have some connexion with the sacred calendar. The literature which survives certainly shows signs of it.

The calendar of the Jews, with its cycle of agricultural festivals, was the same in origin and outline as the pagan calendars previously observed by Gentile converts. In fact, for the great majority of people in the ancient world, the agricultural or ritual year with its periodic holidays was the only one they knew, and by that calendar they regulated their lives. Christians would continue to use it. Indeed there is no instance in the New Testament of an event being dated by the day of the month as established in the Julian or any other calendar. Ignatius of Antioch is the first to do so. The few dates which are mentioned in the New Testament are always points in the agricultural or ritual year; we have Pentecost in I Cor. xvi. 8 and Acts xx. 16 and the Day of Atonement in Acts xxvii. 9, both of them previous to A.D. 64. We see therefore the kind of calendar which was in actual use at that period.

A further question was suggested by what is called 'Form-Criticism'. Without accepting the more sweeping dogmas of this school of literary criticism, we are bound to be grateful for the reopening of the oral theory of the original composition of gospel material, and for the labour on literary detail to which it has given birth. The most striking result of this study is the realization that the gospel material often came into existence in short units generally inculcating a single evangelical message, and marked by opening and closing formulae. Such literary units were capable of standing alone; and it is assumed that they actually did stand alone.

But why was the gospel material first composed in self-sufficient units? And why were the units spliced together into a particular order? What purposes within the ecclesia did these processes serve? Why, above all, was it necessary for the units to have their self-sufficient character retained, and even emphasized, by means of opening and closing formulae *after* their inclusion in a full-length gospel? It looks as if they still had to be used unit by unit in the sequence determined by the plan of the gospel. And that means a predetermined sequence in time, whether of hours, or days, or weeks.

Is the gospel-unit a liturgical gospel, that is to say, a gospel lection prescribed for a set place in the ecclesiastical order? Nothing forbids us to entertain this hypothesis. And what is meant by 'proclaiming a gospel'? What is meant, for instance, by saying, 'Wheresoever the gospel shall be preached throughout the whole world, that also which this woman hath done shall be spoken of for a memorial of her' (Mark xiv. 8)?

The immediate answer to this question is that it refers to general evangelistic activity, and means that wherever the gospel penetrates, this story will be told; but perhaps Mark and Matthew and John are giving a different answer to our question by associating it closely with the Passion Narrative as arranged for the Christian Pascha. Supposing for the sake of argument that the primary meaning of 'proclaiming a gospel' is evangelistic activity in its widest meaning, it is clear that this pretty soon comes down to the 'proclamation' of the death and resurrection of Jesus, and this in its turn is soon embodied in actual forms of words.

The word 'proclaim', 'announce', 'preach', 'publish', 'act the herald'—*kērussein*—often has for its object the name of Christ or the word 'gospel', though there can be a *kērugma* of the kingdom or of repentance. John the Baptist has a *kērugma* (Mark i. 7); Jesus has a *kērugma* (Mark i. 14; Matt. x. 27 and Luke xii. 3); even Jonah has a *kērugma*; it is a very short one: 'Yet forty days and Nineveh shall be overthrown.' It is in each case a brief dramatic announcement delivered with authority.

In I Cor. Paul states that he was sent by Christ to 'preach the gospel' (i. 17). This reads as if it were meant to be understood of general evangelistic activity. His subject-matter was 'Christ crucified' (i. 23), or 'Jesus Christ, and him crucified' (ii. 2). At the end of the epistle, however, he reverts to the same subject, and there is a question of a formula which he had received and which he had delivered to the Corinthians.

> Now I make known unto you, brethren [he says in xv. 1], the gospel which I preached unto you, which also ye received, wherein also ye stand...in what words [*tini logo*] I preached it unto you....For I delivered unto you first of all that which also I received,
>> How that Christ died for our sins according to the scriptures;
>> And that he was buried;
>> And that he hath been raised on the third day according to the scriptures;
>> And that he appeared to Cephas, etc. (I Cor. xv. 1–5)

We are here in the realm of fixed oral documents of an authoritative character, and what is more we seem to get a good idea of the formulae with which they were 'announced' or 'proclaimed' or 'delivered'. Nor is this all. A similar formula is used to introduce a short gospel in xi. 23: 'For I received of the Lord that which also I delivered unto you, How that the Lord Jesus in the night in which he was betrayed', etc.; it is a Paschal gospel, and concludes with the words: 'For as often as ye eat this bread, and drink the cup, ye proclaim the Lord's death till he come'; which could mean, of course, 'Whenever you celebrate the Eucharist you recite the Passion Narrative'.

The word translated 'proclaim' in the last quotation was a different word, *katangellein*, but its meaning is similar as we see from ix. 14: 'Even so did the Lord ordain that they which proclaim [*katangellousin*] the gospel should live of the gospel.'

Our conclusion is that there seems room to include within the meaning of the phrase 'proclaim the gospel', even at this early stage, the delivery of a form of words with some solemnity in the ecclesia. While this procedure seems to be connected with the Passion narrative, there would be nothing to prevent the extension of the phrase to cover the shorter evangelistic units with which the study of 'form-criticism' deals. These gospel-units must have come into existence to be used within the ecclesia, and the theories of the form-critics really require some such procedure as we have been considering.

5. THE MARCAN CALENDAR

A preliminary study of Mark showed that chapters i–x would divide quite naturally into about 60 units of the kind required. This number is rather high for the Sundays of the year, but this was due to over-conscientiousness on our part in dividing up sequences of teaching. In the narrative portions of the gospel it is generally easy enough to decide what makes a single unit; but a long collection of sayings may either be taken as one unit or subdivided in various ways. Later research showed that collections of sayings, however long, were usually taken as a single unit. Our number, therefore, turned out to be too high.

It should also be remembered that the lections in Mark might be arranged for the Liturgical Year without allotting set gospels for every Sunday. It might be sufficient to provide set gospels for the special seasons and give enough to choose from for the other Sundays. On the other hand, if the lections were too few, they could be supplemented from other sources, and perhaps this is the actual intention in some cases. The one-sentence utterances which appear in Mark from time to time may simply be the first line of a whole lection which can be used there if required. Examples of this are

Mark iv. 21:   'Is the lamp brought to be put under the bushel', etc.
Mark iv. 22:   'There is nothing hid, save that it should be mani-
                fested', etc.

and still more likely

> Mark viii. 12: 'Why doth this generation seek a sign?', etc.
> Mark viii. 15: 'Beware of the leaven of the Pharisees', etc.

In two of these cases at least, probably in three, and possibly in all four, the simple Marcan sentence served to introduce a whole section in Q.

It would thus be sufficient support for our theory if we found that there were gospels for the main festivals of the year, and about enough gospel material for the other Sundays. What we do find is that Mark i–x, which we call the Galilean Gospel, can easily be divided into 52 sections more or less.

Supposing we prepare an arrangement of Mark in 52 lections, the question which arises next is whether we have any way of checking this arrangement with regard to the length of the lections. There are two answers here. The first is that so many of the gospel-units are easily identified, that a rough idea of average length is easily established. The second is more exact. If the Feeding of the Five Thousand is a Passover gospel and the Feeding of the Four Thousand is a Pentecost gospel, exactly six gospels should intervene, so as to allow for the seven weeks (or fifty days) of harvest. We find, on trial, that this works out very well, and provides us not only with a scale, but with a test of location. If these lections from vi. 30 to viii. 10 represent the eight Sundays of the Easter-Pentecost season, the rest of I Mark (for so we may call Mark i–x) can easily be arranged in its correct place in the calendar. The test gives one excellent result. The first lection of the gospel falls quite naturally at the season of the Jewish New Year in the month of Tisri (September–October); and we have already mentioned the theory of Levertoff which connects the teaching of John the Baptist with this season.

There is, however, a distinct disappointment. The Transfiguration comes much too early to be equated with the Feast of Tabernacles which closes the calendar in the month of Tisri. It comes about a month after Pentecost, and would about coincide with the midsummer festival. Further research showed there were such festivals in the next month after Pentecost (Tammuz), and in the next month after that (Ab). It became apparent, too, that if the Transfiguration is allotted to a midsummer festival, the Entry into Jerusalem and Cleansing of the Temple with its pendent teaching must be allotted to the Feast of Tabernacles, not to the Passover. This is a surprising result; but after all there is nothing in these Marcan sections to connect them with Passover, and there are numerous contacts with the ritual of Tabernacles. Support for the idea can also be derived from other sources.

The Galilean Calendar which emerges is as follows:

1. New Year: Preaching of John.
2. Spring Sowing: Parable of Sower.
3. Passover: the Five Thousand.
4. Pentecost: the Four Thousand.
5. Midsummer: the Transfiguration.
6. Tabernacles: Entry into Jerusalem, etc., as far as the Discourse on the Mount of Olives.

As the year makes a circle, the final lections are naturally connected with the opening ones; Tabernacles (no. 6) and New Year (no. 1) are the same festival; in fact it could be claimed that New Year came before Tabernacles; what we have done, however, is to use the word 'New Year' for the opening of the Lectionary Year at the conclusion of Tabernacles.

If we now open the Anglican Prayer Book, we will see that the Christian Liturgical Year opens in the autumn, actually about six weeks later than Tabernacles. This opening season is called Advent; the gospel for the First Sunday in Advent is the Entry into Jerusalem; the Second Sunday has the Discourse on the Mount of Olives; and the Third Sunday is concerned with the Preaching of the Baptist. The connexion created by the Marcan system is still in existence, though it has drifted later in the year owing to the attraction of Christmas, a festival which was not thought of when Mark was written. We may add, to forestall some objection, that the Anglican system agrees with that of the Latin lectionary called the *Comes* which may be dated about the seventh century; the modern Roman system varies slightly.

We note, further, that the Sower Parable is still in the spring, or at any rate in the Mediterranean spring. The Five Thousand and the Four Thousand have been displaced; St John's Gospel has taken possession of the period from Passover to Pentecost. The Transfiguration is on 6 August, or in Armenia on 14 July.

6. THE ANCIENT CHAPTER-DIVISIONS

We have now shown the possibility, or perhaps the probability, of our thesis. It must be admitted that Mark i–x can be arranged as a series of lections beginning with the Jewish New Year and placing the Five Thousand at Passover and the Four Thousand at Pentecost. The next step is to discover whether this was actually done. The evidence for this comes from the old manuscripts of the gospels; for almost every ancient manuscript was also a lectionary, and has numbers in its margin indicating the divisions of the text for liturgical purposes, and titles which indicate the subject-matter of each lection.

These figures are to be found in the margin of the recent editions of the Greek Testament of Dr Eberhard Nestle, and we owe him a debt of gratitude for the restoration of this indispensable textual evidence.

We may first place on one side Sinaiticus, the Washington Codex, and the Chester-Beatty papyrus which show no sign of the chapter-divisions, though Sinaiticus has the Ammonian sections and Eusebian canons which are quite another matter. We may then place on one side Vaticanus (B) and its followers which have a special system of their own to which we will return. The remaining mass of Greek manuscripts, headed by Alexandrinus (A), all have the same chapter-divisions and the same titles; these are the official chapter-divisions and titles of the Greek Church as they took form in the fourth century at the latest. We may even associate them with the series of revisions which produced the 'Byzantine' or 'Antiochene' text. This widespread system of enumeration is alluded to by us in the following pages as the 'non-B' system.

Any thorough investigation of this complex subject would have to take into account the chapter-divisions and chapter-titles found in manuscripts of the Vulgate and of the Old Latin; and these will be quoted from time to time. Without the thorough investigation referred to, we can only venture the remark that they seem to be a parallel form of the same kind of chapter-division which we find in the mass of Greek manuscripts. St Jerome tells us in his *De Viris Illustribus* that the titles or summaries were composed by Fortunatianus Afer in the time of Constantine for use with the authorized chapter-divisions (*titulis ordinatis*), so that the chapter-divisions themselves are vouched for as older than Fortunatianus Afer. We shall leave no doubt in the mind of our readers that they were much older than that. These Old Latin and Vulgate divisions are very hard to find as they have been largely ignored in recent scholarship. Indeed the Old Latin Bible of Dom P. Sabatier (1745) seems to be the most recent authority to print the former.

The chapter-divisions in the manuscript Vaticanus (*B*), however, turn out to be completely different from those found in the mass of Greek manuscripts and in the Old Latin (or Vulgate following the Old Latin). They are also found in the Egyptian palimpsest *Xi*; and I owe to Mr T. C. Skeat the information that they also survive in a medieval Greek manuscript numbered 97 in the Bibliothèque Nationale at Paris and published by J. Schmidtke in 1903.

The mass of Greek manuscripts divide Mark into 48 (49) chapters. There are 48 numbered lections; but the first lection or *pro-oimion*, has no number, which is in accordance with common practice at the time.

The number 48 (49) is insufficient for the Sundays of an astronomical solar year; but what we have to consider is a luni-solar year based on twelve actual moons. The number 48 would provide four lections for each of these lunar months. It is true that when one came to the end of the year, there would be two or three Sundays unprovided for; but this always occurred with the old oriental calendar. The year had to be balanced off by the introduction of 'intercalary' days or even months, so that from time to time the Jews had a year of thirteen months, and the month 'Adar' was gone through twice.[1] Adar about coincided

---

[1] There was a second Adar for instance in 1943 and 1946.

with February, and I suppose that our intercalary day, 29 February, is all that is left of the second Adar.

Furthermore a calendar based on twelve lunations would be attractive to the oriental mind. The ancient calendar was a holy order which reflected the course of the sun in the heavens. The twelve months corresponded (inexactly of course) to the twelve 'houses' of the zodiac through which the sun, as the celestial bull, ploughed his furrow during the year. We shall see that the heavenly 'twelve', or 'dodekad', was of some importance in Christian thought; for astral mysticism was exceedingly fashionable at the time. Excavations have brought to light Jewish synagogues with the twelve signs of the zodiac depicted on the floor, the sun-chariot occupying the centre of the circle, and four winged figures at the corners for the four seasons. No doubt Christian churches had the same. It was their calendar until they adopted, or rather half-adopted, the Roman system introduced by Julius Caesar, which dispensed with the moon altogether. It is clear, therefore, that 48 is an attractive number.

The figure 49 is just as good. The sacred unit of the Hebrew Calendar is the week of seven days, which seems not to be of lunar origin. The agricultural and ritual year begins with the full moon of the spring equinox, which was called the Pascha, or as the English say, Passover. The seventh *day* from Passover marks the end of the 'Days of Unleavened Bread'; the seventh *week* brings one to Pentecost; the seventh *month* brings one to Tabernacles; the seventh *year* was the sabbatical year; and the seventh sabbatical year brought in the Year of Jubilee; forty-nine full years crowned with the fiftieth.

The ambiguity of 48 (49) is better still. Liturgy rejoices in the additional day. Pentecost was the fiftieth day which completed forty-nine days; Tabernacles had an eighth day completing seven days; like Pentecost it was called *atzereth*, the completion. The Christians of the first century loved to call Sunday the eighth day; and Christian liturgy still deals in 'octaves'.

The arrangement of all Mark in 48 (49) lections in the non-*B* manuscripts is an important and interesting fact, and is capable of harmonization with oriental calendrical ideas; but it does not fit our theory, which allots the first ten chapters of Mark to the Calendar Year, and the remainder to the Paschal Liturgy. What we want is 48 (49) up to 54 or 55 for the Calendar Year, plus some unknown number for the Passion Narrative.

The manuscript B, to which we return, divides Mark into 62 chapters, which are numbered from the first chapter. If we take our cue from the non-B system, and allot 48 lections to the Calendar Year, we would have 14 left over for the Paschal Liturgy, that is to say two sets of seven. This is very attractive, and we shall find, as we continue our studies, that it works very well, and must come fairly close to the original intention of the author. Indeed it corresponds so exactly with our theory, that the resemblance cannot be regarded as accidental. The discrepancy is that the 48 lections which we have tentatively assigned to the Calendar Year end at xii. 44, thus making the Passion Narrative begin at xiii. 1, which is rather unexpected. Further study, however, shows that this is the right point. We shall therefore abandon any lection-divisions of our own making, and accept the divisions as we find them in B.

We are now in a position to apply the test which we used before, based on the assumption that the Feeding of the Five Thousand (no. 25) is a Passover lection. This gives perfect results. The Feeding of the Four Thousand is no. 32, and falls on Pentecost, exactly seven weeks later. Eight weeks before Passover we have the Parable of the Sower (Lection 17), on Sexagesima Sunday, where it is still to be found in the Roman Missal or Anglican Prayer Book. Lection 1 (the Preaching of John) falls in the month of Tisri, the Jewish New Year month, when the synagogue lectionary ends and begins again. Lections 1–24 fill up Tisri to Nisan, and Lections 25–48 fill up Nisan to Tisri. Lection 37 (the Transfiguration) falls in midsummer. It fits our theory like a glove, and I do not see how it can be accidental.

Lections 43–8, which mark the close of the Calendar Year on this hypothesis, are those which comprise the cure of Blind Bartimaeus, the Triumphal Entry into Jerusalem, the Cursing of the Fig-Tree, the Cleansing of the Temple, the Parable of the

Vineyard, and the Questions in the Temple. Everything in these lections suggests the Feast of Tabernacles, before and during which they must have been read according to this calendrical arrangement; and there is not one word in Mark to contradict this except for these eight words: 'for it was not the season of figs'. We are bound, now, to suggest that it *was* the season of figs, and that these eight words are a gloss. We shall find other authority for placing all these events (with the exception of the Triumphal Entry) at the Feast of Tabernacles.

My view is, however, that not even B preserves the original arrangement, which I believe allowed 48 lections for the Calendar Year, 14 for the Feast of Tabernacles, and 14 for the Paschal Liturgy. All that we need record at this point, however, is that we have found some confirmation; the actual figures of the chapter-divisions in B are in exact agreement with our theory.

In Matthew we find further confirmation. B has a 170-chapter system which does not interest us; but the non-B manuscripts divide Matthew into 68 (69) chapters, and this system of chapter-divisions closely follows the Marcan system which we have found in B; for we may allot 54 (55) chapters to the Calendar Year and 14 to the Paschal Liturgy. In spite of the enormous amount of new material incorporated into Matthew, the correspondence, lection by lection, is extraordinarily close. In fact, there is only one possible inference. The composer of Matthew had before him a copy of Mark in the 62-chapter form, identical with, or closely resembling what we have in B, and arranged all his material to fit this plan.

We would suppose that the increase from 62 chapters in the case of Mark to 68 (69) in the case of Matthew was due to the amount of new material in the latter gospel. We might suppose that three chapters were added for the Nativity stories, and two or three for the Sermon on the Mount, and another for the Resurrection narrative. Nothing of the sort. These additions, and many more, are brought in without serious disturbance of the system of enumeration; or if there is a disturbance, the enumeration of Matthew soon gets back into step with that of Mark.

In the first half of the liturgical year, it is true, there are a number of transpositions of order, which are very perplexing; but these are due to the fact that Matthew has decided to follow the order of some non-Marcan authority, quite probably Q in most of the cases. However, he gets back into step with Mark at Lection 24, which is the half-way point of the year, being the Confession of Peter at Caesarea, just before the Transfiguration. From this point onward the two systems are never far apart, and listeners would hear the familiar gospel-lection in its revised form on the same Sunday, or very nearly the same Sunday, as when the Marcan book had been in use.

Where, then, do the extra lections come in? A glance at the Comparative Table of Lections (p. 97) shows that this begins to occur after the Triumphal Entry into Jerusalem, which is 44 in Mark and 45 in Matthew. When we come to the Discourse on the Mount of Olives, Mark is 49 and Matthew is 57; Matthew is eight lections ahead.

Now we had already conjectured that in B the Marcan lections intended for the Feast of Tabernacles were reduced from 14 to 7; we see now that Matthew was operating with a copy of Mark which had 14 lections at that point, and not 7. We must therefore revise a statement which we made above. Matthew did not have a 62-lection form of Mark before him; he had a 69-lection form of Mark, which was the blue-print which he used for his own 69-lection gospel. The 62-lection Mark of B is a reduced form of the original 69-lection form as used by Matthew.

This 68 (69)-lection Matthew took the place of the 69-lection Mark, which almost disappears from the scene, being fully preserved only in one manuscript (B), and even there it was reduced to 62 lections. The condensed 48 (49)-lection form continued to circulate. There is no evidence of a form of Matthew condensed in a similar way; if it had been so condensed for use throughout a Calendar Year, one supposes that it would have been reduced to 55 lections. This is a good number of lections for the Sundays of the year, and is the number of lections found in the *Diatessaron* of Tatian.

About the year A.D. 160 a Syrian scholar of the name of Tatian wove the whole four gospels into a single composition which he called the *Diatessaron*. It was probably composed in Greek, but was soon translated into Latin and Syriac. Down as late as the century it was still the only liturgical gospel used in the Syrian Church. Its Greek, Latin, and Syrian texts are lost, but in the eleventh century 'the excellent and learned presbyter Abû-l-Faraj Abdullah Ibn-at-Ṭabîb, with whom may God be pleased, translated it from the Syriac into the Arabic tongue'. This translation is what we have.

The *Diatessaron* is not merely a lectionary; it is a calendar. Its beginning falls in the spring equinox, which agrees with the date of 25 March which seems to have become fairly settled in Rome before the time of St Hippolytus, as a sort of ecclesiastical New Year. The first half, Lections 1–27, does not seem to be liturgical, though the lection-numbers correspond fairly well to those of the condensed 48-lection Mark. The change in the New Year has thrown them out of order. But the eight lections of the autumn, 28–35, are identified with the eight days of Tabernacles; [1] these are followed by 36–8, the middle one of which is identified with the Feast of the Dedication (midwinter?); and these are followed by seven weeks prior to Pascha (39–45), seven weeks of Pascha (46–52), and three lections for the Resurrection (53–5).

Furthermore the eight lections which are connected with Tabernacles, 28–35, contain all the Marcan lections (except the Triumphal Entry) which we saw reason to assign to that Festival, and they are allotted to lections with almost exactly the same numbers as those which are given them under the non-B system in Mark; from which we may deduce that when Tatian wrote, he was aware of a strong tradition in the Church which was in favour of reading those lections then.

We have provided on p. 97 a Comparative Table which shows in parallel columns the order of lections in Mark (according to B), Matthew (according to non-B), Mark (according to non-B)

---

[1] The reference to the days of Unleavened Bread in Tatian xxx. 31 must be regarded as an unintelligent gloss. It is certainly not drawn from any of the four gospels, and fails to accord with notes of time in 28 and 35.

and the *Diatessaron* of Tatian. These should be studied as they appear in the actual documents, not merely as they are indicated in the Table, though this will give a good idea of the close connexion which exists between Mark *B* and Matthew non-*B* on the one hand, and Mark non-*B* and Tatian on the other.

Tatian pays considerable deference to some historical statements in John, and follows his order in many instances; but where it is possible to do so, he defers to the order of Mark, or sometimes Matthew, in determining the order of the *Diatessaron*. When one considers what quantities of material he has to take on board from Matthew, Luke and John, it is astonishing that he can preserve it at all. The Sermon on the Mount provides him with three extra lections; additional matter from John is even harder to absorb; yet the enumeration of the lections, however greatly disturbed, soon returns to the Marcan enumeration as found in the non-*B* authorities. Time after time the lection in Tatian is identical with the corresponding lection in Mark to the extent of some part of it. Only at the end does it leave the Marcan enumeration behind, as it fills up its number of 55 lections as compared with the Marcan 48 (49); and even so we have to remember that the three Resurrection lections of Tatian, 53, 54 and 55, are almost entirely additional to the true text of Mark, so that (except for two verses of the original Mark and the so-called spurious ending) we have 52 lections of Tatian corresponding to 48, or actually 49, lections of Mark.

The same phenomena may be found, but with the opposite result, in the Vulgate lections as preserved in Codex Amiatinus. This system has three fewer lections than the non-*B* arrangement of Mark, that is to say 45; the difference being caused by the treatment of the major part of the Passion narrative as a single lection. The Old Latin system is not very different.

The facts which we have reviewed fall naturally into the following order. The 62-lection Mark (or more probably its 69-lection ancestor) is the parent of the 68 (69)-lection Matthew; it was at a later date condensed into the 48 (49)-lection Mark, which was the ancestor of the 55-lection *Diatessaron*. The developments represented by these figures took place before Tatian composed his *Diatessaron* (A.D. 160–70);[1] they were, indeed, completed and accepted in the church before that date. This opinion is confirmed by the reflexion that they could only have taken place at a period when a single gospel had the dominant liturgical position in the Church; indeed the composing of the *Diatessaron* was a belated effort to save the principle underlying the one-gospel system.

We are inclined to think, however, that the whole series of figures and facts can only be explained by the hypothesis that the process to which they bear witness is as old as the gospels themselves. Neither Mark, Matthew, nor Tatian, fall by accident into this complicated mathematical order; our view would be that Matthew replaced Mark at Antioch (or in Syria somewhere) and quite possibly the *Diatessaron* replaced Matthew for a time; all within the same liturgical framework.

7. THE STRUCTURE OF ST MARK

The next step in working out the theory was to prepare a text of Mark which was divided into the 62 lections of the *B* system, and arranged for the weeks of the Hebrew Calendar. The first outline of such an arrangement would naturally be as follows:

First half-year	LECTIONS 1–24	(Mark i. 1–vi. 29)
Second half-year	LECTIONS 25–48	(Mark vi. 30–xii. 44)
Passion narrative	LECTIONS 49–62	(Mark xiii. 1–xvi. 8)

It was not without its surprises. The Passion narrative is usually thought of as beginning at xiv. 1, 'Now after two days was the feast of the passover'; but in the above arrangement it was found to include the Discourse on the Mount of Olives, beginning at xiii. 1. The thirteenth chapter is itself divided. Lection 49 ends splendidly with the words 'Heaven and earth shall pass away: but my words shall not pass away'; Lection 50 begins 'but of that day or that hour' (where a title appears to have slipped into the text?) and ends with xiv. 1 and 2, with their reference to the Pascha

---

[1] We cannot exactly date the *Diatessaron*, which must have been complete before A.D. 173. But it took many years of study and labour.

and the hours of the night. This is obviously right, and it will be noticed, in the notes appended to the text, that this lection, which ignores a modern chapter-division, and passes so boldly from the prophetic to the liturgical, appears intact in every authority (except the Old Latin), and is even preserved in the English Authorized Version.

A literary analysis of the text made it necessary to abandon the divisional point between 24 and 25. As the twelve disciples are sent out by Jesus in 23 and return in 25, we cannot help linking 23, 24 and 25 together, and this makes an excellent divisional point so far as the first half is concerned. The reception of Jesus in a synagogue in Lection 5, with which the Galilean ministry opens, is balanced by a rejection in a synagogue in Lection 22, with which it closes.

The transfer of Lections 23 and 24 to the second half also serves a calendrical purpose. We had supposed that the Feeding of the Five Thousand (Lection 25) was read on the Sunday after the Pascha, which was Nisan 14; if this was so, the two previous lections, 23 and 24, would fall on the first two Sundays in Nisan. The first half, at the rate of four lections a month, would thus begin on the last week of Tisri, as the Jewish lectionary does, and close on Lection 22 prior to Nisan 1; the second half would begin on the first Sunday in Nisan, and extend well into Tisri. We thus get this plan which replaces the one introduced above.

REVISED OUTLINE OF THE MARCAN YEAR

First half-year	Tisri (end) to Nisan 1	LECTIONS 1–22
Second half-year	Nisan 1 to Tisri 23	LECTIONS 23–48
Passion narrative	Paschal Day	LECTIONS 49–62

These conclusions, it must be confessed, are worked out mainly on a basis of literary analysis; and the subjective element in judgement of this kind always leaves the results a trifle uncertain, however convincing the arguments may be. Fortunately, however, these results received confirmation at a later date in a very curious way. A careful study was made of the photographic facsimile of *B*, and script-divisions were found which had not been reported.

We reproduce the majority of these script-divisions in connexion with the text of Mark so that the reader will be in no doubt of what they are. There is an unmistakable sign; the first line of the new lection projects into the left-hand margin by the amount of one letter; sometimes the line above is a short one, but this is not necessarily so. The projecting letter on the left could hardly have failed to catch the eye of the reader, and was obviously intended for a purpose, namely, to indicate the beginning of a new section in the text.

Such script-divisions occur after Lection 22 (Mark vi. 6) and after Lection 48 (Mark xii. 44) at the very points where they are required by our theory, and we may conclude that the manuscript from which the scribe of B made his copy of Mark was divided in accordance with our theory.

It is necessary, however, to ask how many more such script-divisions there are in Mark, and the answer will be found in-structive. At the beginning of the gospel there are three; they come after i. 20, i. 34 and i. 45. There are two (or possibly three) more which come towards the end of the Galilean material; they come after ix. 16, x. 31, and possibly x. 45. There is a curious symmetry about this arrangement which invites attention; for there is no script-division between i. 45 and ix. 16, except for the one after vi. 6 with which the half-year ends.

In our preliminary analysis we had come to the conclusion that x. 45 was the original conclusion of the second half-year and of the Galilean material, because it is the end of the material dependent on the Third Passion Announcement. It is unfortunate, therefore, that we cannot be sure that a script-division was to be found there; the line that should have projected into the margin to the left was omitted by a blunder such as often occurs, and is written in the margin; a photographic facsimile of this page of the manuscript will be found in the text, and reasons are given in favour of the assumption that there was a script-division there; but, after all, the evidence has vanished. We are out of luck. We have to be satisfied with the script-division fourteen verses earlier at x. 31. The following table shows how the script-divisions harmonize with the liturgical theory.

SCRIPT-DIVISIONS IN *B*

Liturgical theory	Script-divisions
Opening Lections	After i. 20, i. 34 and i. 45
First half-year ends at vi. 6	After vi. 6
Galilean material ends at x. 45	After ix. 16, x. 31 (x. 45?)
Second half-year ends at xii. 44	After xii. 44
Passion narrative	No further script-divisions

It would be a pity to leave this point without attempting any explanation of the script-divisions of *B*, which must have served some purpose, and in some way guided the lector in his use of the gospel. Fortunately we came across evidence which seemed to suggest what their purpose was. In the calendar of the Greek Church, the gospels are read in sequence except during Lent, but in Lent special lections from Mark and John are chosen for the Saturdays and Sundays, the five non-liturgical days of the week being given lections from Genesis. It is worth recording these lections which must be very ancient.

LENTEN LECTIONS FOR THE GREEK LITURGY
(from Mark unless otherwise stated)

Saturdays		Sundays	
(1) ii. 23–iii. 5.	On the Sabbath	(1) John i. 44–52.	Nathanael
(2) i. 35–44.	The Leper	(2) ii. 1–12.	The Paralytic
(3) ii. 14–17.	Call of Levi, etc.	(3) viii. 34–ix. 1.	After First Passion Announcement
(4) vii. 31–7.	Epphathah	(4) ix. 17–31.	Second Passion Announcement
(5) viii. 27–31.	First Passion Announcement	(5) x. 32–45.	Third Passion Announcement
(6) John xi. 1–45.	Lazarus	(6) John xii. 1–8.	The Anointing (and at the 'Liten', Mark x. 46–xi.11)

We cannot help noticing at once how frequently the divisional points in these lections agree with the script-divisions of *B*. There are twelve lections of which nine are taken from Mark. In these nine Marcan lections we find four of the eight script-divisions from *B* accounted for, and we note that our sense of the importance of the three Passion announcements is also confirmed. We suggest that we have here a conflict between a twelve-lection system from Mark and a twelve-lection system from John, and that three Marcan lections have given way before Johannine lections. If we turn to the non-*B* system, we shall find that it gives John fifteen lections prior to the Passion, of which Lazarus is number 11 and the anointing by Mary is number 12; these coincide with the eleventh and twelfth lections in the table above.

We cannot help being confirmed in our view that the chapter-enumeration and script-divisions, and whole conformation of Mark in *B*, are due to its being copied from an exemplar which was arranged for liturgical use; and this arrangement and conformation support in a remarkable degree the results which we had obtained simply from literary analysis. The same pattern continues to reappear. We are dealing with a continuous process, the last stage of which is the system of Lenten lections in the Greek Church, which means of course the lections chosen for the training of catechumens; and we remember that the 'Epphathah' lesson, which appears on the fourth Sabbath in Lent, was the basis of a ceremony used at one of the baptismal scrutinies in the Roman Church, probably on the fourth Sunday in Lent.

We may add that a further examination of *B* reveals about 45 script-divisions in Matthew (neglecting those which separate the Beatitudes), 12 in Luke (all prior to the Passion narrative) and none at all in John. As for the rest of the New Testament, we have found one dividing Romans xi from xii. They are frequent in some parts of the Old Testament, especially the Books of the Law; they are less frequent in others.

Once or twice we have something near to a script-division, when a lection begins on a new line without any projection into the margin, and the line above it is unduly short. Such a case is the Epphathah story in the table above. They will be noted in the text.

It now remains to take this outline and adapt it still more precisely to the Hebrew-Syrian Calendar, with its New Year in the autumn. This is the point described in the Old Testament as the 'turn of the year' or *tekūphāh*. There were in fact four such turning points, which appear in the English Prayer Book as the 'ember' seasons; the word 'ember' being derived from an Old English word which means to turn or revolve. They were represented on the synagogue floor by winged figures at the four corners of the zodiac circle. Mosaics of this kind in synagogues have not been found as early as our period; they belong to two centuries later, but the ideas which they represent are of great antiquity in the east. They appear in the Revelation of St John as the four living beings round the throne of God. They mean the four winds, the four points of the compass, or the four seasons of the year.

THE FOUR TEKUPHOTH: 62-LECTION SYSTEM OF *B*

(1) Autumn Equinox (*b*)	Tabernacles	Baptism of Jesus	LECTIONS 1–5
(2) Winter Solstice	Dedication?	—	LECTIONS 12–13?
(3) Spring Equinox	Passover	Five Thousand	LECTIONS 24–5
(4) Summer Solstice	Tammuz	Transfiguration	LECTIONS 36–7
(5) Autumn Equinox (*a*)	Tabernacles	Triumphal Entry	LECTIONS 43–9

In studying the above table two points should be borne in mind. The first is that our theory requires that the opening lections, 1–5, were read at the end of, or after, the Feast of Tabernacles, and that the true lections for Tabernacles will be 43–9 with which the year ends. The second is that it is now apparent that Lection 49 (the seven times' seventh), which is the apocalyptic discourse on the Mount of Olives, had a double function; it was the last of the Calendar Year, being the crown of the agricultural and liturgical system; and it was also the first of the Passion.

The non-*B* system, found in the other Greek manuscripts, which divides *B* into 49 lections, appears to be adapted to the Roman Year, though of course many references and allusions are lost. It is that which is found in the Old Latin and the Vulgate. The Roman Year, which is the one we still use, was introduced by Julius Caesar on the advice of Alexandrian astronomers. It begins on the old Roman New Year, which followed the Saturnalia (1 January, or Kalends of January).

It is remarkable that the Transfiguration should again be brought into connexion with the Summer Solstice, by this alternative system, which revolves on an axis determined by the two Epiphanies, the Baptism and the Transfiguration. It almost looks

THE ROMAN CALENDAR: 48 (49)-LECTION SYSTEM OF NON-*B*

(1) Winter Solstice	Saturnalia	—	—
	Kalends	Baptism of Jesus	LECTIONS 1–5
(2) Spring Equinox	Passover	—	—
	Rites of Attis	—	—
(3) Summer Solstice	Tammuz-Adonis	Transfiguration	LECTIONS 24–5
(4) Autumn Equinox	Tabernacles	Triumphal Entry	LECTION 32
	Dionysus	Vineyard Parable	LECTION 36

as if the gospel were so planned as to make this secondary arrangement a possibility. The figures 24 and 36 are, of course, the points which mark the quarters of the year in a system based on 48 lections. It is interesting that in the older form of chapter-enumeration festal features also occur in connexion with Lection 12.

It has already become apparent that before the end of the second century a third arrangement had superseded the others in Rome; for when Tatian composed his *Diatessaron* about A.D. 160, he arranged it for a calendar which began with the Spring Equinox, returning to an old Hebrew precedent which still rivalled the current autumn New Year.

8. THE PRIMITIVE CHRISTIAN CALENDAR

We have now shown by means of a mathematical calculation that the division of Mark into lections for the Liturgical Year explains a number of phenomena in the composition and textual history of the gospel; and also that such a division had passed through all its main phases well before A.D. 160 when Tatian was composing his *Diatessaron*. Indeed these phases could only occur in an early period when each church was operating a single gospel. I feel sure, however, that the reader would welcome external evidence to show that a 'Christian Year' was itself in operation at so early a date. We have given general grounds for this assumption, but we must proceed to a closer examination of such evidence as may be found in the small number of documents surviving from these times. We may begin with the institution of the weekly Sunday.

The Lord's Day. In Acts xx. 7 we have an account by an eyewitness of a service on the first day of the week which occurred at Troas about nineteen days after the Passover. It was a vigil service; but we must take the night to be Saturday night which was regarded as the beginning of Sunday. There were many lights, much speaking, and the breaking of the bread. We must regard it as an observation of the holy night (the eve of Sunday) on which Christ rose from the dead.

Now there is evidence that the Sunday on which Christ rose from the dead was a holy day of the Hebrew Calendar, in its capacity as a Sunday. It was the Omer or Firstfruits, on which the first sheaf of barley was offered to the Lord in the Temple, a rite which is connected with the resurrection of Jesus in I Cor. xv. 20. It is laid down in Lev. xxiii. 11 that it is to take place 'on the morrow of the sabbath', that is to say on a Sunday; and the Sadducees and the Samaritans took this quite literally, though the Pharisees did not. Where the Samaritans and the Sadducees controlled the ritual (and this may have included both Palestinian temples), what we call Easter Sunday must already have been an important day in the Calendar; furthermore the fifty weeks of Pentecost were counted from Omer, so that the Sadducees and Samaritans made this a Sunday too. And we may go further, and ask whether it was not implied that *any* Sunday was a proper day for offering firstfruits; for it is hardly possible to suppose that all firstfruits of all crops everywhere in Palestine were offered on the two great Sundays specially set aside for the purpose. The account of this in the Mishnah is romantic but unconvincing.

The other reference to the Lord's Day (in I Cor. xvi. 2) fits in well with this supposition, as it directs that offerings shall be laid by on that day, and when we turn to II Cor. ix, where the same subject is continued, we find that the theology of such offerings is worked out from the Hebrew theology of seed-time, harvest, and thank-offering (*eucharistia*). The Corinthian letters were, of course, written in the Easter-Pentecost season.

The Pascha. We have thus found some precedent in the Hebrew Calendar for the observance of the first day of the week, or 'morrow of the sabbath', even if it was not honoured by all parties among the Jews. The observance of the Passover, Pascha, or Easter was also continued among Christians, though there were different traditions about it. The Hebrew system was:

Nisan 14. Full moon. 'Pascha.' The lambs killed.
Nisan 15. First day of Unleavened Bread: 'Mazzoth.' Paschal meal on the eve, i.e. after sunset, Nisan 14.

In the apostolic age a difference arose in chronology. According to John, Jesus suffered on Nisan 14; according to Mark he suffered on Nisan 15, having partaken of the Passover on the previous evening. No doubt a difference of custom with regard to the Christian Pascha is responsible for this difference in the text. It is widely held that the Johannine date is correct, and that the original text of Mark agreed with it. In this case the Pascha was on a Friday and the Omer a Sunday in that particular year; this seems to harmonize with I Cor. v. 7 and xv. 20, which we quote further on. But we have to realize clearly that the Pascha would fall on other weekdays in other years; and, on the Sadducee-Samaritan computation, Pascha and Omer would drift apart; for Pascha might be any day of the week, and Omer, the Resurrection Day, would always come on a Sunday.

The most important controversy between orthodox Christians in the second century turned on this intricate point. The Asiatic Christians, following, as they said, the custom of the disciple John, kept the Pascha on the fourteenth day of Nisan whatever day of the week it might be; their fast coincided exactly with the Passover of the Jews; and they were known as 'Quartodecimans' (fourteenthites). The Roman Christians, on the other hand, took account of the day of the week, and so arranged matters as to keep the fast on a Friday and end it on a Sunday, just as if their thinking was dominated more by the precedent of the Omer as the Sadducees understood it. For this system they claimed the authority of the 'Elders', by which they meant the teachers and presbyters of old, whose tradition had come down to them. Both customs in short were well established in their respective centres, and there was no record or memory of an alternative.

Acute friction arose in Rome where a colony of Asiatic Christians insisted on keeping the Pascha on their own day. This was tolerated for a long time, but about A.D. 190 the Roman Bishop Victor decided to excommunicate the Quartodecimans. Protests came in not only from Polycrates, the Bishop of Ephesus, who was the natural champion of the Asiatics, but also from Irenaeus, the Bishop of Lyons in Gaul, a master of theology, who was also of Asiatic origin, but had spent time in Rome, where he had studied in the school of Justin Martyr. His original master, however, had been Polycarp of Smyrna, the great Asiatic teacher who had actually heard St John.

Irenaeus, in his letter to Victor, did not defend the Asiatic custom about the Pascha, and admitted that there was considerable variation with regard to the length and termination of the fast; but he did protest rather strongly against the excommunication of other churches; and he referred explicitly to the good relations which had existed for so long. He pointed out that when Polycarp had visited Rome (about A.D. 154) the question had been discussed with the Roman Bishop of the time, Anicetus, and, though the two bishops had been unable to agree, this had not prevented them communicating; indeed Anicetus had asked Polycarp to celebrate the Eucharist. This friendly toleration of difficulties, Irenaeus said, could be traced as far back as the time of Xystus, who became Bishop of Rome about A.D. 118–20. (See Eusebius, *Ecclesiastical History*, v, 24, 12–17.)

This evidence shows that the observation of the Christian Pascha was so ancient and so deep-rooted that any violence done to it caused the bitterest resentment. It was established as a Christian institution before A.D. 120, and the two different traditions were already well entrenched at that period.

One of these traditions was that of the Elders of the Asiatic churches, the chief of which was Ephesus, who defended their position by quoting the great name of John the disciple, who had been their master. Now this John cannot be thought of as flourishing much later than the 90's, and may perhaps be assigned to a median date of 85–95. His pupils were quoting his opinions as late as the 140's, or even in the case of Polycarp the 150's; but the tradition which they defend belongs to the first century;

John and his pupils were observing the 14th of Nisan in the 90's. It was presumably earlier than that.

The other tradition was that of Rome. The leading teacher at Rome in the 90's was the Clement who wrote an *Epistle to the Corinthians* about 96. He has something to say about the Calendar, but it is a feature of his style to avoid precise detail. Nevertheless what he does say is interesting: 'Whatever the Lord has commanded us to perform, we ought to do in accordance with the appointed seasons. He commanded the offerings and services to be performed conscientiously and not at random or without order, but at appointed seasons and hours. Where and by whom they should be performed he himself appointed', etc. (I Clem. XL, 1 ff.). Since Clement goes on to refer to the high priests, the priests, and the Levites, it is clear that the 'appointed seasons' which he regards as essential must be those of the Levitical Law, that is to say Pascha, Pentecost, New Year, Day of Atonement, Tabernacles. If words have any meaning at all, a Liturgical Year of the Hebrew type must have been well established in Rome and in Corinth by the 90's. He does not say that this arrangement was made by the apostles; but he does say that the related question *by whom* the offerings were to be made was settled by the apostles (I Clem. XLII and XLIV), so that in his mind and memory apostles intervened in connexion with the system. More we cannot say, except that a calendrical system was established in Rome and Corinth in the 90's just as it was in Ephesus, and we must look for its origin at an earlier date.

We have no contemporary evidence from the 60's, when the apostles suffered martyrdom, and the gospel of Mark began to receive its present shape, but we are fortunate in having evidence from the 50's. We learn from the Epistle to the Romans (A.D. 56–7) that there were divisions in the Roman Church; and these were probably connected with the liturgy or common meal. There were some who refused to eat meat, and only took herbs. Others attached importance to the observance of special days: 'One man esteemeth one day above another; another esteemeth every day alike' (Rom. xiv. 5). Paul is not prepared to condemn either party. He had modified the stronger attitude of his Epistle to the

Galatians, in which he said, 'Ye observe days, and months, and seasons, and years. I am afraid of you, lest by any means I have bestowed labour upon you in vain' (Gal. iv. 10, 11). He has heard of controversy at Rome over the Calendar, and he is not prepared to exclude the observants from the church. His attitude is benign.[1]

And what else can he do? for he has just written his Epistles to the Corinthians in which it is clear that he makes use of Pascha and Pentecost himself:

> For our Pascha also hath been sacrificed, even Christ:
> Wherefore let us keep the feast. (I Cor. v. 7)
> But now hath Christ been raised from the dead,
> The Firstfruits of them that are asleep. (I Cor. xv. 20)

the Pascha being the lamb slain on Nisan 14, and the Firstfruits (Omer) being the offering of the first sheaf of the barley-harvest on Nisan 16 or following Sunday.

I Corinthians is a Paschal letter, a fact which is made particularly clear in its use of Exodus-Numbers, or, more likely, a 'midrash' upon it. Indeed a midrash of this sort should be added to the list of early Christian literature which was current in the 50's, but perished in the course of time. (Was it the *Eldad and Medad* of Hermas, *Vis.* II, 3 ?) These events of the Exodus formed the historical background of the seven weeks from Pascha to Pentecost, and their influence can be traced in Mark as well as in the Corinthian letters.

At the end of I Corinthians, we have a reference to Pentecost as being in the near future; and II Corinthians, or part of it, is a Pentecostal letter. The Exodus-Numbers midrash is followed as far as the giving of the Law on Sinai, which was supposed to have occurred at Pentecost. The mysticism of chapters iii–vi is inspired by the giving of the Law and the shining of Moses' face; and these verses have their own contacts with the Transfiguration story in Mark which we have connected with the Jewish Calendar Year subsequent to Pentecost.

---

[1] The suggestion has been made that this refers to old Roman superstitions of *fas* and *nefas*; but could St Paul say that such days could be observed 'unto the Lord'?

The rich liturgical material of the Corinthian epistles, which is closely connected with a gospel tradition, makes it perfectly evident that a Christianized form of the Hebrew Calendar was even then in existence, so that it would have been possible and even quite natural for Mark to have arranged his gospel for the liturgical year with a view to having it read in the churches. This Christianized Calendar was of course merely a simplified form of the old Hebrew Calendar as used by Jewish Christians in Palestine where the whole Christian tradition had received its primary form. There is no reason to think that there ever was a form of Christianity anywhere which dispensed with this Calendar.

It is not possible in this book to go into detail with regard to the whole New Testament literature, or the whole Old Testament Calendar, both of which would require a great deal of research; but it is possible to fill out the background a little.

The evidence is strong and full, of course, for the Pascha, and the connexion with it of Paul's gospel-proclamations, and the Petrine Passion narrative which we find in Mark. Another document which must be assigned to a paschal occasion is the First Epistle of St Peter. This epistle is readily divisible into three lections, as has been done by a later hand in B; the first of these lections is evangelistic, paschal, and baptismal; indeed it gives us our first clear suggestion of an association between the baptismal rite and the paschal season.

In the Gospel of St Mark, however, we found lections which we felt obliged to associate with the autumn solemnities of the New Year, the Day of Atonement, and the Feast of Tabernacles; but successive revisions of the lection-enumeration seem to have been designed to reduce the importance of this group of holy days. My attention has since been directed to an article by Dr Manson in which he assigns I Corinthians to Pascha and II Corinthians to Pentecost, as I have done on the clear evidence of the documents themselves, but also assigns Romans to the Day of Atonement. If this is correct, these epistles, in succession, provide readings for the whole course of the agricultural year.

The Epistle to the Hebrews also offers a field for study. Here is a restrained and scholarly piece of work, arguing a thesis, but at the same time making use of the old Hebrew liturgical tradition as it has been transformed by the Christian gospel. It would be natural to ask whether it is not a *megillah* (or roll) for the Day of Atonement, the ritual of which it interprets in a Christian sense; xii. 22 is distinctly reminiscent of the 'Shofaroth' of Tisri 1 which is the Day of Trumpets. It may also be suggested that the Epistle of St James was intended for use on the Day of Atonement.

It is in the Johannine literature, however, both Gospel and Apocalypse, that we find the richest storehouse of the evangelistic, the ritual, the apocalyptic, and the mystical. The Gospel is built up on a system of three Passovers in connexion with which the author introduces his Marcan material; these are separated by an unnamed feast in chapter v, which must be Tabernacles, and an elaborate section based on Tabernacles in chapters vii and viii in which Jesus seems to make his final appeal; for at the feast of the Dedication in x. 22, he is walking in Solomon's Porch, and at the final Passover it is not said that he entered the Temple. The Revelation lives and moves in the colour and order of the Temple liturgy glorified and transformed by the Christian gospel and by the superlative imagination of the author; it reflects the Christian worship of the ecclesia of the time, and became the storehouse of liturgy and hymnology for the future. It is clear from both Gospel and Revelation that the Feast of Tabernacles was a living tradition in Johannine circles; it provided a language which Christian prophecy and evangelism could use.

9. THE DODEKAD OF PREACHING

All this literature can be regarded as the fruits of a vigorous and evangelical liturgical tradition stemming from the old Hebrew popular faith and practice. It was all intended to be operated as part of that tradition within the Church. If our theory is correct the gospels were composed to give a Sunday–by–Sunday arrangement of the words and acts of Jesus to be announced or proclaimed at the proper point in the service. There could thus only be one gospel in a given church. Mark was the gospel for Rome based on a calendar in use in Rome. Matthew was the gospel of Antioch, based on the Marcan scheme with certain variations. We have shown that these gospels were divided into lections which fit in with the Calendar Year; we have also shown that the Calendar Year was in operation in the Christian Church; but we have found no actual evidence to show that the one fitted into the other. We have not found a church actually operating a gospel in this way. We must now look more closely into that dark period beginning in the 90's and extending to about the 120's when Xystus was Bishop of Rome and the Paschal controversy was already acute.

The evidence which survives from this period is extraordinarily slight; but we must make some effort to deal with it. About 115–20 Ignatius of Antioch went to his death, and wrote his epistles, which show to the satisfaction of most critics that Antioch was still in the one-gospel stage, and that the gospel so used was Matthew; other gospels, such as John, were also known; but Matthew is '*the* gospel'. In Asia Minor pupils of John preserved his memory and some recollection of his opinions; some of these are recorded by Irenaeus, in his great book *Against Heresies* written about A.D. 180. Others were written down a generation earlier by his pupil Papias, Bishop of Hierapolis, in a book of which we have only a few fragments which happen to be quoted by Irenaeus or Eusebius. Papias was never quite satisfied with written gospels; he could remember hearing the gospel oracles declaimed by those who had heard them from the disciples, and he loved the 'living voice'. Another pupil was Polycarp, whose *Epistle to the Philippians* belongs to the year of the martyrdom of Ignatius. In the same period we place the sources from which the *Didache* was compiled and the *Epistle of Barnabas*.

It was at the end of this period, about A.D. 130 or earlier, that Justin Martyr, a Samaritan by birth, was teaching at Ephesus; and with his career, Christianity passes out of its purely oral and liturgical phase. He went on to Rome, established a school, wrote books, entered into controversy, and died for the faith about A.D. 165. Irenaeus, who had sat at the feet of Polycarp, followed him to Rome and studied there, with Tatian and others. The stream was full and continuous; it is only our record of it that is meagre.

This record can be supplemented from the study of heresy. In the 150's, when Polycarp paid his visit to Anicetus, and Justin was organizing his school, and Tatian the Syrian was studying the problems presented by the prevalence of four gospels, there were other schools and other masters who had separated from the Church after much controversy.

Marcion of Pontus, puritanical and evangelical, was a total anti-Semite; he cut the Hebrew God, the Hebrew Law, the Hebrew scriptures, and every vestige of Judaism out of his church. This does not mean that he had no Old Testament lections in his services. He had a series of extracts arranged by himself in his book called the *Antitheses* with notes of his own composition discrediting the old religion. In addition to this he had a collection of Epistles of St Paul, and a Gospel. This Gospel had no author's name, and he said that it was the original written gospel of the apostles which Paul brought to Galatia. To Marcion the word 'gospel' meant a book containing the words and acts of Jesus. It is obvious that he can only think of *one* gospel. In closing down his canon the way he does, he is already old-fashioned. Just as Papias clung to an oral gospel, so Marcion clung to a single gospel, when the current of church opinion had already passed him by. He arrived in Rome about A.D. 140.

The Gospel of Marcion resembled our Luke, but was considerably cut down and altered. Tertullian and other church writers accuse him of mutilating Luke himself, but his protestations of innocence should surely be accepted. He stoutly affirmed that his abridged Luke was the original apostolic gospel, and that the canonical Luke had been filled out with material which was designed to favour Judaism. Now Irenaeus and Pseudo-Tertullian (who may be regarded as none other than Hippolytus) both provide Marcion with a predecessor Cerdo, whose views he adopted, and whose school he took over; moreover, says Pseudo-Tertullian, Cerdo used a mutilated version of Luke. We have, therefore, some support for the theory that Marcion received his gospel, and it must have been current for some time before that for him to have so high an opinion of it.

Tertullian gives us a continuous commentary on this gospel

in *Adversus Marcionem* IV, which can be checked by the 78 quotations of Epiphanius. Sometimes he notes that a section has been omitted; sometimes he passes over an omission in silence. It is not possible to reconstruct the text of the Marcionite Luke, but there is no great difficulty in making a list of its chapter-divisions. That it had chapter-divisions I judge from the remark of Tertullian in *Adv. Marc.* III, 11: *Et videbimus de his capitulis suo tempore*, 'we will see about these chapters at their proper time'. The number of chapters which I allot to the part of this gospel prior to the Passion Narrative is about 55 or 56. The first half-year down to and including the Transfiguration is 26 or 28; 29 at the outside limit; I really do not think it could be more. The second half-year, down to but not including the apocalyptic discourse, also gives 26 to 29, but this includes a number of literary judgements into which a subjective element must enter. The Passion narrative cannot be estimated; possibly it counted as a single lection.

By adding the two halves together we get a total of 52 to 58 lections for the material preceding the apocalyptic discourse, which we assume to be the first lection of the Passion narrative. It will be remembered that the non-B arrangement of Matthew gave 54 (55) lections for this part of the gospel.

There is a rough way of checking the number of lections in the Marcionite Luke. The non-B manuscripts divide the canonical Luke into 83 (84) lections; 74 (75) of these lections precede the apocalyptic discourse; nineteen of these lections are omitted in Marcion's gospel, or at any rate are not represented in Tertullian or Epiphanius; and this would leave 55 (56) lections for the Marcionite Luke, which agrees with the result mentioned above, obtained by literary analysis of Tertullian.[1]

The suggestion is, therefore, that Luke has been cut down to agree with the Marcan pattern as revealed in the B system; and this is supported by two other considerations. In a number of cases it can be shown that the text of the Marcionite Luke followed the text of Mark, not the canonical Luke; and the title given to it, 'the Gospel', was taken from the first verse of Mark, and does

---

[1] See chapter-numbers and titles of Luke with information about the Gospel of Marcion, p. 103.

not appear in Luke at all. The suggestion is that there was an ultra-Pauline church which had been working for a long time with Mark; the time came when a fuller liturgical 'gospel' was required; Luke was taken and cut down to fill the requirements, the style being assimilated to Mark at some points, and a Marcan title given to the new document. Some of the omissions were obviously made for theological reasons, and others from motives of space. The difficulty in explaining the Marcionite Luke has always been those large omissions, like the Prodigal Son, for which no plausible dogmatic reason could be provided.

This digression, if it is a digression, serves to answer the question, Does Luke partake in the liturgical theory? Does it seem to have the nature of a Calendar? It would appear that it has not. It seems perfectly clear from Irenaeus (*Adv. Haer.* III, 14 and 15) that Luke was not read through continuously, but that everyone made use of characteristic Lucan lections which he calls 'Acts of the Lord' or 'Gospels', many of which he names, though not in any particular order. Such a practice would explain why Tatian shows so little respect for the order of Luke. On the other hand, the abridged 'Docetic' Luke may well have been used in connexion with the Calendary Year in Marcion's one-gospel church.

Our view of the pre-Marcionite Luke is, however, a dim one, and does not help us very far. Better progress can be made along another road. There was another 'heretical' school at Rome in the 140's which rivalled those of Justin and Marcion in importance. Valentinus was the leader of the intellectuals and mystics; he was a widely-read broad-minded man with a talent for weaving myths from many sources into what looked like a philosophy. He brought his peculiar views from Alexandria, and his skill in allegorization was so great that there was no gospel that he could not use. He made use of all four, and his favourite was that of John; but the early Alexandrian Gnosticism out of which he wove his more abstract system was based on Mark, as we shall see.

The earliest form of the Alexandrian heresy has to be pieced together from disconnected statements in Irenaeus and other authors. We have very few fragments written by the 'Gnostics' themselves. A universal feature of their heresy, however, was the separation of the Christus from the Jesus. The Christus was a divine Spirit who descended from heaven and entered the Jesus at his Baptism. Valentinus and similar theosophs had no difficulty in working the Virgin Birth into their system at an early date; but it would appear that the original theology of the Alexandrian heretics did not require it; the incarnation of the divine Christus in a human body took place at the Baptism. Such a view must depend upon a gospel like that of Mark which begins with the Baptism.

This heresy must be carefully distinguished from the view of Marcion, according to which the divine Christus descended into the Capernaum synagogue as a 'life-giving spirit' and was not incarnate at all. The Marcionite Luke is shorn of its Baptism story as well as its Nativity stories. This is the true 'Docetism' which did not allow Christ to have a material body. He only *seemed* to have a body. This must be the teaching controverted by Ignatius of Antioch about A.D. 115–20. It was, perhaps, brought from Syria to Rome by Cerdo, and handed on by him to Marcion.

The form of belief which makes the divine Christus descend into the human Jesus is also called 'Docetism', and sometimes 'Adoptionism'; but both expressions are misnomers; it is a form of incarnation.

The first teacher who is said to have taught this doctrine is Cerinthus, who is said by Irenaeus (*Adv. Haer.* I, 21) to have been a contemporary of the disciple John and to have taught in Asia; but, says Irenaeus, he was 'trained in the Egyptian discipline'. This date is so early that there is no difficulty in thinking that Alexandria (where it may be supposed that Cerinthus received his Egyptian education) had not got beyond the one-gospel stage with Mark as the one gospel.

Various small pieces of evidence fit into the pattern which is now emerging. The tradition that Mark was the founder of Alexandrian Christianity is not one to be lightly dismissed, though we cannot trace it any earlier than the *History* of Eusebius in the fourth century. Where Eusebius found it, we do not know; what we do know is that he worked in the library, and was versed in the learned tradition, of the Alexandrian Origen who was born in the 180's. What Eusebius says is, 'Now it is said that Mark journeyed to Egypt, and was the first to preach there the gospel which he had composed; and he was the first to form churches at Alexandria itself' (*Hist. Eccl.* II, 16). It almost looks as if the important point here was the reference to the Marcan gospel; no long residence of Mark in Alexandria is asserted.

Furthermore, Irenaeus tells us that the gospel of Mark was the favourite gospel of those heretics who separate the Christus from the Jesus, saying that the latter was capable of suffering, but not the former (*Adv. Haer.* III, 11, 10). Who he meant by this seems to be clear from the account which he gives of Cerinthus in I, 21: 'at the end the Christus departed from the Jesus, and the Jesus suffered and rose again, but the Christus remained impassible, being spiritual'; the Christus, therefore, ascended into heaven before the Crucifixion or during the Crucifixion. This may also be the view taken in the apocryphal *Gospel of Peter*, which is a free composition based on all four gospels; it may have been written as early as the 150's, but its place of origin is unknown. Its use of Peter's name, however, suggests a connexion with the Marcan tradition, since Mark was everywhere regarded as a Petrine gospel. It is possible that it was never any more than a Passion narrative, like the second part of Mark, or the harmonized Passion narrative which Rendel Harris thinks preceded the *Diatessaron*.

According to this gospel, Jesus, when crucified, 'remained silent as if feeling no pain', but, before his death, he said, 'My power, my power, why hast thou forsaken me?', perhaps referring to the Christus; but the effect is rather confused.

A quite different theory of the Crucifixion is given by another branch of Alexandrian Gnosticism, whose principal teacher was the austere and philosophic Basilides. According to Irenaeus (*Adv. Haer.* I, 19) their view was that the Jews crucified Simon of Cyrene, and that Jesus adopted the form of Simon and stood by and laughed at them. This extraordinary notion can only be based on a misunderstanding of Mark, who says, 'And they compel one passing by, Simon of Cyrene, coming from the country, the father of Alexander and Rufus,...that he might bear his cross. And they bring him unto the place Golgotha....And they

offered him wine mingled with myrrh....And they crucify him'
(xv. 21-4). This looseness of construction, which is characteristic
of Mark, gives an easy explanation of this peculiar idea.

The form of the Alexandrian heresy which now begins to
emerge is obviously Marcan, and is best explained by a theory of
an early ascendancy of Mark in Alexandria, which went on later
and was perhaps more influential there than elsewhere. It was
responsible for the following heretical opinions:

(a) the idea of the Christus as a heavenly spirit who entered
the world by descending into the body of the man Jesus
at his Baptism;

(b) the idea that the Christus, being impassible, evaded crucifixion, and that the person crucified was only the man
Jesus, or even Simon of Cyrene.

This christology could only arise from a gospel which lacked
Nativity and Resurrection narratives, as Mark does.

The outlines of a pre-Gnostic theology based on Mark do now
begin to appear. The heretical *systems* of Basilides and Valentinus
were not being taught in their elaborated forms before A.D. 120,
perhaps not before 130; but they were both based on traditions
of the previous generation which they swore came to them from
the apostles. Valentinus claimed that his came from Theodas,
a pupil of St Paul; Basilides claimed that his came from Glaucias,
a pupil of St Peter. These traditions, on which Valentinus and
Basilides worked, belong to the dark period from about A.D. 90 to
about 120. We must suppose that Alexandria had its 'apostolic'
tradition in the 90's, with its Marcan gospel, and its school of elders
contemporary with Cerinthus, John, and Clement; among these
elders, we may not be far wrong in placing Theodas and Glaucias.

This is not at all too early a period for the first 'Ophites'
(or serpent-worshippers) who were considered by Hippolytus to
be the original 'Gnostics'. Our knowledge of this very queer
sect is based on late accounts in which their complex and rather
fluid mythology had been greatly elaborated; indeed it is never
the same. We may suppose, however, that Ophite doctrines were
popular in Alexandria before Valentinus composed his system;

for he appears to have made considerable use of them; or, to put it another way, elements common to the Valentinian and Ophite systems must go back to an early period.

The Ophites believed that the Jesus (not the Christus) remained with the disciples for eighteen months after his resurrection, and this would seem to harmonize best with a gospel like Mark, in which no resurrection appearances are actually narrated, and consequently there is no limit to the imagination in this respect. The period of eighteen months is also found in the *Ascension of Isaiah*, and is best explained as part of a fuller chronology.

This chronology is found in Valentinus, who taught that Jesus preached for twelve months from the Baptism to the Passion, and taught his disciples for eighteen months afterwards. These figures reflect the system of thirty 'aeons' or divine existences which emanate from and exist within the divinity of Valentinus. The highest circle is that of the Eight (or Ogdoad); the second is that of the Ten (or Dekad); the third is the Twelve (or Dodekad). The Dodekad corresponds to the twelve signs of the zodiac, which, we remember, were sometimes depicted on the synagogue floor as a visual Calendar. In Valentinus everything on one plane of existence is a copy or image of something on another plane of existence. The twelve months of preaching by Jesus from the Baptism to the Passion correspond to the twelve signs of the zodiac, which correspond to the twelve aeons of the Dodekad; the eighteen months of preaching afterwards correspond to the higher realms of the ten aeons of the Dekad, and the eight aeons of the Ogdoad; the full number of the whole *pleroma* (fulness) is thus completed; it is thirty (the Triakontad) which is the number of days in the month.

The astrological or calendrical interest appears clearly in the central event of the Gnostic myth, as it is adapted by Valentinus. The twelfth aeon of the Dodekad (or thirtieth of the whole pleroma) was a female named Sophia, who fell from her high place into the *kenoma* or void, and this fall set going those causes which led to creation.[1] According to Valentinus the earthly

---

[1] The myth of the Fall of Sophia in Valentinian Gnosis is identical with the psychological 'theory' of S. Freud.

career of Jesus was a reflexion of the Passion of his divine mother, Sophia. He preached for twelve months from the Baptism to the Passion, and was betrayed in the twelfth month by the twelfth apostle. This whole concept of an earthly course of Jesus 'from the Baptism to the Passion' seems to be based on Mark.

We learn from Irenaeus that Ptolemaeus, who was the successor in Rome of Valentinus, relied on a prophecy of Isaiah which is quoted in Luke iv. 19, 'to proclaim the acceptable year of the Lord', in order to prove the one-year ministry. He also made use of the statement in Luke that Jesus was beginning to be about thirty years old (iii. 23) when he began his ministry, equating this with the Triakontad, or full number of aeons. But this hardly seems strong enough to bear the weight which the Gnostics placed upon it. I have no wish to deny that Luke was known in Alexandria when the Gnostic tradition was taking form; I believe that every gospel reached this hive of literary bees at an early date, and was duly worked into the Gnostic tradition. But we are surely handling one of those fundamental traditions which the Gnostics believed to be part of their apostolic tradition.

I suggest that the tradition of the twelve months of preaching was based on something more solid than a couple of allusions in Luke which fit the theory very well once it is established. The Gnostic belief would be satisfactorily explained if the Marcan gospel 'from the Baptism to the Passion' was read in Alexandria as the system of lections for the Calendar Year. If Mark had been read from the earliest times in the Church as an annual cycle of liturgical lessons, the idea would naturally, or even inevitably, grow up that the events which were thus chronicled had taken place within a single year. This would require the second system of chapter-enumeration, which we find in the non-*B* manuscripts, dividing all Mark into 48 (49) lections; and this system fits into the Julian Calendar, which was itself a product of Alexandrian science.

Confirmation for this suggestion comes from the Basilidian School. Clement of Alexandria tells us that the Basilidians invented a festival peculiar to themselves, a festival of the Baptism of Jesus which they celebrated on 6 or 10 January, keeping it as his 'birthday'. This agrees with the peculiar Alexandrian heresy that the divine Christus took flesh or at any rate entered into a human body at the Baptism; it also fits in with the 48 (49)-lection system of the non-*B* manuscripts which is arranged so that the first lection or lections were read at the Roman New Year, 1 January. And we are now deep in the question of Christian liturgical origins; for this 'heretical' festival of the 'Epiphany' became a universal festival throughout the whole Christian Church, commemorating both the Baptism and the Nativity of Jesus. It is rather hard to explain this as a world-wide imitation of the Basilidian heretics; it is quite easy to explain if the 48 (49)-lection arrangement of Mark was used as a Calendar fairly widely at one time.

To anticipate matters a little, we may point out that the substitution of Matthew for Mark as a one-year gospel provides a natural explanation for the Roman Nativity festival of 25 December; for if the Baptism of Jesus had been read by custom for some time on 6 January or thereabouts, and it were found prudent to retain that custom, the reading of the Nativity stories which precede it in Matthew would of necessity be thrown back one or two weeks earlier. The Eastern custom represents a different expedient; for we find that the Nativity and the Baptism were both commemorated on 6 January. As time went on, the connexion of the Epiphany (6 January) with the Baptism receded into the background or was forgotten. In the seventh-century lectionary called the *Comes* the Baptism gospel has been shifted from Epiphany into the Octave, and in the Roman Missal has disappeared.

Irenaeus wrote his great book against heresies in the 180's, and strongly opposed the idea that the preaching of Jesus from the Baptism to the Passion lasted twelve months, coinciding with the thirtieth year of his life; and his line of argument suggests that the controversy was no new one. He first argues from the Fourth Gospel that the ministry of Jesus lasted at least three years. He then admits the Lucan statement that Jesus was beginning to be about thirty years old when he was baptized, but he thinks that some years elapsed between the Baptism and the beginning of the preaching, as Jesus must have reached senior age before he began to teach. In support of this he quotes the unanimous verdict of the Elders of Asia Minor, who had this tradition from John himself; and so we come for the second time to a difference of opinion between a tradition supported by the school of John, and a tradition which is based on, or may be based on, the Marcan gospel.

The idea of a three-year ministry is mentioned by another Asiatic writer, Melito of Sardis, who was a good deal senior to Irenaeus, and quite probably one of his sources of information. Is it possible that Ephesus and Asia had a three-year lectionary, following the Palestinian synagogue system, instead of the one-year Babylonian system which superseded it in the synagogue? We do not know; but I think we will not be far wrong in advancing the opinion that the controversy which agitated the Church on gospel-chronology in the 90's, and drew an expression of opinion from John the Elder, was not merely literary or historical; if this opinion was given and remembered, we may be sure that it related to some controversy which affected the life of the Church. It may therefore have had a connexion with the observance of the liturgical year, like the contemporary debate about the Pascha. Indeed they may be aspects of the same debate, which, as we have observed, became acute in Rome under Bishop Xystus in the 120's. We may note that the authority of John has now been quoted in connexion with (*a*) the heresy of Cerinthus, (*b*) the date of the Pascha, and (*c*) the gospel chronology: in every case against a position which appears to be based on Mark.

We must now return to the Calendar of Valentinus, which may not be the same as that of Basilides in all respects. The Dodekad of Valentinus, which derives from the number of months or zodiacal signs, and his Triakontad, which derives from the number of days in the month, make it abundantly clear that his Calendar would be the old oriental lunar Calendar, which was used by the Hebrews; his New Year, therefore, would be likely to be in the spring or autumn equinox.

Basilides, however, taught a system of 365 heavenly aeons, which implies that he made use of a 'Roman' solar calendar which measured off the year by counting 365 days. This is in

55

accordance with his mental outlook and processes, which were far more rigorous and realistic than those of Valentinus. It also gives additional confirmation to the suggestion that his Calendar began on 1 January, thus causing the Baptism lection to be read at the beginning of that month.

When did the Calendar of Valentinus begin? Fortunately Irenaeus sheds some light upon this question. How can Valentinus place the Passion in the twelfth month, he asks (*Adv. Haer.* II, 33, 3), when everybody knows that it took place in the first month? And as he refers to the Law of Moses (see Exod. xii. 2), there is no doubt that the first month means Nisan or March–April. The twelfth month of the Valentinian Calendar would thus include the Pascha, or as we say, Easter Day.[1] He would read the first lection immediately after the Easter season. This would harmonize well with his myth; for the Passion of Jesus in the twelfth month was a reflexion of the Passion of Sophia, the twelfth aeon; now as the fall of Sophia was the first of the stages which led to the creation of the world, we may think of the Valentinians as commemorating the creation in their twelfth month or on their New Year. And the idea that the Paschal Season was the New Year, and that it commemorated the creation of the world, is an old Jewish idea which lingered in Alexandria, as we learn from Philo.

We have already remarked that a Calendar of gospel lections from spring to spring is given us in the *Diatessaron* of Tatian. We must now include Valentinus, and possibly Irenaeus himself, among the supporters of this third calendrical system. Other support is not lacking. The *Clementine Homilies*, a romantic compilation, the earliest sources of which may not be later than the 170's, state that the preaching of Jesus began in the spring (I, 6) and lasted for a whole year (XVII, 19); but, they add, the news of this spring preaching did not reach Rome until the autumn. This does more than confirm the spring as a date for the commencement of the twelve-month gospel cycle; it looks as if a reason were being advanced for a change in the Roman Church from an autumn New Year to a spring New Year.

---

[1] Nevertheless the non-*B* system would locate the Passion lections in December which is the twelfth month of the Roman Calendar, which we think was that of Basilides.

This is supported, in its turn, by Hippolytus and other sources. Hippolytus wrote in the early third century; but conservatism had settled upon the Roman Church, or at least upon the part of it for which Hippolytus wrote; his evidence can be used, with caution, for the 170's or 180's. He worked on the assumption that 25 March (a conventional date for the spring equinox) was the day of the Annunciation, and therefore of the Conception of Jesus by the Virgin Mary; that is to say, the day when the Logos took flesh. This gives 25 December, nine months later, as the day of the Nativity. The Passion is placed on the same day as the Annunciation, 25 March, thus completing a twelve-month gospel cycle. If we are right in our suggestion that the date of 25 December for the Nativity resulted from the supersession of a Marcan Calendar of the Roman or Basilidian type by a Matthaean Calendar of the same type, we see here an ingenious harmonization of that date with a Lucan Calendar which places the Passion on the same date as the Phrygian festival of Attis, and adopts this day as the New Year. But there are difficulties in establishing the text of Hippolytus, and it may be that March 25 was his date for the Nativity itself.

We now see the outlines of the present Christian Calendar coming into existence, and we can pursue this topic no further. We hope, however, that the considerations which we have laid before our readers will be admitted to shed some light on the early stages of its development, and also on the various chronological speculations which are found in the works of Clement of Alexandria, Epiphanius and others.

We must return to Ephesus and to the period A.D. 90–120. We have found that during this period there was a difference of opinion between the Ephesian and Roman traditions on the subject of the date of the Pascha. The Ephesians, following the example of John, kept the Jewish Passover; the Romans on the authority of their own Elders kept the following Sunday. We also found an opinion of John as handed on by the same Elders, with regard to the age of Jesus, which had a bearing on the liturgical question; it favoured a three-year ministry, and held that Jesus could not have begun teaching before the age of forty, as this would have been contrary to Jewish precedent. We now come to a third opinion attributed to John, this time by his pupil Papias, who wrote it down in his book from which it was quoted by Eusebius in *Ecclesiastical History*, III, 39. It concerns the gospel of Mark.

The Elder, we are told, approved of the accuracy of this gospel, but not of its order. Mark, he explains, accompanied Peter and acted as his interpreter. Peter never made an arrangement of the words (*logoi*) or oracles (*logia*)[1] of the Lord, but 'framed his teachings in view of needs'. Matthew, on the other hand, made an arrangement of the oracles (*logia*); but this compilation was written 'in the Hebrew tongue', so that 'everyone had to translate them as best they could'. Now this gospel of Mark, whose order is disapproved, is the very gospel which we have shown to be the basis of the twelve-month calendar, so that these three Johannine statements may all be connected with the same controversy and with the same circle of ideas. The Elder felt himself bound to oppose certain views which were based rightly or wrongly on Mark; he does not, however, impugn the veracity or accuracy of Mark, but only his order; and there is a simple explanation for his errors in this respect. He is defending Mark, not criticizing him.

What kind of order did the Elder mean? Historical order, or topical order, or calendrical order? If it was the last, much that seems difficult becomes clear. We may begin with the word *logia*, the meaning of which is much canvassed. What does it mean? The dictionary says 'brief utterances' or 'oracles'; and we find it used both of the Law and the gospel. The Hebrew Law was best known to the people through being read aloud at the festivals or in the synagogue service. The *logia* of the Lord might be brief records of the words or acts of Jesus read in the same way in the churches. In fact no better word could be found for the short units of gospel material in their liturgical setting. These *logia*, if we may follow Papias, were originally delivered orally by Peter and other disciples of Jesus; and that is how Papias had loved to hear them, even at second hand. What Mark did was

[1] Surely *logoi* here is a mistake for *logia*. *Logia* is the reading in the case of Matthew.

to write them down; he did this accurately but not in order; that is to say not the order which the Elder approved. His displeasure with the order would be of some consequence if the order were liturgical; it would mean that Mark could not be used, or only used with difficulty, in the Asiatic churches.

There was, however, according to the Elder, a better arrangement, which had been made by Matthew, only it was in the Hebrew tongue. It is agreed on all hands that this was not our canonical Matthew which was composed in Greek. It is something older; and when John spoke it was not available in Greek. We must remember that he was speaking in the 80's or 90's.

There has been a tendency among scholars to assume that the Hebrew Matthew mentioned by the Elder was a document containing different material from that contained in Mark; and this has led to theories which identify it with Q or even with the *Book of Testimonies*. Does not the Elder really imply that it was a collection of the same material as we find in Mark, or very much the same material, the difference being found in the order? The difficulty in reconstituting it from our canonical Matthew might be due to the fact that much of it was identical with our canonical Mark.

The word 'Hebrew' is generally taken to mean Aramaic (West Syrian) which is its meaning in the Johannine books (see John xix. 13 and 20, and probably Rev. xvi. 16). Its place of origin therefore might be in Syria, or perhaps among Palestinian Jewish Christians. The Asiatic tradition associated with John always turns out to be a Hebrew one; it prefers the Jewish day for the Pascha, the Palestinian three-year lectionary (?), the 'Hebrew' arrangement of the oracles of Jesus, the oral method of transmission, and even the correct age according to Hebrew ideas for a teacher.

10. THE FOURFOLD CANON

A survey of the scene is now possible.

We think, to begin with, that we have mathematically demonstrated the liturgical succession of Mark, Matthew and the *Diatessaron*. They are successive forms of an ecclesiastical lectionary.

It is generally agreed that what led to the composition of Matthew was the arrival from Rome of Mark. Though Matthew became the liturgical gospel of Antioch, and reigned alone in that church till the time of Ignatius or later, it does not follow that it was written there. Many scholars think that South Syria is more likely; Tyre or Sidon or even Galilee.

It would be a mistake, however, to suppose that the church where our Matthew was composed had nothing of its own corresponding to Mark. It is not merely common sense that forbids such a proposition; it is actual evidence. There are occasions when Matthew seems to follow a different version of a Marcan passage, and sometimes this Matthaean version is superior as in Matt. xiv. 12–13. More striking is the fact that additions to the narrative are of a subsidiary nature; there are certain additions, for instance, to the Passion narrative which are peculiar to Matthew, but they could never have stood alone without the Passion narrative itself to support them. There must have been a Passion narrative in use before Mark arrived, and that Passion narrative must have been substantially the same as Mark's. In other words a gospel very much like Mark's must have existed in Syria before Mark arrived. No church could have subsisted on the sections of Matthew not found in Mark.

It is convenient to ask whether we are not now thinking of the Aramaic *logia* of Matthew, mentioned by the Elder John. Let us see what happened. The Roman gospel of Mark, when it arrived, carried great weight because it had the authority of Peter behind it; for Peter was elevated to a very high position indeed in the Matthew area: see Matt. xvi. 18, etc. It was combined with what gospel material this church already had, and the omnibus gospel, as we may describe it, was issued under the name of Matthew. This name was not taken out of a hat; it was given for a reason. As it did not apply to the Marcan part of the compilation, it is reasonable to suppose that it referred to the non-Marcan part of the compilation.

Is this Q? Now Q is a symbol with a fluctuating meaning which must be fixed for purposes of discussion. It can only be used scientifically to refer to certain passages in Matthew and

Luke which do not derive from Mark, and yet resemble one another so closely that they must be copied from the same Greek document or documents. The only test we can apply in determining what is Q is identity of words. If we go through our canonical Matthew and obliterate all the words in non-Marcan passages which are identical with the corresponding words in the corresponding passages of Luke, we shall find that it makes much less difference to Matthew than you might suppose. Its Matthaean shape, structure, colour, and character remain, even when Q, so far as we can be sure of Q, is gone. The name 'Matthew' is more likely to be given to this remaining material, which provides a setting and style and colour which give Matthew its own character.

In other words our Matthew may be a combination of our Mark not only with Q but with the old Aramaic Matthew (translated now into Greek) which was itself a full liturgical gospel like Mark, and no doubt identical with it in many of its parts. A theory of this sort makes the best of the evidence which we get from Papias and Irenaeus. The latter says that Matthew wrote his gospel in Hebrew 'while Peter and Paul were evangelizing and founding the church in Rome'. This is perfectly in agreement with the statement of John the Elder reported by Papias. Irenaeus is wrong, of course, if he thinks that the canonical Greek Matthew is a reproduction of the original Hebrew Matthew; and of course he writes as if he does think so. But this error in no way invalidates his statement. No one has ever turned up the least bit of evidence or produced the slightest reason for doubting these plain statements of men who ought to know, that Matthew wrote the gospel for the Hebrews in his own language while Peter and Paul were evangelizing and founding the church in Rome. Nor is there any reason to suppose that it was not a full liturgical gospel; if our theory is correct, the 'Elder' referred to it as having a calendrical order.

The period from A.D. 30 to 60, then, is the formative period of the gospel tradition within the evangelistic and liturgical process. No doubt much was written down. In the 60's two notable forms of the gospel tradition were reduced to writing, the Greek Mark in Rome and the Aramaic Matthew in the East.

We can only make statements about the former, because the latter does not survive in its original form.

The Greek Mark spread widely, but it was insufficient in at least two ways for the growing needs of the Church. Its lack of Nativity and Resurrection narratives made it a favourite among the Docetics of the ultra-Pauline school, and also among the type of Gnostics who 'separated the Christus from the Jesus'.[1] Its omission of the old oral teaching tradition, which was presumably in the hands of some special class of teachers, also told against it. It made on the whole for a non-human, unhistorical Jesus. It had to be enlarged and supplemented.

When it arrived in Syria, it was combined with the 'Matthew' form of the tradition, and with other material too, to form the canonical Matthew which we still have. This probably appeared in the 90's. It travelled westward, carrying all before it. It could easily be substituted for Mark as it had adopted the same liturgical pattern; the 48 lections for the year had been enlarged to a more practical 54 (55); the Passion narrative was still separate. For a considerable time, and in many places, Matthew was the one liturgical gospel. It might have become the universal gospel of the whole Church so far as that Church was not in the hands of heretical teachers, who did not like the strong Jewish colouring which was necessary in order to present the human historical Jesus.

The heretics turned to Luke–Acts, a work which may have been written as early as the 60's, and contained materials drawn from earlier sources still. It was not, we think, a liturgical work. It was a library book in two volumes which gave the history of Christian origins down to about A.D. 62, where it stops short with great abruptness. It has a pleasant Biblical style, and first-hand Palestinian local colour, but it would be easy for a Gentile to read, omitting as it does a great deal of Jewish controversy and other material hard for the Greek mind to assimilate. We have already seen how the first volume of the book was trimmed down to suit the needs of an ultra-Pauline church, which certainly could

---

[1] The addition of a supplementary lection at the end of Mark (about A.D. 90–100) was doubtless designed to offset this disadvantage. See my notes on xvi. 9–end.

not have accepted Matthew, and how it became the liturgical gospel of Cerdo and Marcion.

What was the position of Luke in the great churches of Syria and Asia Minor and Alexandria and Greece and Rome, we simply do not know. It was strong enough, however, to challenge the supremacy of Matthew. We see this in the pages of Justin Martyr whose conversion we placed before A.D. 130. There were two teaching traditions of an oral character in which we can look for it. One is the successive *Books of Testimonies*, or Old Testament extracts to prove New Testament points; this very important propaganda went hand in hand with the progress of Matthew; the influence in point of fact was reciprocal; they must have been developed in the same area; yet by the time of Justin Luke had found its way into this field. More important was the instruction of converts in the teachings of Jesus, the most important element in which was the Sermon on the Mount. When we study Justin and other writers we see clearly that teachers found the existence of two (or more?) texts a problem; quotations in this age were never very exact, and quotations of the words of Jesus are no exception; but the forms we find are due not merely to the looseness of quotation by memory in the oral method, but also to the fact that the texts of Matthew and Luke have been combined. The same is true, Dr Rendel Harris tried to prove, of the Passion narrative. The *Diatessaron*, then, was not without its predecessors. Texts of different gospels had already been combined so far as concerned certain parts of them, and for certain purposes.

But whether the canonical Luke was used as a liturgical gospel in any area in the one-gospel period, we cannot say. We have given evidence to the effect that selected lections were in use.

The Fourth Gospel is obviously liturgical in character, and references are made in it to the Jewish Calendar, but there is no evidence that it ever competed with the Mark-Matthew tradition. Perhaps it was designed for use on special occasions, festal or sacramental or otherwise. This is possibly supported by the quotations in Justin, who is our only writer of any considerable length from this period; he alludes to John iii. 14, and quotes John iii. 3–5

63

in *Apol.* LX and LXI, which are preparatory to his description of the sacrament of Baptism. (iii. 8 is quoted by Ignatius in *Philad.* VII.)

We have already shown how Marcion clung to the mutilated Luke as a single liturgical gospel, while Basilides perhaps continued to use Mark in the same way. In the great church this was impossible. After a period in which Matthew had the pre-eminence (and this was perhaps a very short one), the one-gospel canon came to an end. In his description of the Sunday Eucharist Justin tells us that 'gospels' were read, not 'the gospel', these lections, it would seem, being followed by readings from the 'prophets', which may have been extracts from the *Book of Testimonies*; for there is no evidence either among the Jews or the Christians of any consecutive reading of the Prophets. Justin was writing about the year A.D. 150, and we may suppose that by that time the one-gospel period had been definitely left behind. Valentinus seems to have agreed with the great church on this point.

We have practically no light at all on the formation of the fourfold canon of the gospel. All we can say is that it must have occurred between A.D. 120 and 150, that our four gospels were the only ones to be considered, and that its success within the Roman Empire was complete, in spite of isolated protests. Outside the Roman Empire, Tatian managed to impose his *Diatessaron* upon Syria; the question must arise whether he succeeded in imposing it upon Antioch first, for Syria received its institutions from Antioch. The geographical distribution of the Encratites, a heretical sect which regarded Tatian as their patriarch, suggests that his influence may have radiated from Antioch; and Theophilus Bishop of Antioch (about A.D. 180?) is said by Jerome to have written a commentary on the gospels in a harmonized version. But Antioch is in historical darkness about this period.

The tiny fragment of Tatian's *Diatessaron* discovered at Dura-Europos was part of a parchment roll, showing that this form of book was still used in these parts for the book containing the liturgical gospels. The Chester-Beatty papyrus, discovered in Egypt, belongs to the same period, the first half of the third century, is in codex form, and contains the four gospels and Acts; this codex has no chapter-divisions or enumerations and may not, therefore, have been intended for church use.

Working backwards we learn from the Muratorian Fragment that the four gospels and Acts were still five separate books in the ecclesiastical order of the Roman Church in the period A.D. 175–200. We should picture them as rolls of papyrus (or parchments), each one with a tag bearing some sort of title attached to the 'frons' or top edge of the beginning of the roll; such gospel-books, bearing such titles on the 'frons', are alluded to by Tertullian in *Adv. Marc.* III, 2. The codex form for a single gospel is proved, of course, for the first half of the second century by the existence of the fragment of St John preserved in the John Rylands Library; but this form of book-production may not have spread beyond Egypt, or have been extended to church books even there. Vaticanus in the fourth century is thought to have been copied from rolls.

We may now turn to Irenaeus who is an excellent witness for the same period. In the third book of his work against heresies, and in the first chapter, he gives a short historical account of the four gospels in the order Matthew, Mark, Luke, John, which he regards as the historical order, since Matthew brought out his gospel in written form in the 'Hebrew tongue' when Peter and Paul were evangelizing in Rome, and founding the church. The same order is found in the Muratorian Fragment; for there is no serious doubt that the missing first paragraphs dealt with Matthew and Mark in that order.

In chapter x Irenaeus begins a study of the character of each gospel as deduced from its 'beginning', summarizing the first lection or lections in each case as far as the appearance of John the Baptist, which is the 'beginning' in Mark. These beginnings give the *prosōpon*, face or aspect of the gospel, and indicate its *morphē* or form; the order is still Matthew, Mark, Luke, John. In connexion with this argument, which was drawn from current controversy and has left its marks on the Muratorian document also, he quotes a piece of traditional mysticism which assigns to each gospel as an interpretative symbol one of the four 'beasts', or rather living things (*hayyoth*), of the Revelation; the face (*prosōpon*) of the man is assigned to Matthew, the eagle to Mark, the calf or bull to Luke, and the lion to John.

A good deal of fun has been poked at this piece of mysticism by modern writers; but it may be worth the effort required to investigate its origin and meaning. Irenaeus, or rather his source, knew perfectly well that the four *hayyoth* of Hebrew liturgical symbolism were connected with the four quarters of the earth and the four principal winds or points of the compass; they thus suggested the whole cosmos, so that a fourfold gospel meant a universal gospel for the whole world. Fr. Boll in his commentary on the Revelation has shown that they have an astronomical origin, representing the four corner-points of the zodiac; the bull is the sign of the spring equinox, the lion of the summer solstice, the eagle of the autumn equinox, and the man of the winter solstice. The bull is the constellation Taurus, the lion is Leo, the eagle is Aquila (substituted for the nearby Scorpio because the scorpion is the sign of death), and the man is Aquarius, the water-carrier, the only constellation of the zodiac to be represented by the drawing of a man. These are the four *tekuphoth* or turning-points of the Hebrew year, which were represented in mosaic on the synagogue floor as simple winged figures without any distinction, at the four corners of the zodiac-figure; and if used thus for calendrical purposes in the synagogue, why not in the ecclesia?

The four zodiac figures may therefore have denoted the seasons of the year to which the four gospels were allotted in the new four-gospel lectionary which succeeded the original one-gospel lectionary. This hypothesis gives excellent results. The figure of the man (Aquarius) belongs to the winter solstice, about 25 December, and we have already seen reason to allot the reading of the Nativity stories of Matthew to that season. The figure of the bull or calf (Taurus) belongs to the spring equinox, and this would bring the reading of the Annunciation which is the 'beginning' of Luke to about 25 March, where, as we have seen, Hippolytus placed it, regarding it at the same time as the New Year. The figure of the lion (Leo) belongs to the summer solstice, and would indicate that John began to be read then. The figure of the eagle (Aquila) belongs to the autumn equinox, where as we have seen Mark began to be read in the original Roman order, if our theory is correct. It is possible, therefore, that these zodiacal signs were inscribed on the tag which was attached as a title to the 'frons' or beginning of the gospel, and indicated the season of the year when it began to be read.

This gives us, however, a different order for the four gospels, Matthew, Luke, John, Mark. I have not been able to find any list of the gospels in which this order was adopted, but Clement of Alexandria gives the order Matthew, Luke, Mark, John, and this would be the zodiacal order if we allotted the lion to Mark and the eagle to John, which is actually traditional in the West; for the allotment made by Irenaeus is not heard of again.

The theory that the four zodiacal signs allotted to the gospels indicated the points in the year at which they began to be read lacks documentary proof, but suggests a reason why the signs were allotted to the gospels at all. It brings the mysticism of the source of Irenaeus down from the level of sheer fancy to the level of actual liturgical procedure; and the calendrical order which it establishes, especially in the cases of Matthew and Luke, seems to be due to something more than mere coincidence.

We may add here another possible reference to the Calendar in the Muratorian Fragment. After dealing with four gospels, one book of Acts, a number of epistles, and two apocalypses, it comes to the *Pastor* of Hermas, which it commends for private reading only. It could not be read in church, it states, either among the prophets (that is to say the Old Testament?) because their number is complete, or among the apostles (that is to say the New Testament books which he has been enumerating) *in fine temporum*, 'at the end of the seasons'; that is to say they cannot be squeezed in at the end of the liturgical year.

Before leaving this topic, however, a few remarks may be offered on the arrangement of the gospels in the Calendar of the Greek Church. No doubt the transition to the four-gospel canon created the utmost confusion and variety, as can be seen from the mixture of gospels used in the Roman and Anglican churches; but the Greek Church managed to introduce a fairly orderly system.

The year begins with Easter, and John is read from Easter to Pentecost, a usage which has left its traces in the Roman and Anglican system also. Matthew is then read until the autumn equinox, after which the change is made to Luke, which is read until the Sunday before Septuagesima.

How about Mark? We have already seen that selections from Mark are read on the Saturdays and Sundays of Lent, and there is a Marcan lection on Easter Day; the remainder of Mark is divided into 55 short lections and read on week-days only (Monday to Friday) during the five weeks preceding the autumn equinox and the six weeks preceding the Sunday before Septuagesima. So far as Sundays are concerned, therefore, the Greek order is Matthew, Luke, Mark, John; but so far as week-days are concerned, Mark is given a subordinate position in the Matthaean and Lucan periods respectively. It would hardly be wise to conclude that this betrays a consciousness that it was once set for reading throughout the year.

But the Greek Calendar does betray consciousness of an old connexion of Mark with the period of Lent and Easter, which comes into conflict with an association of John with the same period. The Johannine connexion may well have been from Christmas-Epiphany to Easter, or even to Pentecost; perhaps there was a stage when Mark filled the period from Epiphany to Holy Week, 'from the Baptism to the Passion'.

At any rate we have Marcan gospels set for Lent, and we have seen that some of these Lenten gospels had some special position in the church order when *B* was written; for special attention is drawn to them by the projection into the margin of their first line. Lent everywhere was the set time for the preparation of candidates for baptism, Easter being the baptismal occasion. According to the *Gelasian Sacramentary*, the 'scrutinies' or examination of candidates began in the third week in Lent; the masses for the last three Sundays were called *pro scrutinio*, though unfortunately we are not informed what gospels were set for them; but we are told of 'exorcisms' which took place in the course of the scrutinies, the most striking of which was the *Effeta* ceremony, based on the Epphathah gospel. In the *Gelasian Sacramentary*, this takes place on Easter Eve; but one authority places it in the third scrutiny (of which there came to be seven).

Now the Epphathah gospel in the Greek Calendar is found on the fourth Sabbath, which comes, of course, at the end of the third week, so that we seem to have here a point of contact between the Greek and Roman systems. To appreciate this fully, we should recollect that the Epphathah story is an obscure story from the gospel which came to be the most neglected; it was not thought worth while preserving by Matthew or Luke; its prominence at the same point in the Greek and Roman liturgical systems is more easily explained by liturgical association, going back to the time when Mark was a dominant gospel, than by the long arm of coincidence.

The Greek Lenten gospels, comprising early lections from Mark, the Epphathah, and the three Passion announcements, reproduce a pattern which is also indicated by the 'script-divisions' and near-script-divisions of *B*; it is the same pattern which we found for ourselves in Mark by literary analysis. In that literary analysis, we decided that the Galilean preaching and teaching ended with x. 45; and so does the Lenten sequence of Marcan lections. The Passion follows immediately, as we thought it should.

With regard to the Sundays between Pentecost and the autumn equinox, the following table may be useful for reference:

SUNDAYS AFTER PENTECOST:

	GREEK	NESTORIAN	ARMENIAN
First	Of All Saints	Of the Apostles, I	After the Descent, I
Seventh	—	Of the Summer, I	Of the Transfiguration, I
Thirteenth	—	Of the Assumption, I	—
Fourteenth	—	—	Of Elijah, I
Sixteenth	Before Holy Cross	—	Before Holy Cross
Twenty-first	—	—	Of Moses, I

11. THE DEVELOPMENT OF THE CHRISTIAN CALENDAR

Enough has now been written to show that what began as a study in the making of a gospel has become a study in the origins of the Christian Calendar. This Calendar is, of course, a compromise between two calendars, the old oriental calendar in its Jewish form, and the more modern calendar of Julius Caesar, based on Alexandrian astronomy.

The old oriental calendar is the one followed in the oldest arrangement of Mark which we find preserved in Codex B. The first 48 (49) lections provide gospels for the agricultural and ritual year, beginning at the autumn solstice; the next fourteen lections were composed as a single continuous lection (though subsidiary lections have been added to it) for the special solemnity of the Pascha. This scheme is still reflected in the Western form of the Christian Year; the series of short gospels is read on successive Sundays beginning on Advent Sunday; the long Passion lection is read as a whole in Holy Week.

The Christian Year no longer opens at the autumn solstice; the first Sunday has drifted five or six weeks later owing to the influence of the festival of Christmas, and the Advent season is regarded as preparatory to that festival; but the gospels and other lections for Advent tell a different story. The gospels in the Anglican Prayer Book are as follows:

Advent 1. The Entry into Jerusalem, from Matthew.
Advent 2. The Discourse on the Mount of Olives, from Luke.
Advent 3. The Messengers of John the Baptist, from Matthew.
Advent 4. The Witness of John the Baptist, from the Fourth Gospel.

Though excerpts from the other three gospels have been substituted in the course of time, we can see our Marcan system underlying them; we have the episodes connected with the Feast of Tabernacles with which the old Marcan year ends, and the preaching and baptism of John with which the New Year begins. These gospels can be traced back to the old lectionary called the

Comes which is assigned to about the seventh century. The Roman Missal has a different arrangement, but it would seem to be connected with the same line of thought; the gospel for the Sunday before Advent is part of the Discourse on the Mount of Olives, from Matthew; and the gospel for Advent Sunday is the same lection in its Lucan form.

In the secondary arrangement of Mark which is found in the non-*B* manuscripts, the Roman Year was followed. This arrangement would be the most natural way of explaining the origin of 6 January (Epiphany) as a festival of the Baptism of Jesus. If Matthew was substituted for Mark as a liturgical gospel, the same arrangement would explain the observance of 25 December as a festival of the Nativity. These festivals are fixed firm because they are based upon the solar year; the older festivals of Easter and Whitsun fluctuate to and fro in relation to them because they depend on the phases of the moon. Neither Calendar has won a complete victory.

The change meant that the Feast of Tabernacles was abandoned as a major feature of the liturgical year, leaving only vestigial traces in the autumnal Ember Days and the Advent season; in the Eastern Church this ancient occasion for the New Year is still an important point in the Calendar, and is marked by the festival of the Elevation of the Cross.

It is not suggested that the whole system existed in the second century; far from it. At the end of the second century, as Clement of Alexandria tells us, the observance of Epiphany was a peculiarity of the Basilidians; the observance of Easter, we learn from Tertullian, was universal among Christians. The observance of Easter naturally carried with it the seven weeks or fifty days of Pentecost; but Pentecost was not a festival in its own right yet; it was merely the fifty days of Easter. These days are mentioned in the pseudonymous *Epistula Apostolorum* which is said to have been written about A.D. 160.

Only in one quarter do we find a suggestion of a year containing three festivals. Tertullian in his *De Xerophagia* tells us that the prophets of the Montanist movement had ordered two fasting periods additional to that of Easter. Jerome (in *Ep.* LIV, *ad*

Marcellam) says that they kept three Lents of fourteen days each; one of which was connected with Easter and one with Pentecost. The New Testament writings which the Montanists preferred to all others were the Fourth Gospel and the Revelation; their place of origin was in the high mountains inland from Ephesus in Asia Minor. Their customs may be old.

Our third system is that which began in the spring, which we found first in Tatian, then in Valentinus, then (we think) in the order of the fourfold canon, and then in Hippolytus and other writers. It is a more confident arrangement of the solar year which meets us here; for we find the quarter-days in their Western form; 25 March, a conventional date for the spring equinox, and a high day in the rites of Attis, was fixed for the Annunciation and Passion; 25 December, a conventional date for the winter solstice, and a high day in the Saturnalia, was fixed for the Nativity of Christ. It is natural to ask what happened to the two other quarter-days, and when we examine the Church Calendar, we find that 24 June (virtually midsummer) is the Nativity of St John the Baptist, and 29 September (near the autumn equinox) is Michaelmas. The latter can have no connexion with our studies in the gospel, but the former has a close connexion; the calculations which lead to the idea of 25 March as the Annunciation, and 25 December as the Nativity, depend upon the chronology of Luke i–ii, and would inevitably assign the nativity of the Baptist to midsummer. No one could fail to observe this synchronization: but how soon the day was put into the Calendar we do not know.

Was there a midsummer festival at the end of June? At this time the pagans kept the festival of the lamentation for the sun-god or vegetation-god, called Adonis among the Greeks and Romans, and Tammuz in Syria and Israel; in fact Tammuz is the Semitic name for the hot month of July–August. The Jews could not prevent their young men and maidens from joining in its festivities; so they veiled it with a fast, two fasts in fact, one in Tammuz, and one in Ab; but the veil was a very thin one; Rabbi Simeon ben Gamaliel who perished in the destruction of the Temple in A.D. 70 said there was nothing to be compared with the joy of the fasts of the fifth and seventh months (Ab and Tisri) when the maidens danced in white dresses in the vineyards, and so forth.

Did the Christian Church use this midsummer festival which Gentiles rejoiced in, and Jews could not ignore? According to our liturgical theory the high point of the Galilean part of the Marcan gospel, the great wonder of the Transfiguration, falls at this season, both in the 62-lection system and in the 48 (49)-lection system. Has this vision of the Son of Man in his glory some connexion with the festival of the sun in his strength? Or has the lamentation for John the Baptist, the dead shepherd, some strange connexion with the weeping for Tammuz? As far as the second century is concerned we can do no more than ask the question; but if there was a Transfiguration Festival at midsummer, and if it had commemorations of John the Baptist, and Peter, and Elijah, it would go far to explain some phenomena of the calendars both Eastern and Western. We have the 'weeks' of Elijah and of the Transfiguration in the East; we have the Feast of John the Baptist on 24 June and the Feast of St Peter and St Paul on 29 June in the West.

I do not think we can do more than ask the question, because there is no agreement in the early calendars with regard to the Nativity or the Decapitation of the Baptist. The word Nativity itself of course is an ambivalent word which could mean martyrdom as the birthday into heaven. With regard to St Peter and St Paul, the date 29 June can be traced back to the year 258 when, according to an entry in the *Filocalian Calendar*, the bodies of St Peter and St Paul were 'deposed', the one at the Catacombs and the other at the Ostian Way; hence, we are told, the observation of that day as their festival. But can we be sure that this argument does not place the cart before the horse? Why did the Bishop of Rome choose the midsummer solstice for this solemn act? Was there already a tradition which connected the martyr-apostles with the midsummer season? And could this, possibly, be connected with the known fact that the great fire of Rome in the year A.D. 64 occurred in the month of July, and was followed by the enormous multitude of martyrdoms in the gardens of the Vatican, among which both Peter's and Paul's have sometimes been reckoned?

One is rather haunted by the thought of a midwinter and midsummer festival with a grouping of important commemorations round each. Rome quite definitely had its midwinter festival of the Nativity; but the East gives us the best evidence with regard to the attendant saints. A Syrian calendar of the early fifth century gives us

26 December   Stephen.
27 December   John and James in Jerusalem.
28 December   Paul and Peter in Rome.

Other calendars show that these winter commemorations were widespread by this date even in the West, though they were reduced in time to St Stephen, St John, and the Holy Innocents; Rome had already found a place in her calendar for Peter and Paul.

Our first thought is that these names were deliberately appended to Christmas Day; but this will not do. The old Syrian Church knew nothing of Christmas Day. They appear even now in the calendar of the Armenian Church which has not admitted Christmas Day. Their position must be due simply to some connexion with the winter solstice.

I think we can work back this way. The original list may not have been so long; it may have consisted simply of Stephen and James. I suggest this because these are the only names mentioned in the *Apostolic Constitutions* in connexion with the martyrs and the observation of their days; and the *Apostolic Constitutions* is one of our best authorities on the Eastern form of the calendar at the end of the fourth century. These two saints were Jerusalem martyrs, and if their names did indeed form the original nucleus of the Syrian list, we may hazard the guess that what we have here is a continuation in the Jerusalem church of the old Jewish Festival of Hanukkah (Dedication) which took place on the 'twenty-fifth day of the ninth month', and provided the occasion on which those who gave their lives in the Maccabean wars were solemnly remembered.

It is true that the twenty-fifth day of the ninth Jewish month

(Kislev) is, strictly speaking, too early for the winter solstice; but we have the undeniable fact that the *Apostolic Constitutions* makes the identification. After dealing with the martyrs, it proceeds to consider the Calendar, and begins with Christmas Day, which it calls the twenty-fifth day of the ninth month, regardless of the very real difficulties raised by Mr Rankin in *The Labyrinth*. We see, therefore, that when the Christmas feast was adopted in Syria, it actually was identified with the first day of the feast of Hanukkah, and therefore nothing prevents us from thinking that this feast, too, could be identified with the winter solstice, so that a commemoration of Christian martyrs at the winter solstice could well have been the continuation of a commemoration of Jewish martyrs, in the Syrian tradition for which the *Apostolic Constitutions* speaks; and this could have happened before the adoption of Christmas Day as a festival of the winter solstice.

We thus see a consciousness in the early church tradition that the two solstices were points of importance in the Calendar Year. The Roman Christmas and the Greek Epiphany are both festivals of the mid-winter New Year; the remembrance of the martyrs may have originated independently of Christmas in the East where 25 December was not originally observed as Christmas. By A.D. 258 Rome had its remembrance of Peter and Paul in midsummer; the remembrance of John the Baptist, though it follows logically from the calculations of Hippolytus, is not referred to before St Augustine. As for the Transfiguration we find it on 6 August, but there is no very early authority for this. On the other hand the Armenian Calendar, which resisted many innovations, has a series of seven Sundays named after the Transfiguration, the first of which is the seventh after Pentecost.

12. THE GALILEAN GOSPEL

We now return to the 60's of the first century when the faith made its first public impact on the life of the Roman Empire, and the young Church was being organized in the Imperial City, and the Gospel of St Mark was composed. It will be convenient now to give an analysis of this gospel, showing the Galilean

Calendar which provides its structure and shape. This analysis depends upon a chapter-and-verse study which can only be explained by means of a commentary on the text. It will be seen, however, that it reveals seven sequences of seven lections each; not with complete exactitude because the edges of these 'pentecosts' are sometimes hard to define. The eighth lection, for instance, forms an 'octave' to the first sequence of seven; and the twenty-second is even more clearly a postscript to the first twenty-one, closing a half-year. Lections 23 and 24 look as if they had been put there to cover the first fortnight of Nisan, and the original sequences of seven may have been 25–31 and 32–8.

It is hard to separate Lections 36 and 37, and yet the whole book in the Marcan arrangement divides mathematically and logically into halves at this point.

Lections 37–42 is much too crowded, and so is 43–8. I do not doubt that each of these consists of an original sequence of fourteen lections which has been reduced to seven in the chapter–enumeration of B. This was done, we suggest, when the Feast of Tabernacles ceased to be kept in the Christian Church, and the fourteen special lections for Tabernacles were incorporated with the liturgical year. We cling rather obstinately to our first conclusion that the Galilean liturgical year ended at x. 45.

The reduction of a sequence of fourteen into a sequence of seven seems to have been a natural way of condensing material into a smaller compass. We note that the first fourteen lections of the B system are reduced to seven in the non-B system, and so are the fourteen lections of the Passion narrative; and this is what effects the reduction of the 62-lection system to a 48 (49)-lection system. On the other hand the non-B system does not accept all the reductions made by B in Lections 43–8; and the many variations show that the non-B system was not made out of the B system exactly as we have it in B.

We now give the analysis of Mark suggested by the chapter-enumeration of B.

THE GALILEAN CALENDAR

(arranged in 'weeks' or 'pentecosts', i.e. sequences of seven lections)

Lection nos.

1–7 (8)   *Autumn.* The Lectionary begins on the last day of Tabernacles.
    (*a*) John the Baptist, etc.
    (*b*) Beginnings in Galilee.

8–14   Non-liturgical: Controversies with Scribes.

15–22   *Springtime. The First Mountain.*
    (*a*) The Seed Parables.
    (*b*) Works of Power.

23–9   *The Second Mountain: Pascha:* Nisan 14 and following.
    (*a*) The Five Thousand.
    (*b*) Jesus as Law-giver.

30–35 (36)   The Syrophenician. *Pascha Repeated: i.e. Pentecost.*
    (*a*) The Four Thousand.
    (*b*) The Confession of Peter.

(36) 37–42   *Midsummer. The Third Mountain.*
    (*a*) The Transfiguration.
    (*b*) The Three Passion Announcements and pendent
        teachings.
(Originally the fourteen lections closing the Galilean Calendar (?)
but reduced to seven so as to make room for the inclusion of
43–48 (49).)

43–48 (49)   *Autumn. In Jerusalem: Tabernacles.*
    (*a*) Bartimaeus, Triumphal Entry, etc.
    (*b*) Teaching in the Temple.
    (*c*) The Little Apocalypse.
(Originally fourteen special lections for Tabernacles (?) but
reduced to seven when included with the Liturgical Year in the
B system.)

49–62   *THE PASSION NARRATIVE.* Fourteen special lections for
the Pascha. They are still separate in the B system, but were
incorporated with the Liturgical Year in the non-B system.
(Original nucleus 51–61 (?) forming a single lection?)

This analysis, based on the underlying liturgical pattern, dis-
regards the fact that the gospel as a whole divides between
Lections 36 and 37 into two halves, one of which begins with the

Baptism and the other with the Transfiguration, a study of which is included in the Special Introduction to Lection 37 which will be found at that place in the text. This division at ix. 1 made it possible to arrange the whole gospel for a twelve-month lectionary, and the inference might well be that it was done deliberately for this purpose. If so, it would suit the Roman Year which began in January, which is what we find in the non-B system.

We may suspect here a conflict in the Roman ecclesia in the 60's between the Roman Year and the old Hebrew-Syrian Year which began in the autumn. The Julian Calendar had been in operation for a hundred years, and regulated all the public holidays in Rome with scientific exactness. The Jewish synagogue was tied to an old-fashioned lunar year which was not only variable, but even doubtful; nevertheless the Jews stuck to it, and continued to fix their festivals by looking out for actual new moons, as farmers still do when they plant crops or sow seed or kill hogs. Few members of the synagogue can have been sufficiently independent to follow this Calendar in its entirety with absolute freedom. Slaves, clients, and employees were not masters of their own time; such persons in the great Roman houses would be in difficulties. We know from Latin writers that the Jewish Sabbath had forced itself on their notice, no doubt as a nuisance. On the other hand the great heathen festivals were a time of liberty or even licence for all. At the Saturnalia in December or the Attis festival in March, nobody would inquire too closely how their Jewish or Phrygian or Syrian dependents spent their time, or what gods they cultivated. It would be odd indeed if Jews or Christians did not take advantage of these seasons to resort to their own synagogue or ecclesia.

Experience shows that minority groups cannot entirely resist the impact of the festal system of the majority. There has to be some adjustment or compensation to relieve tension. If the authorities at Jerusalem had been obliged to make concessions in Palestine in regard to the midsummer festivals of Ab and Tammuz, and perhaps in other cases too, it would not be unnatural to find the same sort of thing occurring in Rome. Indeed the conflict between the two Calendars must have been a difficult question in the Jewish synagogue before the arrival of the gospel. There would be a twofold problem; how to observe the old Hebrew fasts and festivals in an alien society, and how to preserve young people from the attraction of the pagan festivals. Many passages in the Epistles show how strong the attraction of the pagan festal worship was; Christian converts easily relapsed into it with its drunkenness and licence and 'jesting and foolish talking which is not convenient'. It might be a wise expedient, therefore, to provide some counter-attraction on these exciting occasions.

Such, we need not doubt, was the background of social and religious conflict into which the gospel with its Palestinian or Galilean Calendar was introduced. We have no special information about the Calendar in Galilee, except that Pascha and Pentecost would come too early for the actual harvests in the Galilean hills. It is not conceivable that harvests would be got in without the celebration of the old rites and the presentation of firstfruits, quite possibly at the local sanctuary. If Jesus took advantage of the city festivals in Jerusalem with their crowds of pilgrims, it is natural to suppose that he would do the same at the rural festivals of Galilee at their high places. Indeed the implication of the gospel is that he identified himself with popular social life and popular feasts or suppers, rather than with the system of the Scribes.

Apart from the Preaching of John, the Baptism of Jesus, and the Temptation by Satan, which may be distinguished from the context in which Mark has placed them, the first part of Mark is a Galilean document, whether oral or written. Its background is that of local pride, local colour, local place-names, and of little journeys by road or by boat. At most it goes no further afield than Tyre or Sidon; and Tyre was nearer than Jerusalem, and may have been economically more important; the agricultural produce of northern Palestine found its market there (Acts xii. 20) and it may have been the port by which the salt fish of Galilee found its way to Rome, though of course Galilee had its own port at Ptolemais.

The attempts which have been made to discredit the accuracy of the local colour are far from impressive. The apparent confusion in some cases is due partly to our own ignorance of local names, and partly to the inevitable blurring of this kind of detail in the course of transmission. On my last Labrador journey, I read Mark carefully along with its synoptic companions; I travelled some three or four hundred miles in little fishing boats, and I reflected that a simple straightforward account of my own voyage in the language of the fishermen would not be understood in the great cities, and could with difficulty be reconciled with the maps and charts; place-names and ways of speech were highly idiomatic.

I Mark is a collection of Galilean material, and was doubtless composed for local consumption; but even in its earliest stages it had some connexion with the Passion Narrative. Even if we count the three Passion announcements with their pendent teachings as a different source, we can still only regard it as a preparation or approach to the Passion narrative. The Passion Narrative could circulate and stand alone without the Galilean narrative, but the Galilean narrative would mean nothing without the Passion Narrative, or at any rate without a Passion Narrative.

The Passion narrative in Mark has been united with the Galilean material by a great number of repetitions, connexions, and correspondences, the key to which is the Table of Major Triads which we give before the text. It has even been Galileanized in an extraordinary manner. The Crucifixion takes place in Jerusalem, but the gospel breaks off without recording the Resurrection appearances which took place there. Indeed, it does not narrate any Resurrection appearances at all. It foretells and announces them six separate times, constituting two major triads, but the words of the final announcements are mystical in character and are not now fully understood. They undoubtedly look forward to appearances in Galilee. Appearances in Jerusalem are not denied; they are ignored.

The easiest explanation, indeed the only explanation I know, is that it was a local gospel for use in Galilee. It is concerned with local happenings. It does not feel an interest in Jerusalem appearances. It opens with the picture of Jesus proclaiming in Galilee the gospel which is to go out to all the nations; it closes (by inference) with the same picture, only glorified by the splendour of the Resurrection. In this gospel Jerusalem only exists to crucify Jesus; it has no other function.

This is very different, of course, from the picture which Luke gives us. He seems to have obtained his information in Jerusalem and its neighbourhood, and represents the Jerusalem church as the mother-church, from which the apostles go out as witnesses to Judaea, Samaria, and the uttermost parts of the earth (Acts i. 8). He gives little space to Galilee and omits the journey to Tyre and Sidon; Mark on the other hand has nothing to say about Samaria, which seems to have been under the jurisdiction of Jerusalem.

All this is very natural if the material with which we are dealing is in each case local history; and we are deeply indebted to E. Lohmeyer for making this most practical and illuminating suggestion. The Galilean document is not a life of Jesus or even an account of his teachings; it is an account of the origins of the Christianity of Galilee and the 'beginning' in Galilee of the gospel which subsequently expanded throughout the world.[1]

As we think of this we find that a number of other curious points in Mark are clarified. It has what must candidly be described as an anti-Jerusalem tone. It stresses the fact that Peter and the Twelve, who were Galileans with one notorious exception, even if they were slow to 'see' and 'hear' and 'understand', were the ones who actually received the mysteries of the kingdom of God. If you want to understand the gospel that is, you must go to the Twelve, or better still to the Three, or best of all to Peter—a Galilean point of view which became in time a Roman point of view. The brothers of Jesus, on the other hand, were without understanding; they were among those who 'stood outside'; and to those who were outside, we are told, everything came in riddles. Now when this Galilean gospel was coming into existence, James, the brother of the Lord, was the bishop of the Jerusalem church, and these words might almost be taken as a direct reflexion on the leadership of that church. James may indeed have had a Resurrection appearance, and been received into the fold at that late date, but so far as the Galilean period was

---

[1] From this point of view the local stories of Mark may be compared with the local stories of Acts.

concerned, he stood outside. This may be one reason why Mark had no use for Jerusalem Resurrection appearances.

It may be asked in this case what view would be taken of the apostolate of Paul; but, as E. Lohmeyer has pointed out, the conversion of Paul took place in Galilee or after passing through Galilee.

Returning again to Mark, we notice that the Judaean origin of the traitor apostle is pointed out three times; it forms a major triad. He was 'one of the twelve' (another major triad); but he was always to this writer *Ish Kerioth*, the man of Kerioth in Judaea.

Even the Scribes and Pharisees who attack Jesus are not Galileans; in two cases (or three as Luke makes it) it is specified that they came from Jerusalem. Their incursions may not have been popular in Galilee. No sign appears in Mark of the unfaith of Capernaum and Bethsaida and Chorazin, which is so clear in Q; though a close study of Mark strongly suggests that the real success of Jesus was in Decapolis. Furthermore, there is no rejection at Nazareth; the rejection takes place in 'his native town', which ought to mean Bethlehem, a place in Judaea not far from Jerusalem. Even if it does mean Nazareth, no Roman hearer of the gospel could tell this; the place is left unnamed, whereas other Galilean localities are named freely.

The idea of a friendly, successful, idyllic ministry in Galilee which many people have must be due entirely to the local pride of the Galilean source which was used in the Marcan gospel. This local pride would not be peculiar to Christian Galileans but to all Galileans. It would be the natural reply to the contempt felt by the city-dwellers in Jerusalem for the rural and fishing people of the north. This feeling would explain the hostile use of the word 'Jews' by John; it meant Judaeans, inhabitants of the southern province. This use of the word explains perhaps the statement of Mark vii. 3 that certain rites of purification were practised by the Pharisees 'and all the Jews'; that is to say, all the Judaeans; but by no means all the Galileans.

The material, therefore, took form in Galilee round a Peter tradition, a tradition which is emphasized even more strongly in Matthew.

If we are at all correct in this analysis of Mark we can see that in its original form it performed a useful function in a Galilean, or possibly south Syrian situation, by indicating what was regarded there as the central and legitimate evangelical authority, and what authority was less central, however good so far as it went. It had the hard practical function of providing credentials for the authority of Peter and the Twelve, and not in the same degree for James and the brethren of the Lord in Jerusalem; so that Peter and the Twelve, or some of them, must actually have been exercising an evangelical and apostolic ministry at some available point; for what use would the Galilean document be to the Galileans in this respect, unless they could add the words, 'And this tradition is ours to-day'?

The contemporary character of this trend in Mark is shown by the fact that it is not laboured. In fact it is not on the surface at all. There is no attempt to glorify Peter; far from it. The centrality of the Petrine tradition is never argued; it is assumed and allowed to speak for itself. In Matthew, which was written a generation later, the opposite is the case; the leading position occupied by Peter is deliberately emphasized.

We have been assuming, on the basis of the indications which we find in Mark and Matthew, that Peter ministered in the Galilean churches after the Passion of Jesus. Strange to say there is no direct evidence of this. According to the evidence of Acts, Peter and his fellow-Galileans settled in Jerusalem and presided over the organization of the church there. We need not assume from the silence of Acts that they never visited Galilee; this would be incredible. Nor is there the least reason to suppose that Peter and the Twelve remained stationary in Jerusalem simply because the author of Acts does not record their travels. He does record one visit to Samaria, perhaps because he had a special interest in the conflict with Simon Magus; he then relates the episode of the Ethiopian eunuch and the conversion of Saul, and after this he goes on to say, 'So the church throughout all Judaea and Galilee and Samaria had peace'; and this is all we learn about Galilee in Acts, for Luke apparently had little contact with Galilee or the Galilean tradition. He adds, however, 'As Peter went throughout all parts'; and 'all parts' must include the land of Galilee mentioned in the previous verse, so that the author of Acts thinks of Peter as travelling round Palestine, including Galilee, at this time; and there is no reason why he should not have done this from the beginning, making Jerusalem his headquarters. At any rate he did it now.

It was in the course of this journey, we are told in Acts, that Peter came to the conclusion, as the result of a dream, that there was no divine authority for the distinction made in the Jewish Law between clean and unclean foods. He also made history by consenting to the baptism of a Gentile of the name of Cornelius, and for this he was called in question by the stricter Jewish Christians at Jerusalem, described as the circumcision party.

In the year 44, more than twelve years after the Passion of our Lord, Herod Agrippa launched a persecution against the church in Jerusalem. Among the victims were two of the Galilean apostles: James the son of Zebedee was killed; Peter was imprisoned. As a result of this action, Peter left Jerusalem for 'another place'; the leadership devolved on James the brother of Jesus, who was apparently in less danger. Now who cannot see clearly the implications of these narratives? The stricter Jerusalem Christians of the circumcision party had been critical of Peter for his liberal policy; how much more would the mass of still more narrow-minded non-Christian Jews? The Galilean leadership over the Jerusalem church came to an end; the leadership of James the brother of the Lord began. We see the background against which the attitude of Mark to the family of Jesus becomes intelligible.

Five or six years later, we learn from Galatians that Peter paid a visit to Antioch, and that he entered into full communion with Gentile Christians there, eating and drinking with them, until 'certain came from James' (Gal. ii. 12) who raised points of order about eating Gentile food. Now here we have something which closely resembles an argument described in Mark. It concerns customs in connexion with meals; there is even a parallel between scribes from Jerusalem coming into Galilee with stricter notions of religious observance, and delegates from Jerusalem arriving in

Antioch with stricter notions of religious observance. The point at issue differs, though both controversies concern the question of social or religious meals; matters have moved on a stage. But when we examine the text of Mark we find a curious phenomenon; the story of the controversy between Jesus and the Jerusalem scribes has a note appended to it which indicates that the words of Jesus can be given a wider application; these things he said, Mark adds, 'making all meats clean' (Mark vii. 19). The Marcan lection has thus been adjusted for use in regard to the Antioch controversy, or, shall we say, the point which was raised there. The same lection, or the teaching of Jesus embodied in it, is thought by many scholars to be alluded to by Paul in Romans xiv. 14.

It would therefore be in accordance with the few indications we have, to think of this lection of Mark as coming into shape in the 40's and having some relation to the great Gentile controversy which came to a climax in A.D. 48/49/50. It is not too early. It is only about fifteen years before St Peter met his death by martyrdom in Rome. The Galilean pattern of evangelical teaching, which was transcribed by Mark in his gospel, must have been fixed, in its main outlines at least, by that time.

The historical points which we have been considering are points along a curve which originates in Galilee and ends in Rome. Its origin is a Galilean tradition in which Peter is the central figure; its end is a Roman tradition in which Peter is the central figure. During the fifteen years between the controversy in Antioch and the martyrdom of the apostle in Rome we have no information at all. During these years the curve becomes invisible. It is visible at the beginning through the literary and critical study of the gospel material itself with additional help from other sources; it is visible at the end through a further study of the completed gospel, and through the evidence of the Church tradition, in which the principal authority is the dictum of John the Elder reported by Papias. The character of the gospel can only be understood when this curve of evangelistic activity is visualized as a continuous unity; the gospel is the final record of that evangelistic activity in time-space.

The gospel documents cannot be understood until they are

related to the apostolic mission and to the ecclesia or church which it created. We cannot conceive the gospel documents as loose pieces of literature casually circulated and carried as literature from place to place; still less can we think of oral documents coming into existence sporadically and threading themselves together spontaneously. What we have to think of is an evangelical activity creating an ecclesiastical technique; we have Peter among the Galilean Christians and we have Peter among the Roman Christians; and we have the forms of teaching which he created in response to actual needs, to use the words of John the Elder. They had no interest for anyone at first when separated from that evangelistic and ecclesiastical situation or the persons who originated them; they would be like the libretto of an opera without the music and action and scenery.

It is for this reason that we find the Galilean colours preserved in the Roman gospel; for the agricultural and ritual order which we have found in Mark was not imposed upon the material in Rome. To take the agricultural first; it is at home in a rural society where the ancient rituals were carried on at the turning-points of the year. These references gravitate entirely in the direction of Galilee and not in the direction of urban Rome. It is probable that many points of Galilean folk-religion have become blurred or smoothed over in the course of accommodation to use in the Roman ecclesia, and the same is true of references to the Hebrew scripture and Hebrew religious customs.

Mark shows many signs of being condensed or simplified. Its use of material from the Old Testament tradition has this submerged appearance. The many parallels between this Galilean document and the Old Testament lections for the three great feasts are by no means easy to detect; yet they are there; Moses and the desert, Moses and the manna, Moses and the mountain, Moses and the sea, Moses and the glory of God, Moses and the cloud, not to mention the shining of Moses' face, are examples of this kind of liturgical derivation which is now no longer on the surface. It cannot all be restored. There are points about John the Baptist and Elijah which are by no means clear. Something has been omitted. Was Elijah a local saint in Galilee? Was he connected with mountain-tops, as he is in the tradition of the Greek Church? Why does he appear 'with Moses' at the Transfiguration?

It does not appear that we are dealing with a text to which a liturgical character has been mysteriously added. We are dealing with a text which is liturgical through and through, though superficially the liturgical character may seem to have rather worn off. Yet when the lections are assigned to their correct liturgical setting, their relevance can be seen, and their significance enhanced. The transcript has this liturgical character because the forms of words which were transcribed had a liturgical use; they took form within a liturgical process. It is 'in grain'. The pattern which appears at the end of the curve in the Roman gospel is the pattern which characterized the beginning of the curve in Galilee.

We turn back to Galilee, therefore, for the origin of this pattern. What brought the crowds together on the mountains to meet Jesus? What simpler hypothesis can be proposed than that they were holy convocations at high places? Ancient sanctuaries continued in use, as we learn from the *Tractate Megilloth*. Men and women could not always go to Jerusalem for the three festivals, but they could go to the local sanctuary. They could not sacrifice a lamb at the Pascha, but they could break bread; and many other rituals could be carried out. They could offer their tithes or firstfruits to the village priest. They could hear the Law of Moses read to the congregation. Prophets could deliver their messages. These festivals are still going on in Palestine at the same holy places. It is all part of an immemorial custom rather like the old village fairs in England.

Festivals of this kind afforded an opportunity for a leader in war or politics or religion to get a hearing; and we know from Josephus that they were occasions when popular demonstrations were likely to occur. Jesus made good use of them in his visits to Jerusalem, and so he may have done in Galilee.

Did these convocations continue after the Passion and Resurrection of Jesus? Was it in connexion with such convocations that the substance of the Petrine gospel came into being as a continuation of the ministry of Jesus in the churches which he had himself created? Apart from the Galilean quality of the tradition, there are two points of literary criticism which confirm this suggestion; the gospel-units have the character of a local tale, and are the work of someone who could tell a story effectively; Peter or Levi or John, perhaps, as the old tradition tells us.

Is the suggestion of a continuation of the gospel ministry in Galilee anything more than a conjecture, based simply on the colour and character of the material itself? I believe that if we look once more at the gospel, we shall find a signpost which points the way rather clearly in this direction. If we open it at the first page, we find that the 'beginning of the gospel' (after the baptism which John preached) was Jesus coming into Galilee; if we turn to the last page, we find a message from the tomb which reads as follows:

> But go, tell his disciples and Peter,
> He goeth before you into Galilee:
> There shall ye see him, as he said unto you.

We do not find the word 'end' balancing the word 'beginning'; for an end of the gospel was not yet (though Matthew manages to end his gospel on this word). We find a continuation, and that continuation is in Galilee; and it is committed to Peter and the disciples. Such is the signpost with which the gospel ends. We cannot ignore it.

Can we go further? Perhaps not. But if our liturgical theory is correct, and it has served us very well, we can. The message from the tomb is the climax of the Passion narrative, which was the gospel text for the Paschal solemnity. On the following Sunday was read Lection 25, the Feeding of the Five Thousand; this Sunday was the great day which Christians call Easter Day, and the Jews called the Omer or Firstfruits. The picture it gives is of a mountain in Galilee and of the people scattered like sheep having no shepherd; Jesus is there and has compassion upon them; he teaches them many things; when evening comes, they bring him the five loaves and the two small fishes; he says a blessing; he breaks the bread; and they all eat and are satisfied. If this kind of convocation went on after the Passion (and the collocation of lections suggests strongly that it did), the occasion might seem incomplete without having one or more of the Twelve stand up and rehearse their memories of Jesus in the presence of many who had also heard and seen; and in this way, perhaps, the liturgical gospel was given to the world.

This would be the gift of Galilee to the world, the gift which Jerusalem could not give. Connected as they were with the old festivals, these memories of the disciples would tend to arrange themselves in the order of the Calendar Year; and seeing that the Lord chose to express himself in these surroundings in the terms of the old agricultural and festal mysticism, and seeing, too, that his Galilean ministry may have lasted for something over a twelve-month period of this kind, it may give us a very good idea of that twelve-month or eighteen-month campaign which was the climax of his life on earth. And, if so, we may ourselves enter into the tradition and gain some understanding of it, not merely by literary and critical study along these lines, but by passing through the devotional course of the Christian Year, as it has come down to us in the Church.

APPENDICES TO INTRODUCTION

Appendix 1

THE TRIADIC STRUCTURE OF ST MARK

Attention is now being given by scholars to the conventional forms of the kind of literature of which Mark is an example, and it is hoped that this study of Mark's triads will be a contribution to this kind of research as well as a clue to the thought-connexions in St Mark.

The convention consists in the arrangement of words or phrases in triads (threes) or pentads (fives) or heptads (sevens). It is no more an artificiality than the use of rhyme and measure in modern poetry, or stress and alliteration in Old English poetry; it is simply a different mode of the rhythm and repetition which give music and form to poetic energy. It is not fully understood until its beauty is experienced by the reader through an added appreciation of the mind and purpose of the author.

The text of Mark is full of triads, and these can be divided into two sorts, the minor or simple triad, and the major or complex triad.

The Minor Triad occurs within a single lection or gospel-unit, though the classification may be extended to a triad covering two successive lections, thereby linking them together and indicating a community of thought, such as the phrase 'Is it lawful?' in Lections 13 and 14. The simplest triad, however, is a word three times repeated within a single lection. There are great numbers of them, and it is hard to find a lection without one, an interesting example being Lection 27. As a rule, however, when we find a lection without a triad, or a triad linking two lections, we should ask whether the lections are rightly divided.

A good case, however, of a triad divided between two lections, with telling effect, is that of 'ears' in Lections 31 and 34, and 'eyes' in 34 and 35.

Of course there are numbers of doubtful cases, some of which have been included in the Table for the sake of completeness. One member of a triad may vary in form as in Lection 4 (follow, follow, come after); or it may appear that one member has dropped out; or a fourth member may have come in; or the decision may rest on a point of textual criticism; or the three may be expanded to a five, or even a seven. Nevertheless there is such an abundance of clear and obvious cases that the general principle cannot be questioned.

Triads are also found in Q, and in I Peter, and are especially frequent in the gospel and epistles of John. They add greatly to the beauty and effectiveness of a literature which is intended for recitation. The music of the Fourth Gospel is largely due to the triadic repetition of selected words which have a poetic and mystical effect.

The convention of triads has several practical advantages. It draws attention to the main subject of a passage, and might take the place of a caption or title for the purpose of finding a paragraph in a manuscript, thus facilitating reference. It is an undoubted aid to memorization. It has a considerable range of variety, extending from the triadic narrative, such as the story of Gethsemane, to such exquisite epigrams as

'The Sabbath was made for the Man, not the Man for the Sabbath: So that the Son of Man is Lord also of the Sabbath',

which is built out of two simple triads.

The Major Triad links together different parts of the gospel, and helps to indicate its structure and leading thoughts. All scholars are familiar with the three Announcements of the Passion in Lections 37, 39 and 42; or with the Announcements of the *Parousia* in Lections 37, 49 and 56; a technique also used by the author of Acts, who narrates the conversion of Paul three times. But there are a great number more of these to be discovered. We have already pointed out the Three Mountains of Galilee in Lections 8, 26 and 37; and the three collections of sayings which follow the three Announcements of the Passion. We shall point out a great number more; the title 'beloved son' given to Jesus, the nickname 'Nazarene' or 'Nazarean', the expression 'that day', and so forth.

There are more difficulties in identifying the major than the minor triads; for we often have to distinguish the significant uses of a word from the non-significant. The word 'mountain', for instance, is used more than three times; but not all its uses are significant. In v. 5 and 11 it refers merely to the mountains on which the demoniac yelled and cut himself with stones; in xi. 23 it is the mountain that is moved by faith; in xiii. 14 the elect are warned to 'flee to the mountains'; there is no thought-connexion in these cases; but six are left which we classify as significant. The Mount of Olives is referred to in xi. 1, xiii. 3 and xiv. 26; and our original triad provides us with the high peaks of the liturgical year in Galilee, iii. 13 for the time of sowing, vi. 46 for Passover, and ix. 2 and 9 for Pentecost.

The reader will note that in the case of the last triad mentioned, the word occurs twice in the last instance, making four occurrences; but these four occurrences take place in three significant contexts. There is, however, a margin of inexactness here; the count is not as perfect as we would like.

A similar case is the word 'go before' or 'lead onward', which is used three times with a special significance, x. 32, xiv. 28, and xvi. 7, being connected with the idea of the shepherd, death, and resurrection. It also occurs in vi. 45 and xi. 9 where it has no special significance.

Sometimes we think we find more complex arrangements. The name David, for instance, is first introduced in Lection 13 without any apparent special significance. It occurs for a second time as a minor triad, divided between 31 and 32, where it expresses the popular feeling. It occurs a third time in a minor triad at the end of 39, where Jesus asks a question about its true meaning. The name is thus repeated seven times and yields a major triad consisting of one single occurrence and two minor triads.

Sometimes a complex effect appears within a single lection. In Lection 24, which is the Passion of the Baptist, the words John and Herod occur exactly seven times each; the word king occurs four times and the word John three times; we would like to think that the intention was to use each word three times. When this lection is placed on one side, we find a major triad consisting of 'Herodians', 'Herod', 'Herodians' in iii. 6, viii. 15, and xii. 13.

Sometimes we feel disposed to recognize a major triad where an expression occurs twice in one lection and only once in another, though this is not strictly either a minor or a major triad. A beautiful case is that of the expression 'one on the right hand and the other on the left' which occurs twice towards the end of Lection 42, and once in 59.

The Table of Triads includes some of the dubious or imperfect examples so as to provide a fairly complete list of possible cases. It is probable that a considerable number have not been detected.

A study of these triads will soon convince the student that it is impossible to classify Mark as an 'artless' and simple composition, put together by a person of no literary skill. This judgement, which has sometimes been passed, is due to the fact that the Greek style is rough and colloquial, and the sentences are not always well constructed;

but this is not the same as saying it has no literary merits. The book as a whole is as carefully designed, balanced, and interlaced as the *Divine Comedy* itself, though its scale of course is much smaller; and yet the creation of so intricate a work of art of such enormous spiritual significance on so small a scale is itself no slight achievement. We are bound to regard this author as a master of the peculiar kind of mystical composition which appealed to him and to his auditors, and perhaps to assume that the kind of Greek he used, which is extremely effective for his purpose, was the regular usage in the circles where his material first took shape. The broad, colloquial, everyday idiom forms a remarkable contrast with the system of spiritual thought-connexions which unite the whole composition by almost invisible repetitions; they express a mystical experience of religion which is at home in the simplest everyday life.

Appendix 2

INDEX OF MAJOR TRIADS

INCLUDING DUBIOUS CASES AND A FEW SIGNIFICANT REPETITIONS (MARKED *)

[NOTE. For Minor Triads see notes to the lections]

Lection no.		First occurrence	Second occurrence	Third occurrence	Notes
1, 2, 3, 4a	*Gospel: occurs seven times in Mark	i. 1			Seven occurrences
	? Christ (Messiah)	i. 1	viii. 29	xiv. 61	i. 1 is textually uncertain: there are seven occurrences without it
	? Son of God	i. 1	xiv. 61	xv. 39	
	Announce repentance	i. 4	i. 15	vi. 12	All cases
	Baptism	i. 4	x. 38, 39	xi. 30	All cases: 'baptize' is frequent
	Come after	i. 7	i. 17, 20	viii. 33, 34	All cases
	Holy Spirit (Ghost)	i. 8	iii. 29	xiii. 11	All except xii. 36
	Beloved Son: My	i. 11	ix. 7	xii. 6	All cases
	Satan	i. 13	iii. 23, 26	viii. 33	All but iv. 15
	Preach gospel	i. 14	xiii. 10	xiv. 9	All cases
	Kingdom of God	i. 15	iv. 11, 26, 39	ix. 1	All cases in first half of gospel
4b	Simon—Andrew—James—John	i. 16, 19	i. 29	xiii. 3	All cases
	? Follow	i. 18	ii. 14, 15	viii. 34	All in first half except iii. 7, v. 24, vi. 1
5, 6, 7	New	i. 27	ii. 21, 22	xiv. 25	All cases
	Nazarene (Nazarean)	i. 24	x. 47	xiv. 67	All but xvi. 6 which is textually doubtful
	? (Holy one) of God	i. 24	iii. 11	v. 7	All cases of recognition by demoniacs
8	Pray (prayer)	i. 35	vi. 46	ix. 29	All cases in first half
9	? Son of Man	ii. 10	ii. 27	iii. 28?	All cases previous to Lection 36: restoring text of iii. 28

	Faith	ii. 5	iv. 40	v. 34	All cases in first half
12	That day	ii. 20	xiii. 32	xiv. 25	All cases
13, 14	David	ii. 25	x. 48, 49; xi. 10	xii. 35, 36, 37	All cases: seven occurrences
	Save (give) life	iii. 4	viii. 35, 36, 37	x. 45	All cases
	Hardness of Heart (*pōrōsis*)	iii. 5	vi. 52	viii. 17	All cases: *sklērokardia* in x. 5 a different word
	Herodians (Herod)	iii. 6	viii. 15	xii. 13	All cases except for seven occurrences of 'Herod' in Lection 24
15	Tyre (and Sidon)	iii. 8	vii. 24	vii. 31	All cases
	Mountain	iii. 13	vi. 46	ix. 2, 9	See 'The Triadic Structure', App. I, p. 90
16	Twelve (of the disciples)				occurs seven times, not counting the expression Judas 'one of the twelve' which is a triad
	Judas Iscariot	iii. 19	xiv. 10	xiv. 43	All cases: always with the word 'betray'
	? Parables	iii. 23	iv. 2	iv. 11–34 (seven times)	Also in vii. 17 (and xii. 1, 12, xiii. 28)
17	He who hath ears, etc.	iv. 9	iv. 23	vii. 16	All cases; but the text of vii. 16 is uncertain
18	Not understand	iv. 12	vi. 52	viii. 17, 21	All cases
19	Slept and rose	iv. 27	iv. 38	v. 39–41	All cases
	*Fear (vb.)	iv. 41	v. 15	v. 33, 36	The first four cases: frequent
21	Power	v. 30	vi. 2, 5	vi. 14	All cases in first half
22	Prophet	vi. 4	vi. 15	viii. 28	All cases of this word applied to Jesus
24	Elijah	vi. 15	viii. 28; ix. 4 ff.	xv. 35	All cases
25	*Shepherd and sheep	vi. 34	xiv. 27	—	No third occurrence
	Broke bread, etc.	vi. 41	viii. 6	xiv. 22	All cases
	Satisfied	vi. 42	vii. 27	viii. 8	All cases
26	I am	vi. 50	xiii. 6	xiv. 62	All cases, but compare viii. 28
	Tempt	viii. 11	x. 2	xii. 15	All cases except i. 13
33	This generation	viii. 12	viii. 38	ix. 19	All cases except xiii. 30

Lection no.		First occurrence	Second occurrence	Third occurrence	Notes
36	Passion announced	viii. 31	ix. 31	x. 32	All cases, but see ix. 12
	Deny (*aparneisthai*)	viii. 34	xiv. 30, 31	xiv. 72	All cases
	Cross	viii. 34	xv. 21	xv. 30, 32	All cases
	In glory	viii. 38	x. 37	xiii. 26	All cases
	Parousia announced: with word 'see'	viii. 38–ix. 1	xiii. 26	xiv. 62	All cases
36	In power	ix. 1	xiii. 26	xiv. 62	All cases
37, 38	Cloud	ix. 7	xiii. 26	xiv. 62	All cases
	Resurrection announced	ix. 9	xiv. 28	xvi. 6	All cases
40	*First and last	ix. 35	x. 31	x. 44	All cases: the third occurrence imperfect
	*Servant (slave) of all (James and) John	ix. 35	x. 44	—	No third occurrence
	*Follow: very frequent in these lections	ix. 38	x. 35	x. 41	All cases; James omitted in ix. 38
42	Enter kingdom of God	ix. 47	x. 15	x. 23, 24, 25	All cases
	Lead onward (go before)	x. 32	xiv. 28	xvi. 7	All cases of this usage
	Right and left	x. 37	x. 40	xv. 27	All told
	Drink	x. 38, 39	xiv. 23, 25	xv. 23	All cases
	Cup	x. 38	xiv. 23	xiv. 36	All cases
	*For many	x. 45	xiv. 24	—	No third occurrence
44	Mount of Olives	xi. 1	xiii. 3	xiv. 26	All cases
46	Parable	xii. 1	xii. 12	xiii. 28	All cases in second half
47	Right hand	xii. 36	xiv. 62	xvi. 5	All cases
49	Building	xiii. 2	xiv. 58	xv. 29	All cases
	Destroyed	xiii. 3	xiv. 58	xv. 29	All cases
	That hour	xiii. 11	xiii. 32	xiv. 35, 37, 41	All cases
50	Evening	xiii. 35	xiv. 17	xv. 42	All cases in the Passion
	Cockcrow	xiii. 35	xiv. 30	xiv. 72	All cases
	Dawn	xiii. 35	xv. 1	xvi. 2	All cases in the second half
51	(my) Body	xiv. 8	xiv. 22	xv. 43	All cases in the Passion
52	One of the Twelve	xiv. 10	xiv. 20	xiv. 43	All cases

Betray: occurs seven times of Jesus and Judas in the Passion; it has occurred three times in the discourse on the Mount of Olives, and will occur three times in connexion with the high priests and Pilate.

Lection no.		First occurrence	Second occurrence	Third occurrence	Notes
56	Temple	xiv. 58	xv. 29	xv. 38	All cases

Appendix 3

COMPARATIVE TABLE OF LECTION NUMBERS AND TITLES

Mark (62) B	Matthew (68) non-B		Mark (48) non-B		Tatian (55)
(No titles)	—		—		(No titles)
—	0	No title	—		1, 2
—	1	Magi	—		3
—	2	Murdered children	—		3
1, 2, 3, 4*a*	3	First John preached (Q)	0	No title	3, 4
4*b*, 5	4	Teaching of Christ	0	No title	5
(5) (15)	5	*Beatitudes* (Q)	—		(8, 9, 10)
5		(missing)	1	Demoniac	6
6		(8)	2	Peter's Wife's Mother	6
6, 7		(9)	3	Various Diseases	6
8	6	Leper	4	Leper	22
—	7	Centurion (Q)	—		(11)
(6)	8	Peter's Wife's Mother	(2)		6
(6, 7)	9	Various Diseases	(3)		6
—	10	Not Permitted to Follow (Q)	—		(11)
(19)	11	Rebuke of the Waters	(10)		(11)
(20)	12	Two Demoniacs	(11)		(11)
9	13	Paralytic	5	Paralytic	7
10, 11, 12	14	Matthew	6	Levi the Publican	7 (also in 6)
13		(20)		(cornfields)	7
14		(21)	7	Withered Hand	7
15		(See 5 and 19)	8	(mountain)	8
16		(19)		*Choice of apostles*	8, 9, 10 (*Beatitudes*)
16		(22)		(Beelzebul)	(14)
16		(23)		(mother and brethren)	(16)
17, 18		(24)	9	*Parable of sower*	(16, 17)
19		(11)	10	Rebuke of Waters	11
20		(12)	11	The Legion	11, 12
21	15	Synagogue-ruler	12	Synagogue-ruler	12
21	16	Haemorrhage	13	Haemorrhage	12
22		(24)		(rejection in *patris*)	(17)
—	17	Two Blind men (?)	—		12
—	18	Dumb Demoniac (Q)	—		12
23	19	*Ordering of apostles* (Q)	14	*Ordering of apostles*	12, 13
—	20	Those sent by John (Q)	—		13, 14
(13)		(cornfields)	(6)		(7)
(14)	21	Withered Hand	(7)		(7)
—	22	Dumb Demoniac (Q)	—		14
(16)		(Beelzebul) (Q)	(8)		14
—	23	Demanded a Sign (Q)	—		16
(16)		(mother and brethren)	(8)		16
(17, 18)	24	*Parables* (Q)	(9)		16, 17
(22)		(rejection in *patris*)	(13)		17
24	25	John and Herod	15	John and Herod	18

END OF FIRST HALF OF CALENDAR YEAR ACCORDING TO MARK (62)

Mark (62) B	Matthew (68) non-B		Mark (48) non-B		Tatian (55)
25	26	Five Loaves	16	Five Loaves	18
26, 27	27	Walking on Sea	17	Walking on Sea	19
28, 29	28	Transgression, etc.	18	Transgression, etc.	20
30	29	Chananaean Woman	19	Syrophenician Woman	20
31	30	Crowds Healed	20	Man with Impediment	21 (Tatian 22 is the Leper of Mark 8 and 4)
32, 33	31	Seven Loaves	21	Seven Loaves	23
34	32	Leaven of Pharisees	22	Leaven of Pharisees	23
35		—	23	Blind Man	23
36	33	Question at Caesaraea	24	Question at Caesaraea	23, 24
37	34	Transfiguration	25	Transfiguration	24
37, 38, 39	35	Lunatic	26	Lunatic	24
—	36	Didrachma		—	25
40	37	Who is Greatest?	27	Who is Greatest?	25
—	38	Hundred Sheep		—	26
—	39	Ten Thousand Talents		—	27
41	40	Divorce Wife?	28	Divorce Wife?	25
42	41	Rich Man	29	Rich Man	28, 29, 30
—	42	Hired Labourers		—	29
42	43	Sons of Zebedee	30	Sons of Zebedee	30, 31
43	44	Two Blind Men	31	Bartimaeus	31
44	45	Ass and Colt (temple cleansed)	32	Colt	39 N.B.
				—	32 (followed by Two Lepta Mark 48 and 41)
	46	Blind and Lame		—	40 N.B.
45, 46	47	Withered Fig-Tree	33	Withered Fig-Tree (temple cleansed)	32, 33
46		—	34	Forgivingness	33
46	48	Chief Priests, etc.	35	Chief Priests, etc.	33
—	49	Two Sons		—	33
46	50	Vineyard	36	Vineyard	33
—	51	Wedding		—	30
47	52	The Tribute	37	The Tribute	34
47	53	Sadducees	38	Sadducees	34
47	54	The Lawyer	39	The Scribe	34
47	55	The Lord's Question	40	The Lord's Question	35
47	56	Scribes and Pharisees	40	—	40 N.B.
48		—	41	The Two Lepta	(32)

END OF CALENDAR YEAR ACCORDING TO MARK (62)

49	57	The Consummation	42	The Consummation	41, 42
50	58	The Day and Hour	43	The Day and Hour	42
—	59	Ten Virgins		—	43
—	60	The Talents		—	43
—	61	Coming of Christ		—	43
51	62	Anointed the Lord	44	Anointed the Lord	39 N.B. (following John)

Mark (62) B	Matthew (68) non-B		Mark (48) non-B		Titian (55)
52	63	The Pascha	45	The Pascha	44
53	64	The Mystic Supper	46	The Betrayal	45
53, 54, 55, 56	65	The Betrayal		—	45, 46, 47, 48, 49
56, 57, 58, 59, 60	66	The Denial	47	The Denial	49, 50
—	67	Repentance of Judas		—	51
61, 62	68	Body of the Lord	48	Body of the Lord	52 (53, 54, 55)

END OF PASSION NARRATIVE ACCORDING TO MARK (62)

NOTES. (1) Where the order of the three documents differs the lection number is given in brackets to facilitate references. The exact limits of the Marcan and Matthaean lections can be checked by the numbers in the margin of Nestle's Greek New Testament. The exact limits of the Marcan lections in both systems are clearly shown in the text as printed in this book, with the titles from Alexandrinus. The Matthaean titles are also given where relevant.

(2) The letter (Q) added to certain Matthaean lections in this table gives some indication of the extent to which the Marcan order has been abandoned by Matthew in favour of Q. It has also been disturbed by his special views as to the appropriate position for the Sermon on the Mount (5), the Choice and Ordering of the Apostles (19), and the Parable of the Sower and other parables (24): these are indicated by the use of italic type.

7-2

Appendix 4

THE DIATESSARON OF TATIAN

Seeing that the arrangement of lections in the *Diatessaron* of Tatian is an essential point in the studies which led to the formulation of our theory, a note on this important book becomes necessary. Tatian was a disciple of Justin Martyr, and himself established a school in Rome after his master's martyrdom (A.D. 163–6); he was adjudged to be a heretic and left Rome for Syria about 173. We have allotted the long course of study necessary for the production of his harmony to the fifteen years previous to 173. It was made out of the four gospels and contains almost every verse of them. A Greek fragment of it has been found at Dura-Europos, and was part of a parchment roll which was necessarily written before 265, so that the original may well have been made in Greek. The technical difficulties in the way of composing it in another language would be very great.

The Arabic 'Diatessaron'. A Syriac form of the *Diatessaron* became, before the end of the second century, the only form of the gospels used liturgically in the Syrian church; indeed it may have been for a time the complete New Testament of that church. We know about it from quotations in Ephraem and Aphraates which enabled Th. Zahn to make a reconstruction of it; this reconstruction was shown to be sound in its main outlines by the publication of the Arabic translation, of which two manuscripts exist. The quotations from Ephraem and Aphraates now serve to confirm the trustworthiness of the Arabic *Diatessaron* so far as its contents and order are concerned. Its text has been adjusted to later forms; but this does not affect our researches which only touch the order of sections. It is possible therefore to make an analysis of it from this point of view.

Its Liturgical Structure. It is divided into 55 sections, a number which is reminiscent of the 54 sections into which the Law of Moses is divided for the one-year system of reading in the synagogue service. It divides in half between 27 and 28. Section 28 begins with John vii. 2, 'At that time the Jews' Feast of Tabernacles was at hand'; Section 35 begins with John vii. 37, 'Now on the great day, the last day of the Festival'; this is the famous eighth day of the Feast of Tabernacles, and Section 35 is of course the eighth lection counting from 28. The Feast of Dedication follows in 37, and the Passover comes in sight at the end of 38; the Passion Narrative follows. The second half of the *Diatessaron* is thus clearly allocated to the half-year from the autumn equinox to the spring equinox; we assume that the first half was read from spring to autumn. We have already pointed out that the system of section-enumeration closely follows the second Marcan system which is found in most Greek manuscripts, and that the Marcan sections which contain the arrival of Jesus in Jerusalem, the cleansing of the temple, and the teaching in Jerusalem, are distributed between Sections 28 and 35, and are thus located at the Feast of Tabernacles.

Tatian and the Fourth Gospel. An analysis of the Johannine sections as they appear in Tatian shows extraordinary dislocations and transpositions. Especially we may note:

(a) The Woman of Samaria (iv. 4–45), and the Visit to Jerusalem (v. 1–47) with the healing miracle at the pool of Bethesda, are placed after the Feeding of the Five Thousand and Discourse on the Bread of Life (vi. 1–71), and before the beginning of the Feast of Tabernacles (vii. 1–31).

(b) The Cleansing of the Temple (ii. 13 *b*–22), and the Nicodemus passage (iii. 1–21), are placed after vii. 31, that is to say in the first days of the Feast of Tabernacles; in the case of the Cleansing of the Temple, Tatian omits the references to Passover.

The effect of these drastic changes is, from our point of view, perfectly clear. They destroy the effect of a three-year ministry in the fourth gospel, and arrange it for a one-year calendar. The reference to the harvest in the Woman of Samaria falls into the pattern; the feast of chapter v becomes Pentecost; and the Cleansing of the Temple is assigned to Tabernacles, the reference to Passover being omitted. Tatian has thus rearranged the fourth gospel so that it could be harmonized with the Marcan calendrical system.

Tatian and Luke. There are very few signs anywhere that Tatian was influenced by the order of Luke. Indeed Luke has little organized structure to it, except what it borrows from Mark; it contains numerous narratives and passages of teaching which Tatian seems to have felt free to place wherever he thinks they may be effective.

Mark and Matthew. The basis of Tatian is a synoptic order founded on Mark-Matthew, which he has little difficulty in combining with his rearranged fourth gospel. It would be hard to state in a paragraph the extent to which he follows Mark in preference to Matthew, or vice versa. He accepts the Matthaean transposition of the Sending of the Apostles and the Collection of Parables; he also follows Matthew in moving from its Marcan position the Beelzebul controversy and associated sayings to a position which seems to have been determined by the sequence of Q. But otherwise he frequently restores sequences of short narratives to the position in which they stood in Mark; the extent to which he has done this is sufficient, as has been pointed out, to enable his system of section-enumeration to run remarkably even with the second system of lection-enumeration of Mark. In the Passion Narrative the influence of John is strong throughout.

The Latin 'Diatessaron'. An old manuscript of a Latin form of the *Diatessaron* of Tatian was discovered by Victor, Bishop of Capua, between A.D. 541 and 554. The Vulgate text of St Jerome has been substituted for the original 'Old Latin' so that it is useless to us for the purposes of textual criticism; on the other hand its variations in order are of interest. It is unique in placing the Sending of the Twelve immediately after the Sermon on the Mount; otherwise its transposition of sections seems to have been motivated by the desire to restore the order of Matthew. It is divided into 182 sections which are clearly designed for reading in churches; the half-way point (at 91) is the section on the Transfiguration which we have seen to be a characteristic of the structure of Mark and Matthew. The number 182, being half the number of days in the year, suggests that it was used as a daily lectionary for half of the year.

The rest of the New Testament is contained in the manuscript with interesting supplementary material. It is known as Codex Fuldensis, and is an excellent authority for the Vulgate text.

Appendix 5

THE CHAPTER-ENUMERATION IN ST LUKE

Codex *B* divides Luke into 152 chapters which is of no interest to us; but Alexandrinus and the other manuscripts divide it into 84 chapters numbered from 0 to 83. As this is twelve times seven, it is possible that it may have some liturgical significance. We have therefore set out the Lucan chapter-divisions in such a way as to emphasize this character. We have also included the eleven script-divisions which occur in *B* in the part of Luke which precedes the Passion, dividing it of course into twelve sections. (It will be remembered that the chapter-enumeration of *B* provides twelve lections in John previous to the Passion.)

For purposes of comparison we have also inserted the main literary or liturgical divisions of Mark: the half-way point between 36 and 37, the end of the Galilean material between 42 and 43, and the opening of the Passion narrative at 49.

It would serve no good purpose to give the list of possible lections in the Marcionite gospel arrived at by a literary analysis of the commentary of Tertullian in *Adversus Marcionem*, IV. The mode of judgement is too subjective. We have, however, indicated whether the Lucan lections are present in the Marcionite gospel, or 'missing', that is to say not alluded to or quoted, either by Tertullian or Epiphanius. We have also given samples of certain literary evidence which we find in Tertullian. Tertullian often passes quite abruptly from one chapter in the Marcionite gospel to another, generally introducing his treatment of it by a catch-phrase which may sometimes be a title, and sometimes the opening words of a lection. Examples are: 'Et curatur paralyticus...'; 'De Sabbato quoque...'; 'In curatione decem leprosorum'. We give some of these catch-phrases (which do not always precisely agree with the Lucan enumeration). A capital letter for the first word indicates that the phrase quoted introduces the treatment of a new chapter.

It will be remembered that Tertullian definitely refers to chapters in the Marcionite gospel (*Adv. Marc.* III, 11); and Irenaeus refers to individual passages in the canonical Luke, which he calls 'gospels' (*Adv. Haer.* III, 14 and 15).

In quoting the Lucan titles from Alexandrinus, the word 'Concerning' is omitted throughout. It is not found in the cases of 55, 56, 70, 71, 73, 75, 79.

The figures in the last column refer to Lucan lections of the non-*B* chapter-system, which are known to have been retained in the Marcionite gospel. Allowing seven lections for the Passion narrative, the reader will observe that the total for the Marcionite gospel is 62 (63) which is the same length as Mark in the arrangement of *B*. This reduction to the Marcan scale involves the loss of 20 (21) lections; that is to say three heptads.

	CANONICAL LUKE	MARCIONITE LUKE	
0.	*Pro-oimion.* No title	Missing	—
		Script-division in B	
1.	The Census	Missing	—
2.	The Watchful Shepherds	Missing	—
3.	Symeon	Missing	—
4.	Anna the Prophetess	Missing	—
		Script-division in B	
5.	The Word of the Lord that came to John	(In Marcion the heavenly Jesus descends into Capernaum.) Missing	—
6.	Those who Questioned John	Missing	—
7.	The Temptation of Christ	Missing	—
8.	The Man who had the Spirit of a Daemon	'The spirit of a daemon shouts out' (Marcion refers to the scene in the synagogue at Nazareth)	1
		Script-division in B	
9.	Peter's Wife's Mother	Missing	—
10.	Those Healed of Various Diseases	Present	2
		'He proceeds into the desert'	3
11.	The Catch of Fish	'At the fishing'	—
12.	The Leper	Present	4
13.	The Paralytic	'A paralytic too is cured'	5
14.	Levi the Publican	'A publican chosen'	6
		'Concerning the sabbath'	—
	Script-division in B *in middle of* 14 *precedes walking through cornfields*		
15.	Him who had the Withered Hand	Present	7
16.	The Choice of the Twelve Apostles	'He ascends a mountain'	8
17.	The Beatitudes	'I come now to his ordinances'	9
18.	The Centurion	'Likewise in extolling the faith of the centurion'	10
19.	The Son of the Widow	'He revived also the dead son of a widow'	11
20.	Those sent by John	'But John is scandalised'	12
21.	Her who Anointed the Lord with Ointment	Present	13
		'That rich women adhered to Christ'	—
22.	The Parable of the Sower (with mother and brethren)	'Similarly concerning parables'	14
		'We come now to...'	—
23.	The Rebuke of the Waters	'Who is this who commands the winds and the sea?'	15
24.	The Legion	Present	16

CANONICAL LUKE	MARCIONITE LUKE	
25. The Daughter of the Synagogue-Ruler	Missing	—
26. The Woman with a Haemorrhage	Present	17
27. The Twelve Apostles	'He sends out his disciples'	18
28. The Five Loaves and Two Fishes	'He feeds the people in the desert'	19

Script-division in B

29. The Questioning of the Disciples	Present	20

(Half-way point in St Mark)

30. The Transfiguration	Present	21
31. The Lunatic	Missing	—

Script-division in B, preceding Second Passion Announcement

32. Those who Disputed Who is the Greatest	Present	22
33. One Not Permitted to Follow	'Refuses the one who offers'	23
34. The Appointed Seventy	'He chose also seventy others'	24
35. The Lawyer who Questioned	'A teacher of the law comes up'	25
36. Him who Fell among Thieves	Missing	—
37. Martha and Mary	Missing	—

Script-division in B

38. Prayer	'When he had prayed in a certain place'	26
39. One who had a Dumb Spirit	'When he had cast out a dumb spirit'	27
40. Her who raised her Voice among the crowd	'A woman cried out from the crowd'	28
41. Those who Asked a Sign	'Gives no sign to those who ask'	29

Script-division in B

42. The Pharisee who Invited Jesus	'He inflicts a Woe upon the Pharisees'	30
43. The Woes against the Lawyers	'The Pharisee who invited him to lunch'	31
44. The Leaven of the Pharisees	'The hypocrisy of the Pharisees'	32
45. Him who Desired to Divide the Property	'The quarrelling brothers'	33
46. The Rich man whose Farm was Profitable	'The rich farmer'	34
47. The Galileans and those in Siloam	Missing	—
48. Her who had the Spirit of Infirmity	'A question again about a cure done on the sabbath'	35
49. The Parables	Present	36
50. Those who Asked whether those who were Saved were Few	Present	37
51. Those who Spoke to Jesus with regard to Herod	Missing	—
52. The Man with the Dropsy	Missing	—
53. Not to Love the First Seats	'At lunch or dinner who to invite'	38
54. Those Invited to Dinner	Present	39
55. The Building of a Tower	Missing	—
56. A Hundred Sheep	'The lost sheep and the lost coin'	40
57. A Son who Departed into a Far Country	Missing	—
58. The Unjust Steward	Present	41

	CANONICAL LUKE	MARCIONITE LUKE	
59.	The Rich Man and Lazarus	'The argument between a rich man in hell and a poor man'	42
		'Turning again to his disciples, "Woe" saith he'	—

Script-division in B

60.	The Ten Lepers	'In the cure of the ten lepers'	43
61.	The Unjust Judge	Present	44
62.	The Pharisee and the Publican	Missing	—
63.	The Rich Man who Questioned Jesus	'Then being questioned by a certain man'	45

(End of Galilean material in St Mark.) Script-division in B preceding Third Passion Announcement

64.	The Blind Man	'When therefore the blind man'	46
65.	Zacchaeus	'The house of Zacchaeus also finds salvation'	47
66.	Him who made a Journey to Receive a Kingdom	Present	48
67.	Those who Received the Ten Pounds	Present	49
68.	The Colt	Missing	—

Script-division in B

69.	The Chief Priests and Elders who Questioned Jesus	'The baptism of John, whence it was'	50
70.	Parable of the Vineyard	Missing	—
71.	Questioning with regard to the Tribute	'Render what is Caesar's to Caesar'	51
72.	The Sadducees	'The Sadducees who deny the resurrection'	52
73.	Question How is Christ the Son of David	Present	53
74.	Her who Gave Two Lepta	Missing	—

(Passion narrative begins in Mark)

75.	Question concerning the Consummation	Present	54

Passion narrative begins in Luke

76.	The Pascha	Present	55
77.	Those who Strove which was the Greatest	Missing: some passages present	—
78.	The Demand of Satan	Missing: some passages present	—
79.	The Scornings of Herod	Present	—
80.	The Lamenting Women	Missing: some passages present	—
81.	The Repentant Thief	Missing: some passages present	—
82.	The Request for the Body of Jesus	Present	—

(End of St Mark)

83.	Cleopas	Present	—

NOTE. In the Passion narrative the passages peculiar to Luke which give their names to the Lucan lections are sometimes missing in the Marcionite gospel, but the remainder of the narrative may be well represented; for instance 80 and 81 contain the story of the actual crucifixion which is not omitted. We have therefore not thought it feasible to number the lections subsequent to 55.

Appendix 6

THE BOOK OF TESTIMONIES

The expression *Book of Testimonies* is used for the successive recensions of the collections of proof-texts from the Old Testament, whether Law, Prophets, or Psalms, which were made for the use of Christian evangelists and teachers at a very early time.

Dr Rendel Harris, to whose short but important books on this branch of study all students of the New Testament are deeply indebted, seems to be the inventor of the title; and with the acquisition of a name, this rather shadowy and hypothetical monument of primitive Christianity also acquired a more concrete, perhaps too concrete existence in the imagination.

Dr Harris believed it to be the first written book of the Christian Church; he thought it was drawn upon by most of the New Testament writers; and in the second century, it was used in increasing quantities by the author of the *Epistle of Barnabas* (A.D. 120?), Justin Martyr (130–65), and Irenaeus (about 180). The *Adversus Judaeos* of Tertullian he regarded as virtually a transcript of the text, which was found even better represented in the similar book of Cyprian. We need not go into the detail of his theory and its connexion with more obscure writers like Aristo of Pella and Papias of Hierapolis.

In using the term *Book of Testimonies*, there is no necessity to adopt the ingenious theory of Dr Harris by which he identified it with the 'Logia of the Lord' written in 'Hebrew' by St Matthew. That identification has had long and sympathetic consideration, but the arguments in its favour are not convincing.

It is better to assume that we are dealing with a variety of successive recensions of Testimony collections, which were all related, and indeed go back to some common source or sources. It is unlikely that the first evangelizers carried about a complete collection of Old Testament books, or that all quoters of the Old Testament were quoting from their own knowledge of the original text. It is more satisfactory to assume that they were quoting from lists of extracts which had been drawn up for this purpose, and that the making of such lists was one of the earliest literary labours of the primitive church, prior to the missionary work of St Paul. Indeed we may regard something of the sort as proved. St Paul makes use of such collections of Testimonies in Romans, and probably also in Galatians.

The *Book of Testimonies*, in its characteristic form, was more than a collection of extracts; it had a purpose, a point of view, and even a theology. Each little group of extracts had a title of some sort which indicated the thesis which the extracts were supposed to prove; these include much more than the proposition that the Messiah must die and rise again 'according to the scriptures' (I Cor. xv. 3 and 4), or that he must be born of a virgin (Matt. i. 23); they also had to explain why he was rejected by the very nation to whom these prophecies had been made. For the rejection of the Messiah, and of the prophets who had preceded him and announced his coming, it was not hard to find proof-texts; and it was equally possible to find authority for the further propositions that the Jews were and always had been a hard-hearted and rebellious people, and that they were devoid of spiritual vision and understanding; the foundations of this theory are found as early as the speech of St Stephen in Acts vii. This in its turn led to the view that the Law of Moses was a special discipline only needed in their case, though this Law, being given by God, must naturally be an expression of eternal principles, which principles were expressed in their eternal form in the Christian revelation.

The Law, therefore, which included in its scope the whole Jewish cultus, was bound to disappear, but it would yield place to the Christian gospel in which all its true values would be preserved in a universal and superlative degree. The general thought which underlies this theology is already contained in the epigram of Jesus about the temple made with hands and the temple not made with hands.

One is not prepared to say how far these lines of thought had advanced before the writing of St Mark's Gospel, but the main elements must have been there. And we must certainly suppose that it had been laid down, in the circles where this kind of literature was being produced, 'that God had rejected his people'. This proposition is quoted by St Paul in Rom. xi. 1, and rejected: 'I say then, Did God cast off his people? God forbid.' One of the most convincing chapters in Dr Harris's book is the one in which he shows that chapters ix–xi of Romans are a critique of the *Book of Testimonies*. We must date it, therefore, before the writing of Romans, and *a fortiori* before the writing of Mark. But, on the other hand, when we talk of the *Book of Testimonies*, it is wise to make a mental reservation; in respect of Paul, we mean the *Book of Testimonies* in the recension in which Paul used it; in respect of Mark, we mean the *Book of Testimonies* in the recension in which Mark used it. Yet these recensions must have been sufficiently alike to afford a substantial identity at least in parts.

It is convenient here to give a list of the documents, oral and written, which were in use in the Church prior to the writing of Mark, and concurrently with the Gentile mission in its earliest stages.

(i) The gospels, both the short units, and the continuous Passion narrative.

(ii) Teachings of Jesus which were growing into collections related to various topics.

(iii) Catechisms.

(iv) Prophecies, both of Jesus himself and of the Church prophets.

(v) The *Book* or *Books of Testimonies*.

The *Testimonies* were never incorporated as a separate unit into the New Testament, but maintained their own existence and had an established position in the church order of the second century. Indeed it would be interesting to investigate the relation, if any, between these extracts and the Old Testament lections of the liturgical tradition. The fact that so learned and literary a bishop as Melito of Sardis (about A.D. 160–70) had to make a journey to Palestine to inform himself as to the 'exact truth concerning the ancient books in regard to their number and order' suggests that neither he nor his church were perfectly sure about the 'canon' of the Hebrew Bible, or possessed a complete Old Testament. Even so he contented himself with making a series of extracts, dividing them into six books (Eusebius, *Hist. Eccl.* IV, 26, 13).

Appendix 7

TESTIMONIES IN ST MARK

NOTE. Not every Old Testament quotation is a Testimony, as for instance those verses which are quoted in order to support legal opinions. On the other hand Testimonies in Mark are seldom quoted in full; sometimes there is no more than a key-word; yet these Testimonies are often the clue to the understanding of the passage.

In the list given below, references are often supplied to the use of the Testimony in the Pauline Epistles or I Peter or Hebrews; sometimes in later writers.

The first two Testimonies are the only ones introduced as such by the composer in the editorial material. We may look upon them therefore as a late touch. The ascription of both Testimonies to Isaiah can be easily understood if they stood together in a *Book of Testimonies*, and were taken to be a single Testimony.

LECTION I

Behold, I send my messenger, and he shall prepare the way before me. Mal. iii. 1. Mark i. 2 and Q (Matt. xi. 10).

The voice of one that crieth in the wilderness, Prepare ye the way of the Lord: make straight in the desert a high way for our God. Isa. xl. 3. Mark i. 3 and Q (Matt. iii. 3).

LECTION 2

Thou art my Son, (this day have I begotten thee). Ps. ii. 7. Mark i. 11 and parallels; Heb. i. 5 and v. 5; Acts xiii. 33.

(Behold my servant, whom I uphold; my chosen) in whom my soul delighteth. Isa. xlii. 1. Mark i. 11 and parallels.

Thine only Son whom thou lovest. Genesis xxii. 2.

LECTION 18

Hear ye indeed, but understand not; and see ye indeed, but perceive not. (Make the heart of this people fat, and make their ears heavy, and shut their eyes;) lest they (see with their eyes, and hear with their ears,) and understand (with their heart) and turn again, (and be healed). Isa. vi. 9, 10. Mark iv. 12 and parallels; frequent in N.T.

LECTION 25

Sheep having no shepherd: see Lection 54.

LECTION 26

Hearts hardened: see Lection 18.

LECTION 28

...this people draw nigh unto me, and with their mouth and with their lips do honour me, but have removed their heart far from me, and their fear of me is a commandment of men which hath been taught them. Isa. xxix. 13. Mark vii. 6, 7.

LECTION 34

Not understand, and hearts hardened: see Lection 18.

(Son of man, thou dwellest in the midst of the rebellious house) which have eyes to see, and see not, which have ears to hear, and hear not. Ezek. xii. 2. Mark viii. 18 and parallel in Matthew.

LECTION 36

Coming of the Son of Man: see Lection 49.

LECTION 37

This is my Son: see Lection 2. Luke reads 'elect' in the parallel passage.

Behold, I will send you Elijah the prophet, etc. Mal. iv. 5. Mark ix. 12.

LECTION 44

(The sceptre shall not depart from Judah...till he come whose it is; and unto him shall the obedience of the peoples be.) Binding his foal unto the vine, and his ass's colt unto the choice vine, etc. Gen. xlix. 10, 11. Mark xi. 2. See Justin Martyr, *Apol.* I, 40 and *Dial.* 52.

Save now, we beseech thee, O Lord [Hoshia-na]:...Blessed be he that cometh in the name of the Lord. Ps. cxviii. 25, 26. Mark xi. 9 and parallels.

LECTION 45

For mine house shall be called an house of prayer for all peoples. Isa. lvi. 7.

Is this house, which is called by my name, become a den of robbers in your eyes? Jer. vii. 11. Mark xi. 17 and parallels.

LECTION 46

(And his feet shall stand in that day upon the Mount of Olives... and the Mount of Olives shall cleave in the midst...and half of) the mountain shall remove, etc. Zech. xiv. 4. Mark xi. 23 and parallels.

Let me sing for my well-beloved a song of my beloved touching his vineyard. My well-beloved hath a vineyard in a very fruitful hill: and he digged it...and built a tower in the midst of it, and also hewed out a winepress therein. Isa. v. 1, 2. Mark xii. 1 and parallels.

The stone which the builders rejected is become the head of the corner. This is the Lord's doing; it is marvellous in our eyes. Ps. cxviii. 22, 23. Mark xii. 10 and parallels; Acts iv. 11, Rom. ix. 33, I Pet. ii. 6–8.

LECTION 47

The Lord saith unto my Lord, Sit thou at my right hand, until I make thine enemies thy footstool. Ps. cx. 1. Mark xii. 36: Heb. i. 13.

LECTION 49

There came with the clouds of heaven (one like unto) a son of man, (and he came even to the Ancient of days)... (and there was given him) dominion, and glory. Dan. vii. 13, 14. Mark xiii. 26 and parallels. See Rev. xiv. 14.

(What is man, that thou art mindful of him? and) the Son of Man, (that thou visitest him? For thou hast made him but little lower than the angels, and crownest him) with glory and honour. Ps. viii. 4, 5. Mark xiii. 26, 27. Heb. ii. 6, 7.

See also special note on quotations from Daniel.

LECTION 53

(Yea, mine own familiar friend, in whom I trusted,) which did eat of my bread, (hath lifted up his heel against me.) Ps. xli. 9. Mark xiv. 18 and parallels.

He poured out (his soul unto death,... and bare the sin of) many. Isa. liii. 12. Mark xiv. 24 and parallels.

LECTION 54

Smite the shepherd, and the sheep shall be scattered. Zech. xiii. 7. Mark xiv. 27 and parallels.

Why art thou cast down, O my soul? Ps. xlii. 6, 11, also xliii. 5. Mark xiv. 34 and parallels. See version of LXX.

LECTION 56

Son of Man with Clouds: see Lection 49.

At the right hand: see Lection 47.

LECTION 59

They part my garments among them, and upon my vesture do they cast lots. Ps. xxii. 18. Mark xv. 24 and parallels.

(All they that see me laugh me to scorn: they shoot out the lip,) they shake the head, saying.... Ps. xxii. 7. Mark xv. 29 and parallels.

My God, my God, why hast thou forsaken me? Ps. xxii. 1. Mark xv. 34 and parallels.

(They gave me also gall for my meat; and in my thirst) they gave me vinegar to drink. Ps. lxix. 21. Mark xv. 36 and parallels.

Note

POINTS OF CONTACT BETWEEN DANIEL AND ST MARK

Lection no.		Mark	Daniel
4	Time...kingdom	i. 15	vii. 22
16	Kingdom divided	iii. 24	v. 28
18	(World-tree)	iv. 30–2	iv. 9–13 and 20–2
36	Death of Messiah	viii. 31	ix. 26
	Son of Man come in glory	viii. 38	vii. 13
39	Death of Messiah	ix. 31	ix. 26
42	Death of Messiah	x. 33	ix. 26
49	Destroy sanctuary	xiii. 2	ix. 26
	Consummation	xiii. 4	ix. 27
	The end	xiii. 7	viii. 19, ix. 26, xii. 4 and 10
	Endure to end	xiii. 13	xii. 12, 13
	Abomination of desolation	xiii. 14	ix. 27, xi. 31, xii. 11
	Affliction such as never, etc.	xiii. 19	xii. 1
	Son of man...cloud	xiii. 26	vii. 13
56	Destroy sanctuary	xiv. 58	ix. 26
	Not made with hands	xiv. 58	ii. 34
	Son of man...clouds	xiv. 62	vii. 13
59	Destroy sanctuary	xv. 29	ix. 26

THE GOSPEL ACCORDING TO ST MARK

arranged according to the chapter-enumeration of Codex Vaticanus (B):

PART I

The Liturgical Year: Lections 1–49

PART II

The Passion Narrative: Lections 49–62

NOTES. 1. The text used is that of the Revised Version of 1881 (text or margin), with a few exceptions, which are noted at the foot of the page.

2. The lection numbers (Lection 1, Lection 2, etc.) are taken from the margin of *B*, and are followed by references to the modern chapters and verses.

3. The paragraphing denoted by small italic letters (*a*, *b*, *c*, etc.) is also taken from *B*, where it is denoted by horizontal bars at the beginning of the line.

4. The 'script-divisions' found in *B* are also indicated in the text, and illustrated photographically; also the cases where a lection ends on a short line.

5. Words printed entirely in small capitals are members of 'triads', and a list of these is given at the foot of the lection. A word with an initial capital is a word which, while it does not seem to form part of a triad, is nevertheless repeated from time to time, and would repay study from this point of view.

6. After the lection number and reference will be found the number of the corresponding lection in Matthew in the non-*B* system of chapter-enumeration, that is, the great mass of Greek manuscripts other than *B*. The titles of these lections are also given. This non-*B* chapter-system in Matthew seems to be based on the *B* system in Mark.

7. The non-*B* system for Mark seems to be a shortened form of the *B* system; it is given in the form of captions introduced into the text indicating the beginning of each non-*B* lection. The titles are also given. (There are no titles in *B*.)

8. The chapter-system of the *Diatessaron* of Tatian seems to be based on the non-*B* system. It is given in the form of captions along with the non-*B* numbers and titles. As the order of Mark is sometimes changed in the *Diatessaron*, the quotation of a number only implies that the lection in question is found somewhere in that chapter of the *Diatessaron*.

9. The Old Latin system of chapter-enumeration is given in the same way, but the quotation of a number means that the Old Latin lection begins at that point. It is closely allied to the non-*B* system. I have relied on the edition of P. Sabatier (1745) based on Colbertinus and Sangermanensis. Some information on the chapter-enumeration of the Vulgate, taken from Amiatinus, is given in the notes.

10. The non-*B* system as found in Alexandrinus has been checked from the Koridethi manuscript (Θ), and some information is given in the notes.

ACCORDING TO MARK

PART I

THE LITURGICAL YEAR

1. THE NEW YEAR

The Jewish New Year began on Tisri 1 with the call to repentance and the blowing of trumpets; Tisri fluctuated between September and October. Tisri (or Tishri) was the 'seventh month'.

Tisri 1. The seventh new moon; counting from the Paschal Moon, the appearance of which decided Nisan 1, the first day of the first month, which still retained some of its ancient features as a New Year.

Tisri 10. The Day of Atonement, on which the High Priest went through a species of renewal or re-consecration on behalf of himself and the people.

Tisri 15–21. The seven days of the Feast of Tabernacles (*Sukkoth*), which marked the end of the agricultural year, the ingathering of all crops, and especially of the vintage. The liturgical features of this day include the 'apocalyptic' ideas of creation, judgement, and new creation.

Tisri 22. The additional day (*Atzereth*) which completed the Festival. According to Hertz, the reading of the Law of Moses in the synagogue lectionary ends and begins at this point. The Law is divided into 54 lections, with 9 for special occasions. (See Hertz, *Pentateuch and Haphtorahs*.)

We have therefore arranged the first lection of Mark for the last week of Tisri. This means that the agricultural and apocalyptic features of Tabernacles are not reflected in these opening lections. We find them in the last lections of the Calendar (42–9), which would be read before and during the first three weeks of Tisri. The reading of these lections at this time seems to explain some features of the Christian Advent season, and of the autumn Ember season.

As the non-*B* system seems to be devised for the Roman Calendar, the first lection of that system would come in the first week in January; and a trace of this may be found in the Festival of the Epiphany, which originally celebrated the Baptism of Jesus by John.

The first 14 lections in *B* (7 in non-*B*) have no further liturgical significance; we have divided them for convenience into two sets of seven: seven New Year lections and seven Winter lections; but see notes on 12 and 13.

In the Jewish agricultural year, the fasts and festivals of Tisri were followed by the season of autumn sowing, and what were called the former (or earlier) rains. If the rain prayed for at Tabernacles had not fallen, or was not plentiful, fasts were ordered in the following months.

NEW YEAR I

Third Week in Tisri (September–October): Seventh Month. The reading of the Law for the year begins in the Synagogue.

LECTION I (Mark i. 1–8).

Matthew non-*B*, Lection 3: 'First John preached the Kingdom of Heaven.'

Mark non-B 'Pro-oimion'. Tatian 3 and 4. Old Latin 1

(*a*) The BEGINNING of the GOSPEL of Jesus CHRIST the SON of GOD. (Cf. Gen. i. 1.) Even as it is written in Isaiah the prophet,

'Behold, I send my messenger before thy face,
Who shall prepare thy way';   (Mal. iii. 1)

'The voice of one crying in the wilderness,
Make ye ready the way of the Lord,
Make his paths straight.'   (Isa. xl. 3)

(*b*) JOHN came, who BAPTIZED in the WILDERNESS and PREACHED the BAPTISM of REPENTANCE unto remission of sins. And there went out unto him all the country of Judaea, and all they of Jerusalem; and they were BAPTIZED of him in the river Jordan, confessing their sins. And JOHN was clothed with camel's hair, and had a leathern girdle about his loins, and did eat locusts and wild honey. And he PREACHED, saying,

There cometh AFTER ME he that is mightier than I,
> The latchet of whose shoes I am not worthy to stoop down
> and unloose.

I BAPTIZED you with Water; but
> He shall BAPTIZE you with the HOLY *SPIRIT.

Triads (for Lections 1–4a): gospel, God, John, preach, wilderness, baptize-baptism, Spirit.

Major Triads: Christ? Son of God? (see Special Introduction to Lection 37), preach repentance, come after, Holy Spirit, beloved Son, Satan, preach gospel, kingdom of God.

NOTES

(1) In every other instance the Matthaean titles begin with the word *peri* (concerning). Is the emphatic word *prōtos* (first), in the title of Matthew non-*B*3, a sign that the Matthaean titles are imitated from old Marcan titles? For in Mark this is the first lection, and the word *prōtos* might simply be a numeral.

(2) The *Pro-oimion* (opening unnumbered lection) of Mark non-*B* is quite long, extending over four lections of *B*. The location of the first script-division in *B* at the end of Lection 4 suggests a lection of similar length. We have suggested that such a lection was once used for the original Epiphany Festival which occurred in the first week of January, and commemorated the Baptism of Jesus by John.

(3) From 1941 to 1946, Tisri 22 came on 13 October, 3 October, 22 October, 10 October, 30 September and 18 October respectively.

NEW YEAR II
Fourth Week in Tisri.

LECTION 2 (Mark i. 9–11).
Matthew non-*B* 3 continued.

Mark non-B Pro-oimion continued. Tatian 4

AND it came to pass in those days that Jesus came from Nazareth of Galilee, and was BAPTIZED of JOHN in the Jordan. And straightway, coming up out of the Water, he saw the heavens rent asunder, and the SPIRIT as a dove descending upon him: and a voice came out of the heavens. (Cf. Gen. i. 2, ii. 7.)

> Thou art my †SON,   (Ps. ii. 7; cf. Gen. xxii. 2)
> The †BELOVED;   (Isa. v. 1; cf. Canticles)
> In thee I am well pleased.   (Isa. xlii. 1)

* R.V. Ghost.   † R.V. my beloved Son.

New Year III

First Week in Marheswan (October–November): Eighth Month.

Lection 3 (Mark i. 12–13).

Matthew non-*B* 3 continued.

Mark non-B Pro-oimion continued. Tatian 4 and 5

AND straightway the SPIRIT driveth him forth into the WILDERNESS. And he was in the WILDERNESS forty days tempted of SATAN; and he was with the wild beasts; and the Angels ministered unto him. (Cf. Ps. xcvii. 7, Heb. i. 6.)

NOTES

(1) Tatian 4 includes the first two temptations of Matthew and Luke.

(2) Tatian 5 begins with the third temptation, at the end of which it appends the sentence from Mark about the angels.

New Year IV

Second Week in Marheswan. Season of Autumn Sowing.

Lection 4 (Mark i. 14–20).

Matthew non-*B* 4, 'Concerning the Teaching of Christ'.

Mark non-B Pro-oimion continued. Tatian 5. Old Latin 2

(a) *AND after that John was delivered up, Jesus came into Galilee, PREACHING the GOSPEL of GOD, and saying,

The time is fulfilled,   (Dan. vii. 22)
And the KINGDOM OF GOD is at hand:
REPENT ye, and Believe in the GOSPEL.

Mark non-B 1, 'Concerning the Demoniac'

(b) AND passing along by the Sea of Galilee, he saw SIMON and ANDREW the brother of Simon, casting (a net) in the Sea; for they were fishers. And Jesus said unto them, Come ye AFTER ME, and I will make you to become fishers of men. And straightway they left the nets, and FOLLOWED him.

(c) AND going on a little further, he saw JAMES the son of Zebedee, and JOHN his brother, who also were in the Boat

* R.V. Now.

ΙΩΑΝΟΥΚΑΙΕΥΘΥϹΑΝΑ
ΒΑΙΝΩΝΕΚΤΟΥΥΔΑΤΟϹ
ΕΙΔΕΝϹΧΙΖΟΜΕΝΟΥϹ
ΤΟΥϹΟΥΡΑΝΟΥϹΚΑΙΤΟ
ΠΝΕΥΜΑΩϹΠΕΡΙϹΤΕΡΑ
ΚΑΤΑΒΑΙΝΟΝΕΙϹΑΥΤΟ
ΚΑΙΦΩΝΗ ΕΓΕΝΕΤΟΕΚ
ΤΩΝΟΥΡΑΝΩΝϹΥΕΙΟΥ
ΙΟϹΜΟΥΟΑΓΑΠΗΤΟϹΕ
ϹΟΙΕΥΔΟΚΗϹΑΚΑΙΕΥ
ΟΥϹΤΟΠΝΕΥΜΑΑΥΤΟ
ΕΚΒΑΛΛΕΙΕΙϹΤΗΝΕΡΗ
ΜΟΝΚΑΙΗΝΕΝΤΗΕΡΗ
ΜΩΤΕϹϹΕΡΑΚΟΝΤΑΗΜΕΡΑ
ϹΠΕΙΡΑΖΟΜΕΝΟϹΥΠΟΤΥ
ϹΑΤΑΝΑΚΑΙΗΝΜΕΤΑΤ
ΘΗΡΙΩΝΚΑΙΟΙΑΓΓΕΛΟΙ
ΔΙΗΚΟΝΟΥΝΑΥΤΩΚΑΙ
ΜΕΤΟΠΑΡΑΔΟΘΗΝΑΙΤ
ΙΩΑΝΗΝΗΛΘΕΝΟΙϹΕΙϹ
ΤΗΝΓΑΛΙΛΑΙΑΝΚΗΡΥϹ
ϹΩΝΤΟΕΥΑΓΓΕΛΙΟΝΤΥ
ΘΥΚΑΙΛΕΓΩΝΟΤΙΠΕΠΛΗ
ΡΩΤΑΙΚΑΙΡΟϹΚΑΙΗΓ
ΓΙΚΕΝΗΒΑϹΙΛΕΙΑΤΟΥ
ΘΥΜΕΤΑΝΟΕΙΤΕΚΑΙΠΙ
ϹΤΕΥΕΤΕΕΝΤΩΕΥΑΓΓ
ΛΙΩ ΚΑΙΠΑΡΑΓΩΝΠΑΡΑ
ΤΗΝΘΑΛΑϹϹΑΝΤΗϹΓΑ
ΛΙΛΑΙΑϹΕΙΔΕΝϹΙΜΩ
ΝΑΚΑΙΑΝΔΡΕΑΝΤΟΝΑ
ΔΕΛΦΟΝϹΙΜΩΝΟϹΑΜ
ΦΙΒΑΛΛΟΝΤΑϹΕΝΤΗΘΑ
ΛΑϹϹΗΗϹΑΝΓΑΡΑΛΙΕΙϹ
ΚΑΙΕΙΠΕΝΑΥΤΟΙϹΟΙϹ
ΔΕΥΤΕΟΠΙϹΩΜΟΥΚΑΙ
ΠΟΙΗϹΩΥΜΑϹΓΕΝΕϹΘΑΙ
ΑΛ ΕΙϹΑΝΟΡΩΠΩΝΚΑΙ
ΕΥΘΥϹΑΦΕΝΤΕϹΤΑ
ΛΙΚΤΥΑΗΚΟΛΟΥΘΟΥΝ
ΑΥΤΩ ΚΑΙΠΡΟΒΑϹΟΛΙ
ΓΟΝΕΙΔΕΝΙΑΚΩΒΟΝΤΥ

ΤΟΥΖΕΒΕΔΑΙΟΥΚΑΙΙΩ
ΑΝΗΝΤΟΝΑΔΕΛΦΟΝΑΥ
ΤΟΥΚΑΙΑΥΤΟΥΣΕΝΤΩ
ΠΛΟΙΩΚΑΤΑΡΤΙΖΟΝΤΑϹ
ΤΑΔΙΚΤΥΑΚΑΙΕΥΘΥϹΕ
ΚΑΛΕϹΕΝΑΥΤΟΥΣΚΑΙ
ΦΕΝΤΕϹΤΟΝΠΑΤΕΡΑΑ
ΤΩΝΖΕΒΕΔΑΙΟΝΕΝΤΩ
ΠΛΟΙΩΜΕΤΑΤΩΝΜΙΣΘ
ΤΩΝΑΠΗΛΘΟΝΟΠΙϹΩ
ΑΥΤΟΥ
ΚΑΙΕΙϹΠΟΡΕΥΟΝΤΑΙΕΙϹ
ΚΑΦΑΡΝΑΟΥΜΚΑΙΕΥΘ
ΩϹΤΟΙϹΣΑΒΒΑϹΙΝΕΙϹΕ
ΘΩΝΕΙϹΤΗΝϹΥΝΑΓΩΓΗ
ΕΔΙΔΑϹΚΕΝΚΑΙΕΞΕΠΛΗϹ
ϹΟΝΤΟΕΠΙΤΗΔΙΔΑΧΗ
ΑΥΤΟΥΗΝΓΑΡΔΙΔΑϹΚΩ
ΑΥΤΟΥϹΩϹΕΞΟΥϹΙΑΝ
ΕΧΩΝΚΑΙΟΥΧΩϹΟΙΓΡΑ
ΜΑΤΕΙϹ ΚΑΙΕΥΘΥϹΗΝ
ΕΝΤΗϹΥΝΑΓΩΓΗΑΥΤΩ
ΑΝΘΡΩΠΟϹΕΝΠΝΕΥΜΑ
ΤΙΑΚΑΘΑΡΤΩΚΑΙΑΝΕΚΡΑ
ΞΕΝΛΕΓΩΝΤΙΗΜΙΝΚΑΙ
ϹΥΙΗϹΟΥΝΑΖΑΡΗΝΕΗΛ
ΘΕϹΑΠΟΛΕϹΑΙΗΜΑϹΟΙ
ΔΑϹΕΤΙϹΕΙΟΑΓΙΟϹΤΟΥ
ΘΥΚΑΙΕΠΕΤΙΜΗϹΕΝΑΥ
ΤΩΟΙϹΛΕΓΩΝΦΙΜΩ
ΘΗΤΙΚΑΙΕΞΕΛΘΕΕΞΑΥ
ΤΟΥΚΑΙϹΠΑΡΑΞΑΝΑΥΤ
ΤΟΑΚΑΘΑΡΤΟΝΚΑΙΦΩ
ΝΗϹΑΝΦΩΝΗΜΕΓΑΛΗ
ΕΞΗΛΘΕΝΕΞΑΥΤΟΥΚΑΙ
ΕΘΑΜΒΗΘΗϹΑΝΑΠΑΝΤϹ
ΩϹΤΕϹΥΝΖΗΤΕΙΝΑΥΤϹ
ΛΕΓΟΝΤΑϹΤΙΕϹΤΙΝΤΟΥ
ΤΟΔΙΔΑΧΗΚΑΙΝΗΚΑΤΕ
ΞΟΥϹΙΑΝΚΑΙΤΟΙϹΠΝΕΥ
ΜΑϹΙΤΟΙϹΑΚΑΘΑΡΤΟΙϹ
ΕΠΙΤΑϹϹΕΙΚΑΙΥΠΑΚΟΥ

ΟΥϹΙΝΑΥΤΩ ΚΑΙΕΞΗΛ
ΘΕΝΗΑΚΟΗΑΥΤΟΥΕΥ
ΘΥϹΠΑΝΤΑΧΟΥΕΙϹΟΛ
ΤΗΝΠΕΡΙΧΩΡΟΝΤΗϹΓΑ
ΛΙΛΑΙΑϹ ΚΑΙΕΥΘΥϹ
ΕΚΤΗϹϹΥΝΑΓΩΓΗϹ
ΞΕΛΘΩΝΗΛΘΕΝΕΙϹΤΗ
ΟΙΚΙΑΝϹΙΜΩΝΟϹΚΑΙ
ΑΝΔΡΕΟΥΜΕΤΑΙΑΚΩ
ΒΟΥΚΑΙΙΩΑΝΟΥΗΔΕ
ΘΕΡΑϹΙΜΩΝΟϹΚΑΤΕ
ΚΕΙΤΟΠΥΡΕϹϹΟΥϹΑΚΑΙ
ΕΥΘΥΟΛΕΓΟΥϹΙΝΑΥΤΩ
ΠΕΡΙΑΥΤΗϹΚΑΙΠΡΟϹΕ
ΘΩΝΗΓΕΙΡΕΝΑΥΤΗΝΚΡΑ
ΤΗϹΑϹΤΗϹΧΕΙΡΟϹΚΑΙ
ΑΦΗΚΕΝΑΥΤΗΝΟΠΥ
ΡΕΤΟϹΚΑΙΔΙΗΚΟΝΕΙΑΥ
ΤΟΙϹ ΟΨΙΑϹΔΕΓΕΝΟ
ΜΕΝΗϹΟΤΕΕΔΥϹΕΝΟ
ΗΛΙΟϹΕΦΕΡΟΝΠΡΟϹΑΥ
ΤΟΝΠΑΝΤΑϹΤΟΥϹΚΑ
ΚΩϹΕΧΟΝΤΑϹΚΑΙΤΟΥϹ
ΔΑΙΜΟΝΙΖΟΜΕΝΟΥϹΚΑ
ΗΝΟΛΗΗΠΟΛΙϹΕΠΙϹΥ
ΝΗΓΜΕΝΗΠΡΟϹΤΗΝΘΥ
ΡΑΝΚΑΙΕΘΕΡΑΠΕΥϹΕΝ
ΠΟΛΛΟΥϹΚΑΚΩϹΕΧΟΝ
ΤΑϹΠΟΙΚΙΛΑΙϹΝΟϹΟΙϹ
ΚΑΙΔΑΙΜΟΝΙΑΠΟΛΛΑ
ΞΕΒΑΛΕΝΚΑΙΟΥΚΗΦΙΕ
ΤΑΛΑΛΕΙΝΑΥΤΟΝΧΝ
ΕΙΝΑΙ
ΚΑΙΠΡΩΙΝΝΥΧΑΛΙΑΝ
ΑΝΑϹΤΑϹΕΞΗΛΘΕΝΕΙ
ΕΡΗΜΟΝΤΟΠΟΝΚΑΚΕΙ
ΠΡΟϹΗΥΧΕΤΟΚΑΙΚΑΤ
ΑΔΙΩΞΕΝΑΥΤΟΝϹΙΜΩΝ
ΚΑΙΜΕΤΑΥΤΟΥΚΑΙΕΥ
ΡΟΝΑΥΤΟΝΚΑΙΛΕΓΟΥϹ
ΑΥΤΩΟΤΙΠΑΝΤΕϹΖΗ

Page 1278 of Codex Vaticanus 1209 (Cod. *B*) from the phototypic edition of Ulricus Hoepli, Milan 1904.

This is the 1278th page of the Codex which is a whole Bible transcribed in the early fourth century, i.e. before A.D. 350, most probably in Alexandria. The plate shows the whole page, except that the caption KATA MAPKON which occurs at the top of each page is not included. These are the second, third, and fourth columns of Mark. The first column is on the back of this page, and the ink has worked its way through the parchment so that the ornamental bar at the top of the column can be distinctly seen on the photograph; and also the title KATA MAPKON, and the enlarged capital (in red) of the first word APXH (*arkhē*, beginning). The dots which appear round the corner of the second paragraph in column 2 are part of the decoration which marks the end of Matthew. The faint marks in the right-hand margin of the page are chapter-numbers of Matthew which have also come through the parchment: 169 and 170.

In the left-hand margin of column 1 we see the third letter of the alphabet, gamma, with a bar over it to show it is being used as a numeral; it indicates the third lection. The delta below it indicates the fourth lection. The epsilon to the left of the third column indicates the fifth. The stigma to the left of the third column indicates the sixth lection; this represents the old letter digamma which is used in Homeric texts, but had fallen out of use as a letter even in classical Greek; the stigma will be found used as a numeral in the text of Rev. xiii. 18. The zeta indicating the seventh lection at the foot of the third column has been omitted by the scribe; its place is where the script-division comes.

A horizontal bar (the *paragraphon*) under the first letter of the line is a further guide to the lector in reading or singing the gospel for the day. This sign serves to subdivide the lections; and these subdivisions are indicated in our English text by small letters, *a*, *b*, *c*, etc. As a rule the horizontal bar means that a lection or subdivision of a lection comes to an end in the line which is so marked. As the new lection or subdivision almost invariably begins with the word KAI, the lector's task is made fairly easy. An exception to this rule is the fourth lection; the KAI with which this lection begins occurs at the end of the line above the delta; but the horizontal bar makes this quite clear. In our English text we have printed the word 'AND' in capitals wherever it has this function. Its almost invariable use for this purpose suggests that the author of the gospel intended it to serve this purpose.

In addition to this there are the usual accents over the vowels. The acute accent (´) denotes a rising pitch or inflexion in the voice, and the grave accent (`) denotes a falling pitch or inflexion; the circumflex (ˆ) denotes a rising and falling pitch or inflexion, and consequently a lengthening of the vowel. These accents would be a great help to the lector, but were added to the manuscript at a later date. They made up in some degree for the absence of punctuation or division between words.

This page shows two of the script-divisions which occur at the beginning of the gospel: one after the fourth, and one after the sixth lection. The third occurs after the eighth lection at the foot of the next column (the fifth column of the gospel), and will be found illustrated in Plate II. Otherwise these script-divisions occur only at wide intervals, and serve to divide the gospel into its four principal sections. There are only four more.

There can be no doubt that these script-divisions were deliberate, and served some purpose. We suppose that they stood in the older manuscript from which the scribe was copying. The unmistakable signs are the short line, followed by a line which projects, by one letter, into the left-hand margin. (The projection of one letter into the left-hand margin of the third column nine lines above the script-division can be explained in this way. At some late period in the history of the manuscript the ink had faded, and the letters were inked in again by a later hand. The letter nu in the left-hand margin at this point represents a small nu which can still faintly be seen at the right-hand end of the line above.)

The shadowy letters which appear here and there are letters which have come through from the other side of the parchment.

mending the nets. And straightway he called them; and they left their father Zebedee in the Boat with the hired servants, and went AFTER HIM.

(*First script-division in* B)

Triads: come after (follow). The word 'nets' only occurs twice in the Greek.

Major Triads: preach the gospel, preach repentance, kingdom of God, come after, follow, Simon (Peter) Andrew James John.

NOTES

(1) Luke places his Preaching at Nazareth after *a*, omitting *b* and *c*, and combines with it the Marcan story of the Rejection at his *patris* (see Lection 22). Tatian divides this Lucan lection into its component parts, restoring the Rejection to its Marcan position.

(2) The script-division in *B* suggests the use of the first four lections of *B* as a single lection, possibly for a Sunday or festival, on the lines of the non-*B* division; for Lections 2 and 3 of *B* were very short. The Marcan material in Section 5 of Tatian also ends at this point.

(3) The word translated 'delivered up' in line 1 has a special use in this gospel; apart from iv. 29 (of yielding fruit) and vii. 13 (of a teaching tradition), it refers to 'delivering' or 'betraying' to the evil powers. It occurs again in this sense in iii. 19 and ix. 31, and frequently in the Passion Narrative. See Special Introduction to Lection 37.

NEW YEAR V
Third Week in Marheswan.

LECTION 5 (Mark i. 21–8).
Matthew omits the story of the Demoniac.

Mark non-B 1 *continued. Tatian* 6

(*a*) AND they go into Capernaum; and straightway on the Sabbath day he entered into the SYNAGOGUE and TAUGHT. And they were astonished at his TEACHING; for he TAUGHT them as having Authority, and not as the Scribes.

(*b*) AND straightway there was in their SYNAGOGUE a man with an UNCLEAN SPIRIT; and he cried out, saying, What have we to do with thee, thou Jesus of Nazareth? art thou come to destroy us? I know thee who thou art, the holy one of God. And Jesus rebuked him, saying, Hold thy peace, and come out of him.

And the UNCLEAN SPIRIT, convulsing him, and crying with a loud voice, came out of him. And they were all amazed, insomuch that they questioned among themselves, saying, What is this? a NEW TEACHING! With Authority he commandeth even the UNCLEAN SPIRITS, and they obey him.

(c) AND the report of him went out straightway everywhere into all the region of Galilee round about.

> *Triads:* synagogue (including Lection 6), teach (4), unclean spirit.
>
> *Major Triads:* Nazarene, (holy one) of God, new.

NOTES

(1) The fourth occurrence of 'Nazarene' is in Lection 62; but some manuscripts omit. In this lection a demoniac addresses Jesus as 'holy one of God'; in Lections 15 and 20 the phrase used by the demoniac is 'son of God'; despite the variation in the title, this seems to make a major triad.

(2) Matthew omits subdivision *b* of this lection, and inserts into *a* his 'Sermon on the Mount'; in the non-B enumeration it remains a single lection in spite of its bulk, and retains the same number, 5; Lection 15 of Mark is included with it (see note to 15). The second half of 5*a* (above) follows the Sermon; then comes the Leper (8*c*) which is given the number 6; and then the Centurion's Servant from Q which is numbered 7.

(3) Tatian does not follow Matthew in these changes; but after this lection he places the Call of Matthew (from Matthew) which he regards as quite distinct from the Call of Levi in Mark.

NEW YEAR VI
Fourth Week of Marheswan.

LECTION 6 (Mark i. 29–34).
Matthew non-B 8, 'Concerning Peter's Wife's Mother'; Matthew non-B 9, 'Concerning those Healed of Divers Diseases'.

Mark non-B 2, 'Concerning Peter's Wife's Mother'. Tatian 6.
Old Latin 3

(a) AND straightway, when they were come out of the SYNA-GOGUE, they came into the House of SIMON and ANDREW, with JAMES and JOHN. Now Simon's wife's mother lay sick of a fever; and straightway they tell him of her; and he came and took her by the hand, and raised her up; and the fever left her, and she ministered unto them.

Mark non-B 3, 'Concerning those Healed of Divers Diseases'

(*b*)   And at even, when the sun did set, they brought unto him all that were sick, and them that were possessed with DEVILS. And all the city was gathered together at the door. And he healed many that were sick with divers diseases, and cast out many DEVILS; and he suffered not the DEVILS to speak, because they knew him.

(*Second script-division in* B)

Triads: synagogue (with Lection 5), devils.
Major Triads: Simon (Peter) Andrew James John.

NOTE

Matthew has omitted Lection 5*b* and *c*, and goes on to omit 7. He retains this double lection, placing it after the Centurion's Servant. It rather suggests that it stood as a single lection in his copy of Mark, as it does in *B*.

NEW YEAR VII
First Week in Kislew (November–December): Ninth Month.

LECTION 7 (Mark i. 35–7).
Omitted in Matthew. The numeral zeta (seven) is missing from the margin of *B*; the assumption is that it was intended to coincide with the script-division.

Mark non-B 3 continued. Tatian 7 begins

AND in the morning, a great while before day, he rose up and went out, and departed into a Desert place, and there PRAYED. And Simon and they that were with him followed after him; and they found him, and say unto him, All are seeking thee.

Major Triad: pray.

NOTES

(1) There seems to have been considerable difficulty and confusion in combining and re-dividing the small Marcan lections here. *B*'s separation of 7 from 8*a* seems indefensible.

(2) The combination of Lections 7 and 8 would seem to be original, and is supported in two ways: (i) the script-divisions of *B* seem to mark off 7 and 8 as a single lection, and (ii) they occur as a single lection in the Greek calendar for the Second Sabbath in Lent. The script-divisions may be related to the latter system.

(3) Tatian supports the division between Lections 6 and 7 by beginning his seventh lection at this point.

WINTER I
Second Week in Kislew.

LECTION 8 (Mark i. 38–45).
Matthew non-*B* 6, 'Concerning the Leper'.

Mark non-B 3 continued. Tatian 7

(*a*) AND he saith unto them, Let us go elsewhere into the next towns, that I may PREACH there also; for to this end came I forth.

(*b*) AND he went into their Synagogues throughout all Galilee, PREACHING and casting out Devils.

Mark non-B 4, 'Concerning the Leper'. Tatian 22. Old Latin 4

(*c*) AND there cometh to him a Leper, beseeching him, and kneeling down to him, and saying unto him, If thou wilt, thou canst make me CLEAN. And being moved with compassion, he stretched forth his hand, and touched him, and saith unto him, I will; be thou made CLEAN. And straightway the Leprosy departed from him, and he was made CLEAN. And he strictly charged him, and straightway sent him out, and saith unto him, See thou say nothing to any man: but go thy way,

'shew thyself to the priest',   (Lev. xiii. 49)

and offer for thy Cleansing the things which Moses commanded, for a testimony unto them. But he went out, and began to PUBLISH it much, and to spread abroad the matter, insomuch that Jesus could no more openly enter into a city, but was without in Desert places: and they came to him from every quarter.

(Third script-division in B)

Triads: preach-publish (same word in the Greek), make clean.

NOTES

(1) This lection has a double function in the *B* system; it completes the first 'heptad' or sequence of seven, and also opens the second heptad. Its unity seems to be shown by the minor triad 'preach, publish' (announce, proclaim). Doubtless Lection 7 should be included with it; see notes on 7.

(2) The Leper story seems to have circulated at an early date quite independently of its context here. Matthew moves it to an earlier point, using it as

FIGURE TWO

ΑΠΗΛΘΕΝΑΠΑΥΤΟΥΗ
ΛΕΠΡΑΚΑΙΕΚΑΘ ΡΙCΘΗ
ΚΑΙΕΜΒΡΕΙΜΗCΑΜΕΝ·
ΑΥΤΩΕΥΘΥCΕΞΕΚΑΛΕ
ΑΥΤΟΝΚΑΙΛΕΓΕΙΑΥ
ΟΡΑΜΗΔΕΝΙΜΗΛΕΝΕΙ
ΠΗCΑΛΛΑΥΠΑΓΕCΕΑΥ
ΤΟΝΔΕΙΖΟΝΤΩΙΕΡΕΙC
ΠΡΟCΕΝΕΓΚΓΠΕΡΙΤΟΥ
ΝΑΘΑΡΙCΜΟΥCΟΥΑΠΡ
CΕΤΑΞΕΝΜΩΥCΗCΕΙC
ΜΑΡΤΥΡΙΟΝΑΥΤΟΙC
ΟΔΕΕΞΕΛΘΩΝΗΡΞΑΤΟ
ΚΝΡΥCCΕΙΝΠΟΛΛΑΚΑΙ
ΔΙΑΦΗΜΙΖΕΙΝΤΟΝΛΟ
ΓΟΝΩCΤΕΜΗΚΕΤΙΑΥ
ΤΟΝΔΥΝΑCΘΑΙΦΑΝΕΡ
ΕΙCΠΟΛΙΝΕΙCΕΛΘΕΙΝ
ΑΛΛΕΞΩΕΠΕΡΗΜΟΙCΤ
ΠΟΙCΚΑΙΗΡΧΟΝΤΟΠΡ
ΑΥΤΟΝΠΑΝΤΟΘΕΝ
θ ΚΑΙΕΙCΕΛΘΩΝΠΑΛΙΝΕΙ· 2·
ΚΑΦΑΡΝΑΟΥΜΔΙΗΜε

Page 1279 of Codex Vaticanus 1209 (Cod. *B*) from the phototypic
edition of Ulricus Hoepli, Milan 1904.

This is a reproduction of the last 23 lines of the first column of the third page of Mark,
being the fifth column of that gospel. It shows the script-division which occurs at the
end of Lection 8. The theta in the left-hand margin under a horizontal bar is the figure
nine. The bent bar to the left and top of the word KAI is of no significance. Somebody
went through this manuscript at a late date and indicated our modern chapter-divisions
in this way. There is a small figure 2 in the right-hand margin which corresponds to it,
indicating that this is verse 1 of our chapter 2.

126

a pendant to his 'Sermon on the Mount'; see notes on 5. Tatian does not hesitate to move it to a quite late point; it occurs in his twenty-second Section before the Feeding of the Four Thousand.

(3) There are no further script-divisions in *B* until after Lection 22. The only suggestion we can make as to their function in these opening lections is that they served to mark off two special lections, (i) the Baptism and Temptation of Jesus, and (ii) the Leper. The importance of the latter lection may be attested by the probability that Marcion had a special text of it, and used it in some special way, and also by the enlarged text of it which seems to underlie the Gospel fragment published by Bell and Skeat.

WINTER II
Third Week in Kislew.

LECTION 9 (Mark ii. 1–12).
Matthew non-*B* 13, 'Concerning the Paralytic'.

Mark non-B 4 continued. Tatian 7. Old Latin 5

(*a*) AND when he entered again into Capernaum after some days, it was noised that he was in the House. And many were gathered together, so that there was no longer room for them, no, not even about the door: and he spake the word unto them.

Mark non-B 5, 'Concerning the Paralytic'

(*b*) AND they come, bringing unto him a man sick of the PALSY, borne of four. And when they could not come nigh unto him for the crowd, they uncovered the roof where he was: and when they had broken it up, they let down the BED whereon the sick of the PALSY lay. And Jesus seeing their FAITH saith unto the sick of the PALSY, Son, thy SINS ARE FORGIVEN. But there were certain of the Scribes sitting there, and REASONING IN THEIR HEARTS, Why doth this man thus speak? he blasphemeth: who can FORGIVE SINS but one, even God? And straightway Jesus, perceiving in his spirit that they so REASONED WITHIN THEMSELVES, saith unto them, Why REASON ye these things IN YOUR HEARTS? Whether is easier, to say to the sick of the PALSY, Thy SINS ARE FORGIVEN; or to say, ARISE, and take up thy BED, and walk? But that ye may know that the SON OF MAN hath Authority on earth to FORGIVE SINS (he saith

to the sick of the PALSY), I say unto thee, ARISE, take up thy
BED, and go unto thy house.

(*c*) AND he AROSE, and straightway took up the BED, and went
forth before them all; insomuch that they were all amazed, and
glorified God, saying, We never saw it on this fashion.

Triads: The repetitions exceed the figure three; sick of the palsy (5), bed (4),
sins forgiven (4), questioning in their hearts (within themselves), rise and take
up (bed).

Major Triads: faith, son of man.

NOTES

(1) The text reads 'except one, God'. According to Rabbinic custom the
scribes probably said 'except the One'; 'God' being an explanatory addition
for Gentile hearers.

(2) This is the Gospel for the Second Sunday in Lent in the Greek Calendar,
including the whole *B* lection.

(3) In the years 1941–6, Hanukkah (Dedication), which occurs on Kislew 25,
fell on 15 December, 4 December, 22 December, 11 December, 30 November
and 18 December respectively.

WINTER III

Fourth Week in Kislew. Kislew 25 was the Feast of the Dedication, probably
connected with the winter solstice.

LECTION 10 (Mark ii. 13–14).

Matthew non-*B* 14. This narrative appears three times in Tatian, twice in 6,
and once in 7.

Mark non-B 6, 'Concerning Levi the Publican'. Tatian 7

(*a*) AND he went forth again by the Sea side; and all the Multitude resorted unto him, and he Taught them.

(*b*) AND as he passed by, he saw Levi the son of Alphaeus,
sitting at the place of toll, and he saith unto him, FOLLOW ME.
And he arose and FOLLOWED HIM.

Triads: follow (completed in 11).

Major Triads: follow.

WINTER IV
First Week in Tebet (December–January): Tenth Month.

LECTION 11 (Mark ii. 15–17).
Matthew non-*B* 14 continued.

Mark non-B 6 continued. Tatian 7. Old Latin 6

(*a*)   AND it came to pass, that he was sitting at meat in his House, and many PUBLICANS and SINNERS sat down with Jesus and his Disciples: for there were many, and they FOLLOWED HIM. And the Scribes of the Pharisees, when they saw that he was eating with the SINNERS and PUBLICANS, said unto his Disciples, He eateth and drinketh with PUBLICANS and SINNERS.

(*b*)   AND when Jesus heard it, he saith unto them,

They that are whole have no need of a physician,
But they that are sick:
I came not to call the righteous,
But Sinners.

Triads: follow him (concluded from 10), publicans and sinners (sinners repeated a fourth time).

NOTES

(1) Lections 10 and 11, combined, are the Gospel for the Third Sabbath in Lent in the Greek Calendar. The minor triad 'follow' confirms their unity.

(2) In *D* and the Latin versions the name of the publican is given as James son of Alphaeus, a reading which must surely have been current in a Marcan area before Matthew became authoritative there. This is supported by Θ so far as the text is concerned, but his title reads 'Concerning Levi the Publican'; in the Gospels of the Emperor Otto in the John Rylands Library, the reverse is the case.

(3) In the Arabic text of Tatian we find the Call of Levi narrated for the second time. It has been conjectured that the duplication arose from a confusion between the Levi of what is no doubt the true text, and the James of *D*, Θ, etc.; that is to say Tatian included a call of Levi and a call of James, but James has been corrected to Levi in the text on which the Arabic is based.

Tatian thus has three versions of this story.

(4) In 1941–6 the New Moon of Tebet fell on 21 December, 9 December, 28 December, 17 December, 5 December and 24 December respectively. It tends to precede rather than to follow the winter solstice.

Winter V

Second Week in Tebet. This week would on the average be near the winter solstice, 21 December.

Lection 12 (Mark ii. 18–22).

Matthew non-*B* 14 continued. The twelfth lection marks the end of the first quarter.

*Mark non-*B* 6 continued. Tatian 7*

(*a*) AND John's DISCIPLES and the Pharisees were FASTING: and they come and say unto him, Why do John's DISCIPLES and the DISCIPLES of the Pharisees FAST, but thy DISCIPLES FAST not?

(*b*) AND Jesus said unto them,
Can the sons of the Bride-chamber FAST, while the BRIDE-GROOM is with them?
As long as they have the BRIDEGROOM with them, they cannot FAST.
But the Days will come, when the BRIDEGROOM shall be taken away from them,
And then will they FAST—in THAT DAY.

(*c*) No man seweth a piece of undressed cloth on an OLD garment: else that which should fill it up taketh from it, the NEW from the OLD, and a worse rent is made.

(*d*) AND no man putteth NEW WINE into OLD WINE-SKINS: else the WINE will burst the SKINS, and the WINE perisheth, and the SKINS.

Triads: disciples (4; but 6 if we include Lection 11), bridegroom, fast (6), old, wine, wine-skins. But R.V. adds, 'But they put new wine into fresh wine-skins'; the text is uncertain.

Major Triads: new, that day.

NOTES

(1) Matthew keeps Lections 10, 11 and 12 together, separating them from 13 and 14 which he places rather later.

(2) The non-*B* system links Lections 10, 11, 12 and 13; but this is going too far. See notes on 13.

(3) The twelfth lection marks the first quarterly turning-point in the Marcan arrangement of forty-eight lections. It may be connected with the winter

solstice. The festal and messianic character of Lections 12 and 13 is obvious. See Commentary.

(4) This lection is not included among the Lenten gospels of the Greek Church.

WINTER VI
Third Week in Tebet.

LECTION 13 (Mark ii. 23–8).
Included in Matthew non-B 20, 'Concerning those Sent by John'.

Mark non-B 6 continued. Tatian 7. Old Latin 7

(*a*) AND it came to pass, that he was going on the SABBATH day through the cornfields; and his Disciples began, as they went, to pluck the ears of corn. And the Pharisees said unto him, Behold, why do they on the SABBATH day that which is NOT LAWFUL?

(*b*) AND he said unto them, Did ye never read what DAVID did, when he had need, and was an hungred, he, and they that were with him? How he entered into the house of God when Abiathar was high priest, and did eat the shewbread, which it is NOT LAWFUL to eat save for the priests, and gave also to them that were with him? (I Sam. xxi. 7; Lev. xxiv. 5.) And he said unto them,

> The SABBATH was made for MAN,
> And not Man for the SABBATH:
> So that the SON OF MAN
> Is lord even of the SABBATH.

Triads: see under Lection 14.

NOTES

(1) The phrase 'when Abiathar was high priest' is not supported by Matthew and Luke, and is inaccurate. It looks like a gloss which has been taken into Mark.

(2) The inclusion of this lection with 10, 11 and 12 by the non-B system is obviously unsatisfactory, and is not adopted by all its supporters. The Vulgate system in Amiatinus combines 13 and 14 in a single lection; Θ combines 13 *b* and 14, but has an alternative method indicated in the margin and at the head of the page. The marginal note draws attention to 13 as a 'beginning'

by the letters 'AP' (*arkhē*); and a title at the head of the page reads 'Jesus was going through the Cornfields on the Sabbath'; and the use of the personal name, rather than the title 'Lord', suggests an early date for this title. Opposite this title are the letters 'TⲰKP'.

(3) In the Greek Calendar, Lections 13 and 14 form the Gospel for the First Sabbath in Lent, and it looks as if Θ were attempting to bring the non-*B* system of chapter-divisions into line with this system of special gospels from Mark for the Sabbaths and Sundays of Lent.

We have a remarkable community of interest between Amiatinus, Θ, and the Greek Calendar.

Winter VII
Fourth Week in Tebet.

Lection 14 (Mark iii. 1–6).
Matthew non-*B* 21, 'Concerning the Man with the Withered Hand'.

Mark non-B 7, 'Concerning the Man with the Withered Hand'.
Tatian 7. Old Latin 8

(*a*)   AND he entered again into the Synagogue; and there was a man there which had his HAND WITHERED. And they watched him, whether he would heal him on the SABBATH day; that they might accuse him. And he saith unto the man that had his HAND WITHERED, Arise into the midst. And he saith unto them,

> IS IT LAWFUL on the SABBATH day to do good, or to do harm? To SAVE a LIFE, or to kill?

But they held their peace. And when he had looked round about on them with anger, being grieved at the HARDENING of their HEART, he saith unto the man, Stretch forth thy HAND. And he stretched it forth: and his HAND was restored.

(*b*)   AND the Pharisees went out, and straightway with the HERODIANS took counsel against him, how they might destroy him.

(*The lection ends on a short line in* B)

Triads (13 and 14): sabbath (7), is it lawful (not lawful), hand (4) withered (2).

Major Triads: son of man, David, save life, Herodians.

(1) The last line of this lection in *B* is short by about two letters, but as the next line does not project into the left-hand margin, we cannot count it as a script-division.

(2) A script-division here, if it existed, would mark the end of the second heptad in *B* and the first heptad in non-*B*; the 14 of one system being reduced to 7 in the other. The section numbers of Tatian are level with those of non-*B*, and so continue except for perturbations produced by Matthew's rearrangement of Mark's order. The Vulgate lections in Amiatinus are two ahead of the non-*B*, this one being number 9; this continues with fluctuations until they become level at 41.

(3) The first four Marcan lections at the beginning of Lent in the Greek Calendar are chosen from this first sequence of 14 lections in *B*, or 7 in non-*B*. The four last are chosen from the last 7 lections of the liturgical year in *B* (36–42) which are also 7 in non-*B*, but were originally 14 if our theory is correct. In between comes the Epphathah lection (31).

2. THE SPRING SEASON

The fourteen weeks counted from the end of Tisri, which occurs some time in October, have brought us to the end of January or the beginning of February, which is the Mediterranean spring. It is marked in our Calendars by the fixed Festival of Candlemas on 2 February, an observation of prehistoric origin. Even in Canada, where unbroken snow still covers the landscape, there is a popular belief that spring stirs on that day.

It is also marked by the beginning of Lent, which is a Middle English word for spring; but the Lenten season of the Christian Calendar is not fixed. It varies in accordance with the date of Easter; and Easter varies by twenty-eight or twenty-nine days in accordance with the incidence of the full moon. You cannot know when Lent begins unless you know when Easter comes. The first Sunday of Lent is a nominal forty days before Easter (actually forty-three) and is called Quadragesima (contracted in French into 'Carême'). The Sundays before Lent, working backwards, are Quinquagesima (fiftieth), Sexagesima (sixtieth), and Septuagesima (seventieth).

Quinquagesima really is the fiftieth day before Easter, just as Pentecost (Whitsunday) is the fiftieth day after Easter. Its earliest possible date is February 1.

There is no sign of a Lent in Hebrew liturgiology; but it was equally necessary for the Hebrews to begin making their calculations at this time with regard to the date of Easter. The calendar, as they had been operating it, would have to be adjusted to the Paschal date. A seven-week period previous to the Pascha would be a natural way of doing this. The pivot on which our theory has turned has been the equation of the Feeding of the Five Thousand with the Sunday after the Pascha and the Feeding of the Four Thousand with Pentecost fifty days later; now fifty days before Pascha we find seed parables on Quinquagesima, and on the previous Sunday (Sexagesima) we find the Parable of the Sower, where it still is in the Roman and Anglican systems. This gives us three high points in the agricultural year:

The Spring	Sexagesima, Quinquagesima	Seed Parables	LECTIONS 17, 18
Barley Harvest	Sunday after Pascha (Easter)	Five Thousand	LECTION 25
Wheat Harvest	Pentecost (Whitsunday)	Four Thousand	LECTION 32

The lection-system of *B*, allotting as it does 49 lections to the liturgical year, is built up on the basis of seven sevens; but these sevens are not exact, nor are they in step with the series given above. The arrangement adopted in our text gives two sets of seven (1–14) followed by a set of eight (15–22); while the script-divisions suggest a set of eight (1–8) followed by a set of fourteen (9–22). Nevertheless it must be recognized that the system of pentecosts, or sequences of seven lections, is a normative principle in the system of chapter-enumeration, and probably in the composition of the gospel.

There are several reasons why it does not keep step with the agricultural series based on Pascha. For one thing confusion is created by the fact that the weeks counted forward from the autumn equinox have to be accommodated to the weeks counted backward from the Pascha; an adjustment which is provided for in the Christian Calendar by the provision of more Sundays after Epiphany than are commonly required. But in the Hebrew Calendar there was worse confusion than this; for the number of twelve lunar months was inadequate to the solar year, and there were always weeks which were not accounted for; these were left to accumulate over a period of years, and then compensated for by the introduction of a thirteenth month. And in addition to all this the 48 or 49 lections provided for the Sundays of the year were inadequate to the actual number in the solar year, though this may have been pretty well made up by the special lessons for special Sundays; we have rather assumed, however, that the special lections for Pascha and Sukkoth (if this conjecture is correct) were not Sunday lections.

We must, therefore, on all accounts, assume that the Marcan Calendar was elastic, even more elastic than our Christian Calendar. And it is likely to have been elastic at this very point where the difficulty made itself felt. Our suggestion is that the extra-long lections like 16 and 18 were readily divisible if more Sundays were required to fill out the pre-Paschal period; and that the short sentences like 18 d and e may have been the initial lines of well-known lections, which were within the repertoire of the lector, and could be brought in if required.

It only remains to be added that while the point which we have reached has been described by us as the Mediterranean spring, it was not the season when most of the sowing was done. The great season for sowing was in the autumn as we have pointed out; but sowing also took place in the spring, and the clods were loosened over the seed which had been sowed in the autumn. Growth was looked for from the seeds at this time.

SUNDAY BEFORE SEPTUAGESIMA
First Week in Shebat (January–February): Eleventh Month. Season of Spring Sowing begins about now.

LECTION 15 (Mark iii. 7–13).
Absorbed into Matthew non-B 5.

Mark non-B 7 continued. Tatian 8 begins

(a) AND Jesus with his Disciples withdrew to the Sea: and a GREAT MULTITUDE from Galilee Followed: and from Judaea, and from Jerusalem, and from Idumaea, and beyond Jordan, and about TYRE and Sidon, a GREAT MULTITUDE, hearing what great things he did, came unto him.

Old Latin 9

(*b*) AND he spake to his Disciples, that a little Boat should wait on him because of the *MULTITUDE, lest they should throng him: for he had healed many; insomuch that as many as had plagues pressed upon him that they might touch him. And the Unclean Spirits, whensoever they beheld him, fell down before him, and cried, saying, Thou art the SON OF GOD. And he charged them much that they should not make him known.

Mark non-B 8, 'Concerning the Choice of the Apostles'

(*c*) AND he goeth up into the MOUNTAIN, and calleth unto him whom he himself would: and they went unto him.

Triads: (great) multitude.

Major Triads: Tyre (and Sidon), Son of God (see Lection 5, note), mountain.

NOTE

Matthew takes this lection to be the occasion on which the 'Sermon on the Mount' was delivered; but he moves it into Lection 5 where he places that discourse. Luke also takes this lection to be the occasion of the Sermon on the Mount, which he places after 16 *a*.

SEPTUAGESIMA
Second Week in Shebat.

LECTION 16 (Mark iii. 14–35).
Dispersed in Matthew: see non-*B* 19, 22, 23.

Mark non-B 8 continued. Tatian 8, 14, 16

(*a*) AND he appointed TWELVE, that they might be with him, and that he might Send them forth to Preach, and to have Authority to cast out DEVILS: and he appointed TWELVE; and Simon he surnamed 'Peter'; and James the son of Zebedee, and John the brother of James; and them he surnamed 'Boanerges', which is, 'Sons of thunder': and Andrew, and Philip, and Bartholomew, and Matthew, and Thomas, and James the son of Alphaeus, and Thaddaeus, and Simon the Cananaean, and Judas ISCARIOT, which also BETRAYED him.

* R.V. crowd.

136

Old Latin 10

(*b*) AND he cometh into a HOUSE. And the Multitude cometh together again, so that they could not so much as eat bread. And when his friends heard it, they went out to lay hold on him: for they said, He is beside himself. And the Scribes which came down from Jerusalem said, He hath Beelzebub, and, By the prince of the DEVILS casteth he out the DEVILS.

(*c*) AND he called them unto him, and said unto them in Parables, How can SATAN cast out SATAN?

> And if a kingdom be DIVIDED against itself,   (Dan. v. 28)
>   That kingdom CANNOT STAND.
> And if a HOUSE be DIVIDED against itself,
>   That HOUSE will not be ABLE TO STAND.
> And if SATAN hath risen up against himself, and is DIVIDED,
>   He CANNOT STAND, but hath an end.

But no one can enter into the HOUSE of the strong man, and spoil his goods, except he first bind the strong man; and then he will spoil his HOUSE.

(*d*) Verily I say unto you,

> All their sins shall be FORGIVEN unto the sons of men,
>   And their BLASPHEMIES wherewith soever they shall
>   BLASPHEME:
> But whosoever shall BLASPHEME against the HOLY SPIRIT
>   Hath never FORGIVENESS, but is guilty of an eternal sin:

(Because they said, He hath an Unclean Spirit.)

(*e*) AND there come his MOTHER and his BRETHREN; and, STANDING WITHOUT, they sent unto him, calling him. And a Multitude was sitting about him; and they say unto him, Behold, thy MOTHER and thy BRETHREN without seek for thee. And he answereth them, and saith, Who is my MOTHER and my BRETHREN? And looking round on them which sat round about him, he saith, Behold, my MOTHER and my BRETHREN!

> For whosoever shall do the will of God,
>   The same is my BROTHER, and sister, and MOTHER.

Triads: twelve (with 18*a*), devils, Satan, divided, not stand, blaspheme (blasphemy), house (five times), mother and brethren (five times), forgive (forgiveness), (stand) outside (with 18*a*).

Major Triads: parable?, Satan, Iscariot with the verb betray, Son of man (men)?, Holy Spirit.

NOTES

(1) Luke retains *a* in this position and makes it an introduction to his version of the 'Sermon on the Mount' after which he places the Centurion's Servant and other material of a non-Marcan character. Tatian follows Luke in doing this.

(2) Matthew moves *a* to a later point, and makes it an introduction to the Sending of the Twelve.

(3) The remaining subdivisions, *b* to *e*, are dispersed in Matthew and Luke, owing to the influence of Q, which seems to have had a more elaborate version of some of this material. In Luke, *e* does not lose its connexion with the parables, but is placed after them.

(4) The words 'whom he also named apostles' in *a* are omitted in some manuscripts, and must be regarded as doubtful.

(5) The words 'Everything shall be forgiven to the sons of men' appeared in Q in some such form as this: 'Whoever shall speak a word against the Son of Man shall be forgiven'; if it is considered permissible to restore the text of Mark to this form, then there are three repetitions of the words 'son of man' in the first half of the gospel, forming a major triad.

(6) This lection is obviously composite. The second part of *b*, with *c* and *d*, would appear to be an insertion into the text.

SEXAGESIMA

Third Week in Shebat.

LECTION 17 (Mark iv. 1–9).

Matthew non-B 24, 'Concerning the Parables'.

Mark non-B 8 continued. Tatian 16. Old Latin 11

(*a*) AND again he began to TEACH by the SEA side. And there is gathered unto him a very great Multitude, so that he entered into a Boat, and sat in the SEA; and all the Multitude were by the SEA on the land.

And he TAUGHT them many things in PARABLES, and said unto them in his TEACHING,

Mark non-B 9, 'Concerning the Seed, a Parable'

(b) *HEAR: Behold, the SOWER went forth to SOW: and it came to pass, as he SOWED, some seed fell by the way side, and the birds came and devoured it. And other fell on the rocky ground, where it had not much EARTH; and straightway it sprang up, because it had no deepness of EARTH: and when the sun was risen, it was scorched; and because it had no root, it withered away. And other fell among the thorns, and the thorns grew up, and choked it, and it yielded no Fruit. And others fell into the good †EARTH, and yielded Fruit, growing up and increasing; and brought forth, thirtyfold, and sixtyfold, and a hundredfold. And he said,

WHO HATH EARS TO HEAR, LET HIM HEAR.

(Cf. Ezek. xii. 2.)

Triads: teach, sea, sow, earth, hear.

Major Triads: he who hath ears, etc.

NOTES

(1) According to Θ, non-B9 begins at the words 'And he taught them'.

(2) The fact that this lection was originally conceived as a separate unit becomes clear when we note that 17 and 19 form a continuous narrative. He is still in the boat at the commencement of 19. Lection 18 has been sandwiched in.

QUINQUAGESIMA

Fourth Week in Shebat. The fiftieth day before Easter Sunday, allowing that to be the Sunday after the Pascha.

LECTION 18 (Mark iv. 10–34).

Matthew non-B 24 continued.

Mark non-B 9 continued. Tatian 16, 9, and 17

(a) AND when he was alone, they that were about him with the TWELVE asked of him the PARABLES. And he said unto them,

Unto you is given the Mystery of the KINGDOM OF GOD:
But unto them that are WITHOUT, all things are done in PARABLES:

That 'Seeing they may See, and not Perceive;

* R.V. hearken.   † R.V. good ground.

And HEARING they may HEAR, and not understand,
  Lest haply they should turn again, and it should be FOR-
    GIVEN them'. (Isa. vi. 9–10)

(*b*) AND he saith unto them,

  Know ye not this PARABLE?
  And how shall ye Know all the PARABLES?

(The sower soweth the word. And these are they by the way side,
where the word is sown; and when they have heard, straightway
cometh Satan, and taketh away the word which hath been sown
in them. And these in like manner are they that are sown upon
the rocky places, who, when they have heard the word, straightway receive it with joy; and they have no root in themselves,
but endure for a while; then, when tribulation or persecution
ariseth because of the word, straightway they stumble.

(*c*)   And others
are they that are sown among the thorns; these are they that have
heard the word, and the cares of the world, and the deceitfulness
of riches, and the lusts of other things entering in, choke the word,
and it becometh unfruitful. And those are they that were sown
upon the good ground; such as hear the word, and accept it, and
bear fruit, thirtyfold, and sixtyfold, and a hundredfold.)

(*d*) AND he said unto them,

  Is the lamp brought to be put under the bushel or under the bed,
    And not to be put on the stand?
  For there is nothing hid, save that it should be manifested;
    Neither was anything made secret, but that it should come
      to light.
IF ANY MAN HATH EARS TO HEAR, LET HIM HEAR.

Old Latin 12

(*e*) AND he said unto them,

  Take heed what ye HEAR:
    With what MEASURE ye *MEASURE, it shall be MEASURED
      unto you;

        * R.V. ye mete.

And more shall be given unto you.
For HE THAT HATH, to him shall be given:
And HE THAT HATH not, from him shall be taken away
even THAT which HE HATH.

(*f*) AND he said,

So is the KINGDOM OF GOD, as if a man should cast SEED
upon the EARTH; and should SLEEP and RISE night and day,
and the SEED should spring up and grow, he knoweth not how.
The EARTH beareth fruit of herself; first the blade, then the ear,
then the full corn in the ear. But when the Fruit is ripe, straightway
> 'he sendeth forth the sickle
> because the harvest is come'.   (Joel iii. 13)

(*g*) AND he said,

How shall we liken the KINGDOM OF GOD? or in what
PARABLE shall we set it forth? It is like a grain of mustard (seed),
which, when it is Sown upon the EARTH, though it be less than
all the SEEDS that are upon the EARTH, yet when it is Sown,
groweth up, and becometh greater than all the herbs, and putteth
out great branches;

> 'so that the birds of the heaven
> can lodge under the shadow thereof'.   (Dan. iv. 12)

(*h*) AND with many such PARABLES spake he the word unto
them, as they were able to HEAR it: and without a PARABLE
spake he not unto them: but privately to his own Disciples he
expounded all things.

Triads (neglecting the bracketed portions of (*b*) and (*c*)): twelve, outside,
and forgiven, complete triads begun in Lection 16: kingdom of God, hear
(six times), parable (seven times), measure, he who has, seed, earth. Note:
see—see—perceive.

Major Triads: kingdom of God, not understand, he who hath ears, etc., sleep,
rise (wake).

NOTES

(1) Part of *b* and all of *c* are bracketed because they look like a later addition
to the text.

(2) According to Amiatinus a new lection began at *d* in the Vulgate.

(3) The minor parabolic sayings are moved by Matthew into the Sermon on the Mount, where Tatian also places them. We suggest that they are first lines of whole lections which could be used in case of necessity.

(4) The word 'parable' occurs once in Lection 16, once in 17, and seven times in 18: making a triad of a sort. It also occurs in vii. 17, and in xii. 1, xii. 12, xii. 28.

(5) Instead of 'those who were around him, with the twelve', D has 'his disciples'.

(6) Compare 'know not' in f with 'know not' in Lection 50.

LENT I

First Week in Adar (February–March): Twelfth Month.

LECTION 19 (Mark iv. 35–v. 1).

Matthew non-B 11, 'Concerning the Rebuke of the Waters'.

Mark non-B 10, 'Concerning the Rebuke of the Waters'. Tatian 11. Old Latin 13

(a) AND on that day, when even was come, he saith unto them, Let us go over unto the other side. And leaving the Multitude, they take him with them, even as he was, in the BOAT. And other boats were with him. And there ariseth a great storm of WIND, and the waves beat into the BOAT, insomuch that the BOAT was now filling. And he himself was in the stern, ASLEEP on the cushion: and they AWAKE him, and say unto him, Master, carest thou not that we perish? And he AWOKE, and rebuked the WIND, and said unto the SEA, Peace, be still. And the WIND ceased, and there was a great calm.

(b) AND he said unto them, Why are ye fearful? Have ye not yet FAITH? And they FEARED exceedingly, and said one to another, Who then is this, that even the WIND and the SEA obey him?

Old Latin 14

(c) AND they came to the other side of the SEA, into the country of the Gerasenes.

Triads: boat (of Jesus), wind, sea.

Major Triads: sleep and wake (rise: same word in Greek), faith, fear.

NOTE

According to Θ, Lection 10 of non-B began at 'And leaving the', and Lection 11 at 'And they came' (19c).

LENT II
Second Week in Adar.

LECTION 20 (Mark v. 2–20).
Matthew non-*B* 12, 'Concerning the Two Demoniacs'.

Mark non-B 11, 'Concerning the Legion'. Tatian 11 and 12

(*a*) AND when he was come out of the Boat, straightway there met him out of the TOMBS a man with an UNCLEAN SPIRIT, who had his dwelling in the TOMBS: and no man could any more bind him, no, not with a CHAIN; because that he had been often bound with fetters and CHAINS, and the CHAINS had been rent asunder by him, and the fetters broken in pieces: and no man had strength to tame him. And always, night and day, in the TOMBS and in the mountains, he was crying out, and cutting himself with stones.

(*b*) AND when he saw Jesus from afar, he ran and worshipped him; and crying out with a loud voice, he saith, What have I to do with thee, Jesus, thou SON OF the Most High GOD? I adjure thee by God, torment me not. For he said unto him, Come forth, thou UNCLEAN SPIRIT, out of the man.

(*c*) AND he asked him, What is thy name?

(*d*) AND he saith unto him, My name is Legion; for we are many. And he besought him much that he would not send them away out of the country. Now there was there on the Mountain side a great herd of SWINE feeding. And they besought him, saying, Send us into the SWINE, that we may enter into them. And he gave them leave. And the UNCLEAN SPIRITS came out, and entered into the SWINE: and the herd rushed down the steep into the SEA, in number about two thousand; and they were choked in the SEA.

(*e*) AND they that fed them fled, and told it in the city, and in the country. And they came to see what it was that had come to pass.

(*f*) AND they come to Jesus, and behold him that was POSSESSED WITH DEVILS sitting, clothed and in his right mind, even him that had the Legion: and they were AFRAID. And they that saw it declared unto them how it befell him that was POSSESSED WITH DEVILS, and concerning the SWINE. And they began to beseech him to depart from their borders.

(g) AND as he was entering into the Boat, he that had been POSSESSED WITH DEVILS besought him that he might be with him. And he suffered him not, but saith unto him, Go to thy house unto thy friends, and tell them how great things the Lord hath done for thee, and how he had mercy on thee.

(h) AND he went his way, and began to PUBLISH in Decapolis how great things Jesus had done for him: and all men did marvel.

Triads: tombs, unclean spirit, swine (4), possessed with devils, sea (two occurrences only: but see first verse of Lection 21).

Major Triads: fear (afraid); for 'publish' see note on Lection 8; Son of God.

LENT III
Third Week in Adar. Adar 13 was the 'Fast of Esther' or 'Fast of Nicanor'; Adar 14 and 15, the 'Feast of Purim'.

LECTION 21 (Mark v. 21–43).
Matthew non-*B* 15, 'Concerning the Daughter of the Synagogue-Ruler', and 16, 'Concerning the Woman with the Haemorrhage'.

Mark non-B 11 continued. Tatian 12. * Old Latin 15?*

(a) AND when Jesus had crossed over again in the Boat unto the other side, a great MULTITUDE was gathered unto him: and he was by the Sea.

Mark non-B 12, 'Concerning the Daughter of the Synagogue-Ruler'

(b) AND there cometh one of the RULERS OF THE SYNAGOGUE, Jairus by name; and seeing him, he falleth at his feet, and beseecheth him much, saying, My little daughter is at the point of DEATH: I pray thee, that thou come and lay thy hands on her, that she may be SAVED, and live.

(c) AND he went with him; and a great MULTITUDE followed him, and they thronged him.

* Old Latin 15: number omitted by Sabatier.

Mark non-B 13, '*Concerning the Woman with a Haemorrhage*'

(*d*) AND a woman, which had an issue of blood twelve years, and had suffered many things of many physicians, and had spent all that she had, and was nothing bettered, but rather grew worse, having heard the things concerning Jesus, came in the *MULTI-TUDE, behind, and TOUCHED HIS GARMENT. For she said, If I TOUCH but HIS GARMENTS, I shall be SAVED.

(*e*) AND straightway the fountain of her blood was dried up; and she felt in her body that she was healed of her plague.

(*f*) AND straightway Jesus, perceiving in himself that the POWER proceeding from him had gone forth, turned him about in the *MULTITUDE, and said, Who TOUCHED MY GARMENTS?

(*g*) AND his Disciples said unto him, Thou seest the MULTITUDE thronging thee, and sayest thou, Who Touched me? And he looked round about to see her that had done this thing.

(*h*) BUT the woman FEARING and trembling, knowing what had been done to her, came and fell down before him, and told him all the truth.

(*i*) AND he said unto her, Daughter, thy FAITH hath SAVED thee; go in peace, and be whole of thy plague. While he yet spake, they come from the RULER OF THE SYNAGOGUE's house, saying, Thy Daughter is DEAD: why troublest thou the Master any further?

(*j*) BUT Jesus, overhearing the word spoken, saith unto the RULER OF THE SYNAGOGUE, FEAR not, only BELIEVE. And he suffered no man to follow with him, save PETER, and JAMES, and JOHN the brother of JAMES.

(*k*) AND they come to the house of the RULER OF THE SYNA-GOGUE; and he beholdeth a tumult, and many weeping and wailing greatly. And when he was entered in, he saith unto them, Why make ye a tumult, and weep? the CHILD is not DEAD, but SLEEPETH. And they laughed him to scorn.

* R.V. crowd.

(*l*) BUT he, having put them all forth, taketh the father of the CHILD and her mother and them that were with him, and goeth in where the CHILD was. And taking the CHILD by the hand, he saith unto her, TALITHA CUMI; which is, being interpreted, DAMSEL, I say unto thee, ARISE. And straightway the DAMSEL ROSE UP, and walked; for she was twelve years old. And they were amazed straightway with a great amazement.

(*m*) AND he charged them much that no man should know this:

(*n*) AND he commanded that something should be given her to eat. And he went out from thence.

Triads: ruler of the synagogue (4), at the point of death—is dead—is not dead, multitude (5), saved, touch garments, child (4), talitha—damsel—damsel, cumi—awoke—rose up.

Major Triads: power, fear, faith (believe), Peter and James and John, sleep, rise (awake).

NOTES

(1) The insertion of the story of the Woman with a Haemorrhage into that of the Synagogue-Ruler makes subdivision difficult, and suggests that *B* is correct in making the combined story into one long lection. The Marcionite gospel appears to have omitted the cure of the daughter of the Synagogue-Ruler.

(2) There is no bar under the line to indicate the subdivision which we have lettered as *j*; but there is an oblique stroke in the margin, the purpose of which would seem to be to warn the lector of the resumption of the story of the Synagogue-Ruler.

(3) Purim was the Jewish Spring Festival, but we have very little information about its character. The Book of Esther was read. In the years 1942–7, Purim fell on 3 March, 21 March, 9 March, 27 February, 17 March and 6 March respectively.

LENT IV
Fourth Week in Adar.

LECTION 22 (Mark vi. 1–6).
Appended to Matthew non-*B* 24, 'Concerning the Parables'.

*Mark non-*B* 13 continued. Tatian 17. Old Latin 16*

(*a*) AND he cometh into his own country; and his Disciples follow him. And when the Sabbath was come, he began to Teach in the Synagogue: and many hearing him were astonished,

146

Page 1285 of Codex Vaticanus 1209 (Cod. *B*) from the phototypic
edition of Ulricus Hoepli, Milan 1904.

This is a reproduction of the bottom of the first column of the page. The kappa gamma in the margin under the horizontal bar is the number 23, so that fourteen lections have passed without any break in the continuity of the script. Again we argue that this division is deliberate and has some significance. It marks the point which we had arrived at by literary analysis as the end of the first half of the Calendar Year. It is probable that it indicated some important division in the text of Mark in the manuscript which lay before the scribe of *B*, or in its ancestor.

The figure 23 is on the line below the projecting first line of the new section of *B*, and there is a horizontal line under the first letter of the line opposite to it. If we suppose that this is carefully and deliberately done then we have a discrepancy between the lection-division and the script-division from which we might argue that they are independent systems.

147

saying, Whence hath this man these things? and, What is the Wisdom that is given unto this man, and what mean such POWERS wrought by his hands? Is not this the carpenter, the son of Mary, and brother of James, and Joses, and Judas, and Simon? and are not his sisters here with us? And they were Offended in him.

(*b*) AND Jesus said unto them, A PROPHET is not without honour, save in his own country, and among his own kin, and in his own House. And he could there do no POWER, save that he laid his hands upon a few sick folk, and healed them. And he marvelled because of their Unbelief.

(*Fourth script-division in* B)

Major Triads: power, prophet, unbelief (see 'faith').

NOTES

(1) Matthew has moved Lections 19, 20 and 21 to an earlier point in his gospel. This lection comes after his collection of parables, and previous to the story of Herod and John (see Lection 24) after which Matthew follows the order of Mark.

(2) Luke has already combined this lection with his own story of a preaching at Nazareth at the beginning of the ministry in Galilee: see note to Lection 4. It should be noted that Mark does not mention the name of Nazareth here, or anywhere else in his gospel except in Lection 2.

(3) The script-division marks the end of the first half-year, according to our theory. The 22 lections extend from the last week in Tisri to the last week in Adar, that is to say the non-liturgical part of the year. Lections 23–48 (49) are for the liturgical part of the year from Nisan 1 to Tisri 22.

3. THE FIRST MONTH: NISAN

Even though the official New Year was now on Tisri 1, the months were still counted from Nisan 1. This is because the observance of months, or moons, is agricultural, and has its bearing on the harvest, which is not completed until the Feast of Tabernacles. Students should bear in mind that millions of farmers still sow or plant when the moon is increasing, kill hogs when it is at the full, and reap when it is diminishing. The first moon of the year would be of especial potency.

Nisan 1. Appearance of the New Moon: the old New Year, still used in numbering the regnal years of kings. Regarded in Jubilees, Philo, and other authorities (by the Montanists?) as the day of creation.

Nisan 10. The Paschal Lamb chosen and set aside.

Nisan 14. The slaying of the Lamb in the temple during the afternoon; it should be remembered that the Jewish day ends at sunset, and the new day begins then.

Nisan 15. The Feast of the Passover (Pascha) held immediately after sunset of the 14th. This night would be the full moon.

The first day of the Feast of Unleavened Bread (Mazzoth) which went on from Nisan 15 to 21: seven days.

Nisan 16. The Firstfruits of the Barley Harvest (Omer). The first sheaf was cut on the eve, as soon as the sun of Nisan 15 had set. It was then offered in the Temple, or presumably at the local sanctuary if such existed. The Sadducees and Samaritans observed Omer on *the Sunday following Pascha.*

This Calendar of days should be compared with the Passion Narrative. According to Mark, Jesus kept the Passover on the eve of Nisan 15, and was crucified on the day of Nisan 15; this is corrected by the Johannine chronology according to which the Last Supper took place on the eve of Nisan 14, and Jesus suffered on the day of Nisan 14.

Pascha and Mazzoth coincided, but were different festivals. The seven days of Mazzoth were Nisan 15 to 21. The pattern of the days should be compared with that of Tisri (p. 117). Passover has no eighth day of completion, *Atzereth*, as Tisri does, on the 22nd; the completion of Passover is Pentecost. Besides, the completion of Tabernacles in Tisri closes the whole agricultural and liturgical year.

This year is counted from Nisan. The seven days from Nisan 15 to 21 were the days of Mazzoth; seven weeks brought one to Pentecost; seven months to Tabernacles; seven years to the sabbatical year; seven times seven years to the year of Jubilee. This is the natural liturgical-ritual-agricultural-apocalyptic method of measuring time.

When Herod celebrated his *genesia* (birth rites) we can by no means assume that what is meant is his natural birthday. It might mean his accession-day, and this would be counted as Nisan 1. The Mishnah reprobates the keeping of *genesia* along with *saturnalia* and *kalends* as heathen.

LENT V
First Week in Nisan (March–April): First Month. Nisan 1 was an old 'New Year's Day', and was still so used for certain purposes.
LECTION 23 (Mark vi. 7–13).
Matthew non-*B* 19, 'Concerning the Ordering of the Apostles'.

Mark non-B 14, 'Concerning the Ordering of the Apostles'. Tatian 12 and 13. Old Latin 17

(*a*) AND he went round about the villages Teaching.

(*b*) AND he called unto him the TWELVE, and began to Send them forth by two and two; and he gave them authority over the Unclean Spirits; and he charged them that they should take nothing for their journey, save a staff only; no bread, no wallet, no money in their purse; but to go shod with sandals: and, said he, put not on two coats. And he said unto them,

> Wheresoever ye enter into a House,
>   There abide till ye depart thence,
> And whatsoever place shall not receive you, and they hear you not,
>   As ye go forth thence, shake off the dust that is under your feet
> For a testimony unto them.

And they went out and PREACHED that men should REPENT. And they cast out many Devils, and anointed with oil many that were sick, and healed them.

Major Triads: (twelve), preach repentance.

NOTES

(1) The connexion of this lection with the following is indicated not only by the script-division which precedes it, but by the logical connexion with 25 *a*. See note to 25.

(2) In Q the Sending of the Twelve was preceded by a liturgical formula, 'Pray ye the lord of the harvest', etc. This would be perfectly applicable to the position of this lection just before Pascha, which is the beginning of barley-harvest; and it would be in perfect correlation with the parable of the sower, seven weeks before.

(3) In the years 1942–7 the New Moon of Nisan fell on 19 March, 6 April, 25 March, 15 March, 2 April and 22 March respectively.

LENT VI

Second Week in Nisan. The Sunday before the Pascha. The Pascha was Nisan 14, that is to say, the full moon of Nisan, falling next after the Spring Equinox, which is 21 March.

LECTION 24 (Mark vi. 14–29).

Matthew non-B 25, 'Concerning John and Herod'. This Lection is the last of the second quarter.

Mark non-B 15, 'Concerning John and Herod'.
Tatian 18. Old Latin 18

(*a*)   AND KING Herod heard thereof; for his name had become known: and they said, John the BAPTIST is Risen from the dead, and therefore do these POWERS work in him. But others said, It is ELIJAH. And others said, It is a PROPHET, even as one of the Prophets. But Herod, when he heard thereof, said, John, whom I beheaded, he is Risen.

(*b*)   For Herod himself had sent forth and laid hold upon John, and bound him in prison for the sake of HERODIAS, his brother Philip's wife: for he had married her. For John said unto Herod, It is not lawful for thee to have thy brother's wife. And HERODIAS set herself against him, and desired to kill him; and she could not; for Herod feared John, knowing that he was a righteous man and a holy, and kept him safe. And when he heard him, he was much perplexed; and he heard him gladly.

(*c*)   AND when a convenient day was come, that Herod on his birthday made a supper to his lords, and the high captains, and the chief men of Galilee; and when the daughter of HERODIAS herself came in and danced, she pleased Herod and them that sat at meat with him; and the KING said unto the DAMSEL, ASK of

me whatsoever thou wilt, and I will GIVE it thee. And he sware
unto her, Whatsoever thou shalt ASK of me, I will GIVE it thee,
unto 'the half of my kingdom'. (Esther v. 3)

(*d*) AND she went out, and said unto her mother, What shall
I ASK? And she said, The head of John the BAPTIST. And she
came in straightway with haste unto the KING, and ASKED,
saying, I will that thou forthwith GIVE me in a charger the head
of John the BAPTIST. And the KING was exceeding sorry; but
for the sake of his oaths, and of them that sat at meat, he would
not reject her. And straightway the KING sent forth a soldier of
his guard, and commanded to bring his HEAD: and he went
and beheaded him in the prison, and brought his HEAD in
a charger, and gave it to the DAMSEL; and the DAMSEL gave it
to her mother.

(*e*) AND when his disciples heard thereof, they came and took
up his corpse, and laid it in a tomb.

Triads: king (4), Herodias, ask and give, head (4), damsel. John and Herod
seven times each.

Major Triads: powers, Elijah, prophet.

4. THE PASCHA

The great difficulty in Paschal chronology arises from the failure
to remember that the Jewish day began at sunset; 'And the evening
and the morning were the first day'; 'Heaviness may endure for
a night, but joy cometh in the morning'; 'Slept and rose night
and day'; and so forth, where we naturally say 'day and night'.

The Pascha (Passover) was Nisan 14, but it began on what
we would call the evening of Nisan 13. The Passion Narrative,
apart from certain preliminaries, fills this 24-hour space, from
evening to evening; there may be some reminiscence here of the
queer direction in Exodus xii. 6 that the Paschal lamb is to be
slain 'between the evenings', for which the Rabbis have a quite
different explanation.

THE PASSION LECTIONS (*see* pp. 204 ff.)

Lections 49–62 (Mark xiii. 1–xvi. 8)

49. The Apocalyptic Discourse on the Mount of Olives.
50. Now Concerning the Day and the Hour: with reference to the coming Pascha.
51. The Supper at Bethany: 'Wherever this gospel, etc.'
52. The Disciples Prepare for the Pascha.
53. The Last Supper.
54. Gethsemane.
55. The Arrest.

56. Trial before High Priest and Denial of Peter.
57. Trial before Pilate.
58. The Soldiers.
59. The Crucifixion.
60. The Centurion and the Women.
61. The Burial.
62. The Message from the Tomb.

NOTES

(1) These lections are printed in full in their correct Marcan position; but a note should be made of the 'breaking of the bread' in 53 and of 'the shepherd and the sheep' which occurs in 54, both of which are found again in 25. 53 and 54 would be read on the Pascha, and 25 on the Sunday following, according to our theory.

(2) Similarly the names of the women who ministered to Jesus in Galilee occur in Lections 60, 61 and 62, and would therefore be read at this point.

(3) The message of the angel, with which Lection 62 concludes, points forward to Galilee.

(4) The Passover occurred as follows in the years 1942–7: 2 April, 20 April, 8 April, 29 March, 16 April and 5 April.

(5) These *B* lections have no titles: we have supplied titles for the convenience of the reader.

PASCHA I

Third Week in Nisan. The Sunday following the Pascha (our Easter Day) which was the Jewish Festival of Omer, or Firstfruits.

LECTION 25 (Mark vi. 30–44).

Matthew non-*B* 26, 'Concerning the Five Loaves and the Two Fishes'.

Mark non-B 15 continued. Tatian 14 and 18

(*a*) AND the Apostles gather themselves together unto Jesus; and they told him all things, whatsoever they had done, and whatsoever they had taught. And he saith unto them, Come ye yourselves apart into a DESERT PLACE and rest a while. For there were many coming and going, and they had no leisure so much as to eat.

(*b*) AND they went away in the Boat to a DESERT PLACE apart. And the people saw them going, and many knew them, and they ran there together on foot from all the cities, and outwent them.

Mark non-B 16, 'Concerning the Five Loaves and the Two Fishes'. *Old Latin 19*

And he came forth and saw a great Multitude, and he had compassion on them, because they were

'as SHEEP not having a SHEPHERD': (Num. xxvii. 17)

(*c*) AND he began to teach them many things.

(*d*) AND when the day was now far spent, his DISCIPLES came unto him, and said, The PLACE is DESERT, and the day is now far spent: send them away, that they may go into the country and villages round about, and buy themselves something TO EAT.

(*e*) BUT he answered and said unto them, GIVE ye them TO EAT. And they say unto him, Shall we go and buy two hundred pennyworth of *LOAVES, and GIVE them TO EAT?

(*f*) AND he saith unto them, How many LOAVES have ye? Go and see. And when they knew, they say, FIVE, and TWO FISHES. And he commanded them that all should recline by companies upon the green grass. And they sat down in ranks, by hundreds, and by fifties. And he took the FIVE LOAVES and the TWO FISHES, and looking up to heaven, he BLESSED, and BRAKE the LOAVES; and he GAVE to the DISCIPLES to set before them; and the TWO FISHES divided he among them all. And

* R.V. bread.

they did all eat, and were FILLED. And they took up broken pieces, twelve basketfuls, and also of the FISHES. And they that ate the LOAVES were five thousand men.

Triads: disciples (including Lection 26*a*), desert place, (something) to eat, give, loaves (5), five, two, fishes (4).

Major Triads: shepherd and sheep (imperfect), blessed—broke—bread, filled.

NOTE

In Matthew it is the disciples of the Baptist who come to Jesus in *a*; and this may be the correct text. The word 'apostle' does not occur otherwise in Mark except for the uncertain case of Lection 16*a*.

PASCHA II
Fourth Week in Nisan.

LECTION 26 (Mark vi. 45–52).
Matthew non-B 27, 'Concerning the Walking on the Sea'.

Mark non-B 16 continued. Tatian 18 and 19

(*a*)   AND straightway he constrained his DISCIPLES to enter into the BOAT, and to go before him unto the other side to Bethsaida, while he himself sendeth the Multitude away. And after he had taken leave of them, he departed into the MOUNTAIN to PRAY.

Mark non-B 17, 'Concerning the Walking on the Sea'.
Old Latin 20

(*b*)   AND when even was come, the BOAT was in the midst of the SEA, and he alone on the land. And seeing them distressed in rowing, for the wind was contrary unto them,

(*c*)   About the fourth watch of the night he cometh unto them, walking on the SEA; and he would have passed by them:

(*d*)   But they, when they saw him walking on the SEA, supposed that it was an apparition, and cried out: for they all saw him, and were troubled. But he straightway spake with them, and saith unto them, Be of good cheer: IT IS I; be not afraid. And he went up unto them into the BOAT; and the wind ceased: and they were sore amazed in themselves; for they UNDERSTOOD NOT concerning the Loaves, but

'their HEART WAS HARDENED'.   (Isa. vi. 10)

Triads: boat, sea; for 'disciples' see Lection 25.

Major Triads: mountain, pray, it is I, not understand, hearts hardened.

NOTES

(1) According to Θ the non-*B* Lection 17 begins with *a*, thus agreeing with the *B* system.

(2) Luke omits Lections 26–35.

PASCHA III
First Week of Iyyar (April–May): Second Month.
LECTION 27 (Mark vi. 53–6).
Part of Matthew non-*B* 27 continued.

Mark non-B 17 continued. Tatian 14

AND when they had crossed over, they came to the land unto Gennesaret, and moored to the shore. And when they were come out of the Boat, straightway the people knew him, and ran round about that whole region, and began to carry about on their beds those that were sick, where they heard he was. And wheresoever he entered, into villages, or into cities, or into the country, they laid the sick in the marketplaces, and besought him that they might touch if it were but the border of his garment: and as many as touched him were made whole.

Triads: nil.

PASCHA IV
Second Week in Iyyar.
LECTION 28 (Mark vii. 1–16).
Matthew non-*B* 28, 'Concerning the Transgression of the Commandments of God'.

Mark non-B 18, 'Concerning the Transgression of the Commandments of God'. Tatian 20. Old Latin 21

(*a*) AND there are gathered together unto him the PHARISEES, and certain of the Scribes, which had come from Jerusalem, and had seen that some of his DISCIPLES ATE their BREAD with DEFILED, that is, UNWASHEN, HANDS. For the PHARISEES, and all the Jews, except they WASH their HANDS diligently, EAT NOT, holding the TRADITION OF THE ELDERS: and when they come from the marketplace, except they wash themselves, they EAT NOT: and many other things there be, which they have received to HOLD, washings of cups, and pots, and brasen vessels.

(*b*)　AND the PHARISEES and the Scribes ask him, Why walk not thy DISCIPLES according to the TRADITION OF THE ELDERS, but EAT THEIR BREAD with DEFILED HANDS?

(*c*)　AND he said unto them, Well did Isaiah prophesy of you hypocrites, as it is written,

> 'This people honoureth me with their lips,
> > But their heart is far from me.
> But in vain do they worship me,
> > Teaching as their doctrines the *Commandments of Men'
> > > (Isa. xxix. 13)

Ye leave the COMMANDMENT OF GOD, and HOLD fast the TRADITION OF MEN. And he said unto them, Full well do ye reject the COMMANDMENT OF GOD, that ye may keep YOUR TRADITION. For Moses said,

> 'Honour thy Father and thy Mother';
> > (Exod. xx. 12; Deut. v. 16)

and, 'He that speaketh evil of Father or Mother,

> Let him die the death':　　　　(Exod. xxi. 17)

but ye say, If a man shall say to his FATHER or his MOTHER, That wherewith thou mightest have been profited by me is Corban, that is to say 'Given to God'; ye no longer suffer him to do aught for his FATHER or his MOTHER; making void the WORD OF GOD by YOUR TRADITION, which ye have delivered: and many such like things ye do.

(*d*)　AND he called to him the Multitude again, and said unto them,

> HEAR me all of you, and Understand:
> There is nothing from Without the MAN,
> > That GOING INTO him can DEFILE him:
> But the things which †GO OUT from the MAN
> > Are those that DEFILE the MAN.

IF ANY MAN HATH EARS TO HEAR, LET HIM HEAR.

Triads: see under Lection 29.

* R.V. precepts.　　　　　　† R.V. proceed out of.

PASCHA V
Third Week in Iyyar.
LECTION 29 (Mark vii. 17–23).
Matthew non-*B* 28 continued.

Mark non-B 18 *continued. Tatian* 20

AND when he was entered into the House from the Multitude, his DISCIPLES asked of him the Parable. And he saith unto them, Are ye so without Understanding also? Perceive ye not, that
Whatsoever from Without GOETH INTO the MAN,
It cannot DEFILE him;
Because it GOETH not INTO his Heart, but into his belly,
And GOETH OUT into the draught?
(This he said, making all meats clean. And he said,)
That which *GOETH OUT from the MAN
That DEFILETH the MAN.
For from Within, out of the Heart of MEN,
Thoughts that are evil †GO OUT,
Fornications, thefts, murders,
Adulteries, covetings, wickednesses,
Deceit, lasciviousness, an evil eye,
Railing, pride, foolishness:
All these evil things ‡GO OUT from Within,
And DEFILE the MAN.

(The lection ends on a short line in B)

Triads (for 28 and 29). The repetitions are irregular and exceed the number three; the following count is established without using occurrences of words within quotations from the Old Testament; different results would be obtained if they were counted in. Pharisees, disciples, (not) eat (bread) (4), defile (7), commandment (word) of God, hands, elders, tradition (5), father or mother (2), hear, go into, man (8), go out (5).

Major Triads: if any man hath ears, etc; but some textual authorities omit.

NOTES

(1) 'This he said', etc., is an amplification of three Greek words, 'cleansing all foods': it appears to be a comment by the evangelist.

(2) The lection ends on a short line in B.

* R.V. proceedeth out of.   † R.V. proceed.   ‡ R.V. proceed.

PASCHA VI
Fourth Week in Iyyar.

LECTION 30 (Mark vii. 24–30).
Matthew non-B 29, 'Concerning the Chananaean Woman'.

Mark non-B 19, 'Concerning the Phoenician Woman'.
Tatian 20. Old Latin 22

(*a*)   AND from thence he arose, and went away into the borders of TYRE and Sidon. And he entered into a HOUSE, and would have no man know it: and he could not be hid. But straightway a woman, whose little DAUGHTER had an Unclean Spirit, having heard of him, came and fell down at his feet. Now the woman was a Greek, a Syrophoenician by race. And she besought him that he would cast forth the DEVIL out of her DAUGHTER. And he said unto her, Let the CHILDREN first be FILLED: for it is not meet to take the CHILDREN's Bread, and cast it to the dogs.

(*b*)   But she answered and saith unto him, Yea, Lord: even the dogs under the table eat of the CHILDREN's crumbs.

(*c*)   AND he said unto her, For this saying go thy way; the DEVIL is gone out of thy DAUGHTER. And she went away unto her house, and found the child laid upon the bed, and the DEVIL gone out.

(The lection ends on a short line in B*)*

Triads: daughter, devil, child; in the fourth use of the word 'child', a different Greek word is used.

Major Triads: Tyre (and Sidon), filled.

NOTES

(1) This lection ends on a short line, but as the succeeding line does not project into the left-hand margin, it has not been classified as a script-division. It might, however, be a trace of such a division in the original from which B copied. This conjecture may be thought to be confirmed by other data with regard to 30 and 31.

(2) In Tatian it concludes Section 20.

(3) According to Θ the non-B Lection 19 begins at the words, 'Now the woman was a Greek'; this is surely an error of the copyist.

PASCHA VII

First Week in Siwan (May–June): Third Month. The Sunday before Pentecost; according to the Pharisee reckoning, it might occasionally fall on Pentecost itself or the day following.

LECTION 31 (Mark vii. 31–7).

Matthew has omitted this narrative, and substituted Matthew non-B 30, 'Concerning the Crowds who were Healed'.

Mark non-B 20, 'Concerning the Man with an Impediment'.
Tatian 21. Old Latin 23

AND again he went out from the borders of TYRE, and came through SIDON, unto the Sea of Galilee, through the midst of the borders of Decapolis. And they bring unto him one that was deaf, and had an impediment in his speech; and they beseech him to lay his hand upon him. And he took him aside from the Multitude privately, and put his fingers into his EARS, and he spat, and touched his tongue; and looking up to heaven, he sighed, and saith unto him, EPHPHATHA, that is, Be OPENED. And his EARS were OPENED, and the bond of his tongue was loosed, and he spake plain. And he charged them that they should tell no man: but the more he charged them, so much the more a great deal they PUBLISHED it. And they were beyond measure astonished, saying, He hath done all things well: he maketh even the deaf to hear, and the dumb to speak.

Triads: opened (including Ephphatha), ears (see Lection 34 for third occurrence).
Major Triads: Tyre (and Sidon), published (see Lections 5, 20).

NOTES

(1) This lection is distinguished in Θ by the same marginal notes which we described in the case of Lection 13. Like 13 it is a Lenten Gospel in the Greek Calendar, being set for the fourth sabbath, that is to say the sabbath in the third week.

(2) This gospel is the basis of the Epphathah ceremony used in the Roman ritual during the preparation of candidates for baptism; it takes place in the existing ritual on the vigil of Easter, but in more ancient times it may have been carried out at an earlier scrutiny. The 'scrutinies', at which the candidates were prepared for baptism, began in the third week in Lent, so that we have found a second possible connexion between this lection and the third week in Lent; and, of course, a reason for its special importance.

(3) It is not found in Luke, being omitted along with the other lections of this series. Matthew omits it in favour of a scene at a mountain at which many cures took place, which is obviously intended as an introduction to 32. The liturgical usage for the third week in Lent is therefore based on a Marcan system.

5. PENTECOST

Pentecost was the fiftieth day (or seventh week) counting from the Omer which was the Sunday after Pascha (or according to the Pharisees Nisan 16). Hence its name *Shabuoth* (weeks) and *Atzereth* (completion). From this point of view it was little more than the end of the Paschal season in its extended sense; it is thought of as having little significance of its own; and of course has only one day of special rituals. In the Christian calendar of the second century it was probably little more than this; in fact the word Pentecost in Tertullian is equivalent to the whole extent of the fifty days which followed Easter, and were all suitable for baptism.

In some authorities, however, we find it has greater importance. It is *Kazir*, the harvest, or *Bikkurim*, the firstfruits. On the Omer, in the days of Unleavened Bread, a sheaf of barley was offered in the temple; at Pentecost two cakes of wheat-bread were offered. These marked the beginning of the wheat harvest. While the Old Testament texts pass over these natural rituals of the soil, the existing liturgical texts show that it was a midsummer festival connected with the idea of the sun in his glory. (Incidentally the ritual text from Habbakuk which is used in this connexion is quoted by Tertullian in connexion with the Transfiguration.)

In order to counteract this natural aspect of the festival, a historical commemoration was found for it, which must be as old as the composition of the Pentateuch. Pascha commemorated the deliverance from Egypt and the passage through the Red Sea; Pentecost commemorated the arrival at Mount Sinai, the giving of the law, and the covenant made between Jehovah and his people. The latter was often thought of as a marriage ceremony.

In the *Book of Jubilees*, which is an elaborate story of the adventures of the Patriarchs, there are many calendrical references. Much stress is laid upon Pentecost which is regularly called

'Firstfruits', and it is identified not only with the day of the Mosaic covenant on Mount Sinai, but also with the Covenant of Noah on Mount Ararat. It was, therefore, a much more important popular festival than the official references to it might imply.

The word *Atzereth* is something of a mystery. In Hebrew, the root seems to mean 'to compress, restrain, or compel'; its use for Pentecost and for Tisri 22 may therefore be derived from the notion of closing or rounding off the festal season. In Aramaic, however, the verb is used of treading the grapes in the wine-press, and in this way has a close connexion with Tisri 22 which concludes the vintage festival of Tabernacles.

PENTECOST I
Second Week in Siwan. The Sunday after Pentecost, if not Pentecost itself. It is fifty days from the Sunday after the Pascha.

LECTION 32 (Mark viii. 1–9).
Matthew non-*B* 31, 'Concerning the Seven Loaves'.

Mark non-B 21, 'Concerning the Seven Loaves'. Tatian 23.
Old Latin 24

(*a*) IN THOSE DAYS, when there was again a great MULTITUDE, and they had nothing to EAT, he called unto him his DISCIPLES, and saith unto them, I have compassion on the MULTITUDE, because they continue with me now three days, and have nothing to EAT: and if I send them away fasting to their home, they will faint in the way; and some of them are come from far.

(*b*) AND his DISCIPLES answered him, Whence shall one be able to FILL these men with LOAVES here in a Desert Place? And he asked them, How many LOAVES have ye? And they said, SEVEN. And he commandeth the MULTITUDE to sit down on the ground: and he took the SEVEN LOAVES, and having Given Thanks, he BRAKE, and gave to his DISCIPLES, to SET before them; and they SET them before the MULTITUDE. And they had a few small fishes: and having BLESSED them, he commanded to SET these also before them. And they did EAT, and were FILLED: and they took up, of broken pieces that remained over, seven baskets. And they were about four thousand: and he sent them away.

Triads: multitude, disciples, eat, set before, loaves, seven.

Major Triads: fill, took—bread—blessed—broke ('give thanks', *eucharistein*, occurs twice in the three passages; 'bless', *eulogein*, occurs three times).

NOTE

In the years 1942–7, the 'Feast of Weeks' (Pentecost) fell on 22 May, 9 June, 28 May, 18 May, 5 June and 25 May respectively.

PENTECOST II
Third Week in Siwan.

LECTION 33 (Mark viii. 10–12).
Matthew non-*B* 31 continued.

*Mark non-*B* 21 continued (22 in* Θ*). Tatian 23. Old Latin 25*

(*a*) AND straightway he entered into the Boat with his Disciples, and came into the parts of Dalmanutha. And the Pharisees came forth, and began to question with him, seeking of him a SIGN from heaven, TEMPTING him.

(*b*) AND he sighed deeply in his spirit, and saith,
Why doth THIS GENERATION seek a SIGN?
Verily I say unto you,
There shall no SIGN be given unto THIS GENERATION.

Triads: sign.
Major Triads: tempt, this generation.

NOTES

(1) The reading of Θ is Magdala; several authorities are in favour of 'Magadan'; *B* has 'Dalmanutha' but with small support; this is the reading of Matthew.

(2) According to Θ, Lection 22 of non-*B* begins at 33 *a*, and includes both 33 and 34. Its title is 'Concerning the Leaven of the Pharisees'. We have found something of the same sort in Θ in connexion with Lection 13. Both cases have to do with disputes with the Pharisees.

(3) 'No Sign' in Lection 33, and 'Beware of the Leaven' in 34, look like first lines of well-known lections, the whole of which could be used by the lector if need arose for extra lections: see introduction to 15 and note on 18. The five lections after Pentecost could thus be expanded into seven, if required before the Transfiguration.

PENTECOST III
Fourth Week in Siwan.

LECTION 34 (Mark viii. 13–21).
Matthew non-B 32, 'Concerning the Leaven of the Pharisees'.

Mark non-B 21 continued. Tatian 23

AND he left them, and again entering into (the boat) departed to the other side. And they forgot to take BREAD; and they had not in the Boat with them more than one LOAF.

Mark non-B 22, 'Concerning the Leaven of the Pharisees'

AND he charged them, saying, Take heed, beware of the Leaven of the Pharisees and the leaven of HEROD. And they reasoned one with another, saying, We have no BREAD. And Jesus perceiving it saith unto them, Why reason ye, because ye have no BREAD?

Do ye NOT yet Perceive, neither UNDERSTAND?
Have ye your HEART HARDENED?   (Isa. vi. 10)
Having EYES, See ye not?
And having EARS, Hear ye not?   (Ezek. xii. 2)
And do ye not remember?

When I brake the Five LOAVES among the five thousand, how many baskets full of broken pieces took ye up? They say unto him, Twelve. And when the Seven among the four thousand, how many basketfuls of broken pieces took ye up? And they say unto him, Seven. And he said unto them, Do ye NOT yet UNDERSTAND?

Triads: bread—loaves (the same word in Greek: five times).

Major Triads: not understood, hearts hardened; for 'eyes' and 'ears' see Lections 31 and 35.

PENTECOST IV
First Week in Tammuz (June–July): Fourth Month.

LECTION 35 (Mark viii. 22–6).
Omitted by Matthew.

Mark non-B 23, 'Concerning the Blind Man'. Tatian 23

AND they come unto Bethsaida. And they bring to him a Blind man, and beseech him to touch him. And he took hold of the Blind man by the hand, and brought him out of the village; and when he had spit on his EYES, and laid his hands upon him, he asked him, SEEST thou aught? And he Looked up and said, I SEE men; for I Behold them as trees, walking. Then again he laid his hands upon his EYES; and he Looked stedfastly, and was restored, and SAW all things clearly. And he sent him away to his home, saying, Do not even enter into the village.

Triads: There are five different Greek verbs used in this lection; *blepein, anablepein, blepein* (again), *horan, diablepein,* and *emblepein.* For the word 'eyes', refer to Lection 34.

NOTE

Matthew omits this lection; it is the last of the ten lections omitted by Luke.

PENTECOST V

Second Week in Tammuz: the week following Tammuz 17, the 'Fast of the Fourth Month', which coincided with the Canaanite Midsummer Festival.

LECTION 36 (Mark viii. 27–ix. 1).

Matthew non-B 33, 'Concerning the Questioning in Caesaraea'. The last lection of the third quarter.

Mark non-B 24, 'Concerning the Questioning in Caesaraea'. Tatian 23, 24. Old Latin 26

(*a*)   AND Jesus went forth, and his DISCIPLES, into the villages of Caesaraea Philippi: and in the way he asked his DISCIPLES, saying unto them, Who do men say that I AM? And they told him saying, John the Baptist: and others, ELIJAH; but others, One of the PROPHETS. And he asked them, But who say ye that I AM?

(*b*)   PETER answereth and saith unto him, THOU ART the CHRIST. And he *WARNED them that they should tell no man of him.

* R.V. charged.

165

And he began to Teach them, that

The SON OF MAN must Suffer many things
And be rejected by the elders, and the chief priests, and
the scribes,
And be KILLED,
And AFTER THREE DAYS RISE AGAIN.

And he spake the saying openly.

(c)   AND PETER took him, and began to *WARN him. But he
turning about, and seeing his DISCIPLES, *WARNED PETER, and
saith,

Get thee BEHIND ME, SATAN [literally, 'after me']:
For thou mindest not the things of God,
But the things of men.

(d)   AND he called unto him the Multitude with his DISCIPLES,
and said unto them,

If any man would come AFTER ME, let him DENY himself,
And take up his CROSS, and FOLLOW ME.
For whosoever would SAVE his LIFE shall LOSE it;
And whosoever shall LOSE his LIFE for my sake and the
Gospel's shall SAVE it.
For what doth it profit a man, to gain the whole world and
†LOSE his LIFE?
For what should a man give in exchange for his LIFE?
For whosoever shall be ashamed of me and of my words
In THIS adulterous and sinful GENERATION,
The SON OF MAN also shall be Ashamed of him,
When he COMETH in the GLORY of his Father with the
holy Angels.

And he said unto them,

Verily I say unto you,
There be some here of them that stand by,
Which shall in no wise taste of death,
Till they SEE the KINGDOM OF GOD COME with POWER.

* R.V. rebuked.   † R.V. forfeit his life.

Triads: disciples, I am (thou art), warn, behind me—after me—follow me, lose, life, Peter.

Major Triads: I am, Elijah, prophet, announcement of the Passion, deny, cross, follow, save life, this generation, announcement of *parousia*, glory. See Special Introduction to the Transfiguration, following this lection.

NOTES

(1) In Lection 36*b* we have the First Passion Announcement, and in 36*d* the teachings of Jesus which are appended to it. This is the first of three Passion Announcements (see Lections 39 and 42*h*) which are the most striking features of the seven lections which are numbered 36 to 42. It will be noted that the B enumeration is coming back into step with its series of heptads. (See Introduction to Spring Season, p. 134.)

(2) The question must arise whether these three Announcements with their pendant sayings are not drawn from some source other than the main Marcan narrative (possibly a Petrine source); they may have had their own use on three Sundays or three other ritual occasions; it is pointed out in the notes to 42 that they lead into the story of the Last Supper.

(3) This suggestion derives some support from what may be doublets in the present lection. The advent in glory of the Son of Man appears to be a doublet of the advent with power of the Kingdom of God; 'me and my words' looks like a doublet of 'my sake and the gospel's'. Furthermore the surprise occasioned by the reference to the resurrection in 37*c* is rather hard to understand in view of the reference to the resurrection in 36*b*. Some reference to the Passion must have stood in the original Marcan narrative in 36*b*, but perhaps not so detailed a reference as we find there now. These slight discrepancies disappear if we assume that a new source is here interlaced with the Marcan narrative.

We may add, what is purely a literary judgement, that the style and rhythm of the new sayings are rather different; they suggest couplets and quatrains, rather than triads. Both the style and the subject-matter which appear here seem to be continued in the sayings appended to the two later Passion Announcements.

(4) Marginal notes in Θ indicate the 'beginning' of a lection at the words 'For whoever wishes' in *d*, and add an opening formula, 'The Lord said'. The Vulgate Lection 27 in Amiatinus begins at the same point, but goes on to include the Transfiguration. As in the cases of 13 and 31, we find that the marginal indications in Θ correspond with special Marcan lections of the Greek Calendar; 36*d* is the gospel for the Third Sunday in Lent.

We have already noticed that the Epphathah story is the gospel for the Fourth Sabbath; we may add now that the First Announcement of the Passion (36*a* and *b*) is the gospel for the Fifth Sabbath; while the Second Announcement is the gospel for the Fourth Sunday, and the Third Announcement is the gospel for the Fifth Sunday. It is not only literary analysis, therefore, that finds a relation between the three Announcements and the sayings which they introduce; liturgical tradition points to the same thing. They are connected with the Saturdays and Sundays of the third, fourth and fifth weeks in Lent. Everywhere in Christendom Lent was primarily concerned with the preparation of candidates for baptism; in Rome the third, fourth and fifth Sundays had special services *pro scrutinio*, that is for the passing of candidates; see note on Lection 31.

SPECIAL INTRODUCTION TO THE GOSPEL OF THE TRANSFIGURATION

(1) The Gospel of St Mark divides mathematically into halves between Lections 36 and 37 according to the enumeration of B. In the non-B system, which divides all Mark into 48 gospels only, the dividing point comes between 24 and 25; the 36 lections previous to the Transfiguration fit into the Syrian year. The 24 lections of non-B fit into the Roman year. In both cases this half-way point in the gospel coincides with the midsummer solstice.

(2) Every day, beginning from the midwinter solstice, the sun rises higher in the firmament and makes his way farther north. The midsummer solstice marks his highest point of glory. From this moment he must decline; he turns and begins to retreat southward. Mark's story follows a similar course. The Transfiguration is its highest peak of glory; the movement of the story turns and moves southwards towards Jerusalem. The Son of Man must go there to die.

(3) Apart from any calendrical theory, this dividing point is the most striking feature of the Marcan Gospel. The first half opens with the mystical narrative of the Baptism with its voice from heaven, and closes with the Passion of the Baptizer and the breaking of the bread upon the mountains. The second half opens with the mystical narrative of the Transfiguration which has a similar voice from heaven, and closes with the breaking of the bread in Jerusalem and the Passion of the Baptized. The narratives of the Baptism and the Transfiguration have several points in common.

(4) The following features of the Baptism and associated narratives are repeated in the Transfiguration narrative (including Lection 36 with 37):

    (a)   the interest in John and Elijah; for, while Elijah is not mentioned in the Baptism narrative, the description of John and the quotation from Malachi are meant to connect John with Elijah;

(b)   the voice from heaven, and the words 'This is my beloved Son';

(c)   temptation by a Satan;

(d)   a special interest in Peter, James, and John, and the call to follow Jesus; Andrew is mentioned after the Baptism but not at the Transfiguration;

(e)   the use of the words 'gospel', 'kingdom', and 'angels'.

The word 'Satan' may constitute a major triad; for we can dismiss the occurrence in iv. 15 as irrelevant, occurring as it does in an explanatory addition to the text. Its first occurrence is at the Temptation (i. 13); its second at the conflict with the Pharisees from Jerusalem (iii. 23 and 26); its third is previous to the Transfiguration when Peter protests against the idea of the cross. The words 'Get thee behind me, Satan' in viii. 33 seem to echo the words used in the Temptation story; and yet Mark has not recorded those words; it rather looks as if Mark expected his auditors to be familiar with them even though he has left them unwritten.

The expression 'go behind' or 'go after' also has its interesting connexions, and may be regarded as a major triad. Its first occurrence is in i. 7 where it strongly suggests that Jesus was first of all a follower of John, walking behind him as a disciple walked behind his master; the second in i. 17 and 20 is used of Peter and others in their capacity as disciples of Jesus; the third is the present instance, viii. 33 and 34. The word alternates with another word which is translated 'follow', but has not perhaps so strong a sense of subordination; it can almost be translated 'accompany'. Now nothing was said in those earlier lections as to the meaning of the word 'follow'; but it is said now. It is brought into connexion with the word 'cross' and the word 'deny' which recur of course in the Passion Narrative, the latter being closely connected with the story of Peter.

The narrative of the Baptism and Temptation was closely connected with announcing the gospel, the subject of which was the 'kingdom of God'. This expression, too, seems to be part of a major triad so far as the first half is concerned; it occurs first shortly after the Baptism, then in the Seed Parables, and then here. It was not explained at all at its first occurrence; it was explained in mysteries in the Seed Parables; it is only now that its true implications begin to appear 'openly'. Both expressions, 'kingdom of God' and 'gospel', begin to take up their true meanings by association with the doctrine of the death and resurrection of the Son of Man; *after* this connexion has been made clear, the 'eschatological' vision is allowed to appear.

The half-way point in Mark is, therefore, a point at which various lines of thought, which were introduced in the first four lections, converge; their true meaning is seen in the light of the gospel of the cross; they then diverge to be picked up again and woven into the Passion Narrative.

(5) The thought of the death and resurrection of the Son of Man was introduced in parables after the choice of the Twelve; it was enacted in a sacrament after their sending out; it is expressed openly in the conversation at Caesaraea prior to the Transfiguration. What is quite new is the 'eschatology'; the vision of the 'coming' of the kingdom, or son of man, in power, or in glory, or with the angels,[1] expressions which we may suppose have much the same meaning. There is none of this in the first half of the Gospel. We may associate this imagery in some degree with current apocalyptic literature; and there is a strong emphasis on the word 'to see'.

Several major triads of great importance branch out from this point, the most obvious being the announcement that the Son of Man must suffer many things and be killed and after three days rise again. This triad is recognized by all students of the gospel; it provides the structure for the remaining twelve lections in the Galilean part of Mark, leading from Caesaraea to Jerusalem. Each announcement is followed by a collection of sayings of Jesus dealing with the life in the kingdom in the light of the doctrine of the cross.

Equally important are the three announcements that men then living would 'see' the coming of the Son of Man or kingdom of God in power or in glory. The first is made before the crowds previous to the Transfiguration; the second to the four disciples on the Mount of Olives; the third before the high priest at the trial. They thus serve to connect this half-way point with the Passion Narrative itself.

The third example is less obvious. After the Transfiguration there is a statement about the Resurrection in ix. 9 by itself, that is to say separate from the announcement of the Passion. There is a second announcement of the Resurrection after the Last Supper in xiv. 8, and the third, of course, is that given at the tomb in xvi. 6-8. It is abundantly clear, in any case, that we have reached the turning-point of the book, and that great new trains of thought radiate from Lections 36 and 37.

---

[1] The expression 'with the clouds' is not used yet.

(6) It may be worth while now to point out where the narratives of the Baptism and Transfiguration differ. In the Baptism the heavens open and the Holy Spirit descends on Jesus in the form of a dove; in the Transfiguration a cloud overshadows him which causes fear to the three disciples; the voice comes out of the cloud. This mention of the cloud initiates a major triad which is completed by the two announcements that he will be seen coming with the clouds.

There are obscurities and reticences here. Prior to his Baptism, Jesus was designated as the one who will baptize his people in the Holy Spirit; but what comes of this? There is no reference to the Holy Spirit in Lections 36 or 37; the cloud seems to take its place. Both ideas imply the descent on earth among men of the effective energy of Almighty God; but the Holy Spirit of the Baptism is more the creative energy of God entering Jesus, while the cloud at the Transfiguration is more the glory of God surrounding Jesus. The former has been connected with the creation story in Genesis; the latter must be connected with the story of Moses and the Exodus.

For completeness' sake we may mention that there is a major triad of the Holy Spirit, if we reject xii. 36 as simply formal, which perhaps we should not do. There is first the statement by John that a 'stronger one' who was coming 'after him' would baptize with the Spirit, which was followed by the descent of the Spirit on Jesus, and the Spirit driving him into the wilderness; there was secondly the statement that there was no forgiveness for those who 'blasphemed against the Holy Spirit' (Lection 16); and thirdly there is the promise of the Holy Spirit in Lection 49 to help those who are undergoing trial on account of their faith. We cannot help noting that the Holy Spirit is mentioned in connexion with conflict with evil powers. (Compare I Peter iv. 15.)

(7) There is also some important connexion which has to do with the figure of John the Baptist conceived as Elijah. At the Baptism, John in the role of Elijah designates Jesus as the one who is to 'come'; in the Transfiguration it is Elijah who appears in glory 'with Moses', but the idea of John is not far behind; the connexion between Jesus and Elijah occurs again at the Crucifixion (xv. 35-6), thus forming a triad which is beyond the scope of our imagination.

Nevertheless these connexions help us to see that there is a sublime architecture about this book in which all the parts are related together by trains of mystical thought which may be much simpler than we think. On the other hand our difficulties may arise from the fact that we do not possess the book in its earliest form. References to the Old

Testament seem to have been whittled down to suit a Gentile congregation, and often the merest hint is given of some important train of thought which depends for its understanding on a thorough acquaintance with the texts referred to. John in his role as Elijah represents all that was best in the old religion; I believe that if we had a fuller and older recension of Mark, we would find that it contained more about John and more about Elijah.

(8) The occurrences of the word 'Messiah' or 'Christ' are also not easy to deal with. There are seven in all; and of the seven, three seem to have been of major importance. The first occurs in i. 1 which is the title of the book; it does not occur in the Baptism narrative itself. The second is in Lection 36 where Peter salutes Jesus with this title; the third is the question of the high priest; but in none of these cases does Jesus of his own accord apply it to himself. In the last case, however, he accepts it by using the words 'I am' which may themselves be a divine name of high sanctity; a sense in which it is thought by some to be used in the Walking on the Waters (vi. 50) and the Apocalyptic Discourse (xiii. 6), thus making a triad. It is faintly suggested by the dialogue at the beginning of Lection 36: 'Who do men say that I am?'—*me einai*, however, not *ego eimi*.

(9) There are two expressions which might be used here, but are not. The first is the expression 'Son of God' which is not found here, though the Matthaean version of the text contains it; yet this passage is obviously intended to correspond in a dramatic way to the moment in the trial before Caiaphas when Jesus confesses that he is 'the Messiah, the Son of the Blessed'. Here Peter confesses; there he denies.

The other expression is the word 'betray', which has appeared in i. 14 and iii. 19; yet it is absent from the first Passion Announcement. It occurs in the second and third Passion Announcements, ix. 31 and x. 32, and copiously in the Passion Narrative from Lection 49 on.

MAJOR TRIADS AND OTHER CONNEXIONS IN LECTIONS 36 AND 37

viii. 28	The Baptist	i. 4, 6, 9 (i. 14, ii. 18); vi. 14 ff.	xi. 30, 32
viii. 28	Elijah (6)	(Hinted at in i. 2 and 6)	xv. 35, 36
viii. 28	prophet	vi. 4 and 15 (of Jesus) (i. 2 of Isaiah)	xi. 32 (of John); xiii. 4 (Daniel)
viii. 29	Messiah	i. 1	xiv. 61 (ix. 41; xii. 35; xiii. 21; xv. 32)
viii. 31	*Passion Announced* (including Resurrection):		ix. 30; x. 32
viii. 33	go (come) after	i. 7; 1. 17, 20	
viii. 33	Satan	i. 13; iii. 23, 26; (iv. 15)	xiv. 13, 54, 54; xv. 41

viii. 34	follow	i. 18; ii. 14, 14, 15; (iii. 7; v. 24; vi. 1)	ix. 38; x. 21, 28, 32, 52; xi. 9
viii. 34	cross		xv. 21, 30, 32
viii. 34	deny (*aparneisthai*)		xiv. 30, 31, and xv. 72
viii. 35–6	soul (life)	iii. 4	x. 45; (xii. 30, 33; xiii. 14)
viii. 35	gospel	i. 1; i. 14, 15	x. 29; xiii. 29; xiv. 9
viii. 38	generation (this)	viii. 12	ix. 19; xiii. 30
viii. 38–ix. 1	*Parousia Announced*		xiii. 26; xv. 62
viii. 38	in glory		xiii. 26; xv. 62
viii. 38	angels	i. 13	xii. 25; xiii. 27, 32
ix. 1	kingdom of God	i. 15; iv. 11, 26, 29	ix. 47; x. 14, 15, 23, 24, 25; xi. 10; xii. 34; xiv. 25; xv. 43
ix. 2	Peter–James–John	v. 37	xiv. 33
ix. 1	in power		xiii. 26; xiv. 62
ix. 2–9	mountain	iii. 13; (v. 5 and 11); vi. 46	xi. 1; xiii. 3; xiv. 26; (xi. 13; xiii. 14)
ix. 4–5	Elijah (see above)		
ix. 7	cloud		xiii. 26; xiv. 62
ix. 7	son—beloved	i. 11	xii. 6
ix. 9	*Resurrection Announced*		xiv. 28; xvi. 6
ix. 11–13	Elijah (see above)		
ix. 19	generation (this) (see above)		

SOME WORDS IN LECTIONS 1–4 NOT OCCURRING IN 36 AND 37

beginning	i. 1	(x. 6); xiii. 9, 19
desert	i. 35; i. 45; vi. 31, 32, 35	
baptize(-ism)	i. 4, 4, 5, 8, 8, 9; (vi. 14)	x. 38, 38, 39, 39; xi. 30
repent(ance)	i. 4; i. 15; vi. 12	
Spirit (holy)	i. 8, 10, 12; iii. 29	(xii. 36); xiii. 11
heaven(s)	i. 10, 11; birds of, iv, 4, 32; looking up to, vi. 41; vii. 34; sign from, viii. 11	
	treasure in, x. 21; father in, xi. 25, 26; John's baptism, xi. 30, 31; angels in, xii. 25; apocalyptic discourse, xiii. 25, 25, 27, 31, 32; clouds of, xiv. 62	
betray	i. 14; iii. 19	ix. 31; x. 32, and the Passion narrative

6. MIDSUMMER

The Feast of Pentecost, whether as an old harvest festival of the people of the land, or as a commemoration of the Covenant on Mount Sinai, demands to be continued. It marks the beginning of the harvest, and the offering of firstfruits; but such beginnings and such offerings cannot have all occurred simultaneously. In Galilee things were a full month later than in certain places in the neighbourhood of Jerusalem. The festival in the temple on Siwan 6 initiated the wheat harvest for all Israel, and fitted into the temple-cultus; but it would not satisfy the feelings of Palestinian peasants getting in actual harvests, and still less the village priests who were dependent on the firstfruits of the threshing-floor and of the wine-press for their living.

As a midsummer festival, too, Pentecost is disappointing. It comes too early. Everything goes to suggest that under actual rural conditions, and especially in the 'mountains' of the north, old harvest rites would tend to go on, and real midsummer festivals would take place at the appointed time when Syria in general was celebrating the death of the god of the harvest, Tammuz-Adonis.

From the point of view of historical commemoration, too, there was a necessity to continue the memorials of Pascha and Pentecost, as these memorials are indicated in Exodus:

Nisan 14	Exod. xii. 1		The Deliverance from Egypt. Crossing the Red Sea.	*Pascha.*
Nisan 16			Crossing the Desert.	*Omer.*
Siwan 1		xix. 1	Arrival at Sinai.	
		xix. 11	Three Days Preparation.	
Siwan 6	*The fiftieth day from Omer:*			*Pentecost.*
		xx–xxiv	The Appearance of God, the commandments, and Covenant.	
		xxiv. 15	Moses goes up into the mountain; God calls to him on the seventh day (xxiv. 16).	
		xxiv. 18	Moses was in the mountain forty days and forty nights.	
Tammuz 17		xxxii	Golden calf: descent of Moses: tables of the Law broken.	*Fast of Tammuz.*

The date Siwan 1 is taken from Exod. xix. 1, or that is how the Rabbis interpret the text according to Dr Hertz.[1] The date Siwan 6 is not obtained from Exodus but by adding fifty days to Nisan 16. Forty days from Siwan 6 bring us to Tammuz 17, allowing thirty days for the month; and that is the 'fast of the fourth month', on which, *Tractate Taanith* tells us, the Tables of the Law were broken.

---

[1] *Pentateuch and Haftorahs.*

In order to get this result the Rabbis include the seven days of
xxiv. 15 in the forty days of xxiv. 18. This may be right, but if we
do not want to do this, we would arrive at Tammuz 24. Perhaps
there was a Tammuz festival, then, which ran for a week, from
the 17th to the 24th. These calculations are based of course on
the Pharisee date for the Omer. The Sadducee date (the Sunday
after Nisan) would make it even more uncertain.

In any case the Jews had a fast at this point which served to veil
or mask an old popular festival, and the pagan origin of that
festival is alluded to by identifying the day with the day on which
Israel worshipped the golden calf or bull; a sun symbol if ever
there was one. The fast was instituted, we are told, to serve as
a memorial of the day on which Nebuchadnezzar entered
Jerusalem. (Jer. xxxix. 2 says it was the 9th of Tammuz.)

A second fast occurred three weeks later in the month of Ab.
The 9th of Ab was kept as the day on which Nebuchadnezzar
burned the temple, and this too became a memorial fast. (II Kings
xxv. 8 says this was the 7th of Ab.)

When the temple was rebuilt, however, the prophet Zechariah
decreed that these fasts were to become 'joy and gladness and
cheerful feasts' (viii. 19); and so no doubt they continued until
the destruction of the temple in A.D. 70 when, curiously enough,
the burning of the temple again took place on the 9th (or 10th)
of Ab. From that day it once more became a doleful fast and for
centuries the lamentations have taken place on that day at the
'wailing wall'; so tenacious is religious custom. See also II Esdras
and the *Tractate Taanith* of the Mishnah.

Before A.D. 70, however, in the days of Jesus and even perhaps
while this gospel was being written, it was still a cheerful feast.
It, too, went on for more than one day, as we learn from Simeon
ben Gamaliel quoted in the *Tractate Taanith*: 'Never were more
joyous festivals than the fifteenth of Ab and the Day of Atonement, for on them the maidens of Jerusalem used to go out
dressed in white garments...and thus they went out and danced
in the vineyards saying, Young men look and observe well whom
you are about to choose'; and so forth. The whole passage is
most important. But for our immediate purposes, we have

established the reality of these midsummer festivals, not only for rural places but even for Jerusalem. Pentecost introduced a harvest season within which there were further festivals; among them a definite midsummer festival on Tammuz 17–24, or thereabouts, and another in the following month.

In the years of 1942–7, the 'Fast of Tammuz' fell on 2 July, 20 July, 8 July, 28 June, 16 July, and 5 July respectively. The Fast of Ab was twenty-one days later.

The great fire at Rome which led to the Neronian persecution occurred on 6 July. Tradition associates the martyrdom of St Peter with this persecution.

PENTECOST VI: THE TRANSFIGURATION
Third Week in Tammuz. This week would probably follow the midsummer solstice, 21 June, and include the holy day of Tammuz 17.

LECTION 37 (Mark ix. 2–27).
Matthew non-B 34, 'Concerning the Transfiguration of Christ'; Matthew non-B 35, 'Concerning the Lunatic'.

Mark non-B 25, 'Concerning the Transfiguration of Jesus'.
Tatian 24. Old Latin 27

(a) AND after six days Jesus taketh with him PETER, and JAMES, and JOHN, and bringeth them up into a high MOUNTAIN apart by themselves: and he was transfigured before them: and his garments became glistering, exceeding white; so as no fuller on earth can whiten them. And there appeared unto them ELIJAH with Moses: and they were talking with Jesus. And Peter answereth and saith to Jesus, Rabbi, it is good for us to be here: and let us make three tabernacles; one for thee, and one for Moses, and one for ELIJAH. For he wist not what to answer; for they became sore afraid. (Cf. Exod. xxiv and xxxiv.)

(b) AND there came a CLOUD overshadowing them: and there came a Voice out of the CLOUD, (Exod. xxiv. 15 f. and xxxiv. 5 f.)

This is my *SON,	(Ps. ii. 7; Gen. xxii. 2)
*The BELOVED:	(Isa. v. 1; Canticles)
HEAR ye him.	

* R.V. My beloved son.

And suddenly looking round about, they saw no one any more, save Jesus only with themselves.

(c) AND as they were coming down from the MOUNTAIN, he charged them that they should tell no man what things they had seen, save when the Son of Man should have RISEN again from the DEAD. And they kept the saying, questioning among themselves what the RISING AGAIN from the DEAD should mean. And they asked him, saying, How is it that the Scribes say that ELIJAH must first come? And he said unto them,

> ELIJAH indeed cometh first,
> And restoreth all things:　　(Mal. iv. 5; Ecclus. xlviii. 10)
> And how is it written of the Son of Man,
> That he should suffer many things and be set at nought?
> 　　　　　　　　　(Cf. Lection 36b and Isa. liii. 3.)
> But I say unto you, that ELIJAH is come,
> And they have also done unto him whatsoever they listed,
> Even as it is written of him.

Old Latin 28

(d) AND when they came to the DISCIPLES, they saw a great MULTITUDE about them, and Scribes questioning with them. And straightway all the MULTITUDE, when they saw him, were greatly amazed, and running to him saluted him. And he asked them, What question ye with them?

Mark non-B 26, 'Concerning the Lunatic'

(e) AND one of the MULTITUDE answered him, Master, I brought unto thee my son, which hath a DUMB SPIRIT; and wheresoever it taketh him, it dasheth him down: and he foameth, and grindeth his teeth, and pineth away: and I spake to thy DISCIPLES, that they should CAST IT OUT; and they were NOT ABLE.

(f) AND he answereth them and saith,

> O Faithless GENERATION, how long shall I be with you?
> How long shall I bear with you?
> Bring him unto me.

And they brought him unto him: and when he saw him, straightway the SPIRIT convulsed him grievously; and he fell on the ground, and wallowed foaming. And he asked his father, How long time is it since this hath come unto him? And he said, From a child. And oft-times it hath cast him both into the fire and into the waters, to destroy him: but IF THOU CANST do anything, have compassion on us, and help us.

(g) AND Jesus said unto him, IF THOU CANST! all things ARE POSSIBLE to him that BELIEVETH. Straightway the father of the child cried out, and said, I BELIEVE; help thou mine UNBELIEF.

(h) AND when Jesus saw that a MULTITUDE came running together, he rebuked the UNCLEAN SPIRIT, saying unto him, Thou DUMB and deaf SPIRIT, I command thee, COME OUT of him, and enter no more into him. And having cried out, and convulsed him much, he CAME OUT: and the child became as one DEAD; insomuch that the more part said, He is DEAD. But Jesus took him by the hand, and raised him up; and he AROSE.

Triads: Elijah (2 in *a*, 3 in *c*), dead, rise up, disciples (with Lection 38), multitude (4), dumb or unclean spirit (4), if you can (twice) with 'all things possible' (which uses the same Greek root), belief and unbelief, cast out and come out: but see Lection 38.

Major Triads: see Special Introduction to Lection 37.

NOTES

(1) We can hardly suppose that Lection 37*c* is still in its original shape. The surprise shown with regard to the resurrection is hard to understand after the statement in 36*b*. Is the question about the Son of Man a displaced reply to 36*b*, or to some forecast of the Passion of a simpler nature than 36*b*; or may it be itself the simpler utterance which has been replaced by 36*b*?

(2) The lection in *B* is unduly long, but even so it is cut short; 39 is clearly a part of 38 which has become a separate lection in *B*. This division is quite artificial. *B* makes a division wherever Jesus gives teaching in a house (29) or 'alone' (18) to his disciples. Sometimes he does so with notes of time which have a liturgical significance; see Lections 7 and 19; but *B* misses many cases where this would be obvious, e.g. 25*d* which must surely have been meant as the beginning of a lection; and 26*b* which non-*B* adopts. For 'In those days' see 2 and 32; these must have been intended to mark the beginnings of lections by the composer of the gospel.

(3) The long lection of non-B (including 38 and 39) is marked as 'beginning' by marginal notes in Θ, and is set in the Greek Calendar for the Fourth Sunday in Lent.

PENTECOST VII *or* TRANSFIGURATION II
Fourth Week in Tammuz.
LECTION 38 (Mark ix. 28–9).
Matthew non-B 35 continued.

Mark non-B 26 continued. Tatian 24

(*a*) AND when he was come into the House, his DISCIPLES asked him privately, saying, We COULD NOT CAST IT OUT.

(*b*) And he said unto them, This kind CAN COME OUT by NOTHING, save by PRAYER.

Triads (to be taken with previous lection): disciples, could not and cannot, cast out, come out.

Major Triad: prayer.

NOTE

The minor triads show that this little lection should not be separated from 37.

TRANSFIGURATION III
First Week in Ab (July–August): Fifth Month.
LECTION 39 (Mark ix. 30–2).
Matthew non-B 35 continued.

Mark non-B 26 continued. Tatian 24. Old Latin 29

AND they went forth from thence, and passed through Galilee; and he would not that any man should know it. For he Taught his Disciples, and said unto them,

The SON OF MAN is delivered up into the hands of men,
And they shall KILL HIM; And when he is killed,
AFTER THREE DAYS he shall RISE AGAIN.

But they understood not the saying, and were afraid to ask him.

Major Triads: see Special Introduction to Lection 37.

NOTE

This lection which is independent in *B* was also independent in some old arrangement of Matthew which is preserved in the script-divisions of that gospel in *B*. In the non-*B* chapter-enumeration and in the Greek Calendar it is combined with the story of the Epileptic in Lections 37 and 38; Tatian also includes it in his twenty-fourth Section with the Transfiguration. On the other hand it begins a new lection in the Vulgate according to Amiatinus, and includes 40*a* and *b*.

TRANSFIGURATION IV

Second Week in Ab. The Fast of the Fifth Month was on Ab 10, commemorating the burning of the temple by Nebuchadnezzar; it had, however, become a joyful feast.

LECTION 40 (Mark ix. 33–50).

Matthew non-*B* 37, 'Concerning those who said, Which is the Greatest?'.

Mark non-B 27, 'Concerning those who Disputed,
Which is the Greatest?'. Tatian 25

(*a*) AND they came to Capernaum: and when he was in the House, he asked them, What were ye reasoning in the way? But they held their peace: for they had disputed one with another in the way, Who was the greatest.

(*b*) AND he sat down, and called the Twelve; and he saith unto them,
    If any man would be FIRST,
    He shall be LAST of all, and MINISTER of all.

And he took a LITTLE CHILD, and set him in the midst of them: and taking him in his arms, he said unto them,

    Whosoever shall RECEIVE one of such LITTLE CHILDREN
    IN MY NAME, RECEIVETH me:
    And whosoever RECEIVETH me, RECEIVETH not me, but
    him that Sent me.

(*c*) [JOHN said unto him, Master, we saw one casting out devils IN THY NAME: and we forbade him, because he Followed not us.

(*d*) But Jesus said, Forbid him not: for there is no man which shall do a Power IN MY NAME, and be able quickly to speak evil of me. For he that is not against us is for us.

(*e*)   For whosoever shall give you a cup of water to drink, because ye are Christ's, verily I say unto you, he shall in no wise lose his reward.]

And whosoever shall cause one of these LITTLE ONES that
believe on me to STUMBLE,
It were better for him if a great millstone were hanged about
his neck, and he were cast into the sea.

[And if thy hand cause thee to STUMBLE, cut it off: it is GOOD
for thee to ENTER into Life maimed, rather than having thy
two hands to go into GEHENNA, into the unquenchable FIRE.

(f) AND if thy foot cause thee to STUMBLE, cut it off; it is
GOOD for thee to ENTER into Life halt, rather than having thy
two feet to be cast into GEHENNA.

And if thine eye cause thee to STUMBLE, cast it out: it is GOOD
for thee to ENTER into the Kingdom of God with one eye,
rather than having two eyes, to be cast into GEHENNA;

> 'where their worm dieth not,
> and the FIRE is not quenched'.
> (Isa. lxvi. 24; Judith xvi. 21)

For every one shall be Salted with FIRE.]

SALT is good: but if the SALT have lost its Saltness, wherewith
will ye season it? Have SALT in yourselves, and be at peace one
with another.

Triads: the lection is imperfectly triadic. 'Little children' (twice) seems to
make up a triad with 'little ones'. 'In my name' is a triad; but 'because ye are
Christ's' is literally translated 'in the name that ye are Christ's'. 'Stumble'
with the expression 'it is good (better)' comes four times, but its last three
occurrences are part of a triadic passage, which, however, is not logically
carried out; yet we have 'enter into', 'gehenna', 'fire', and 'salt'.

Major Triads: first and last, John (and James), enter into the kingdom of God.

NOTES

(1) We regard this lection as giving the teachings of Jesus to which the
Second Passion Announcement in 40 was an introduction. The literary connexions with the teachings after the Third Passion Announcement (42 h) are
obvious.

(2) The lection is composite. The sayings in *c, d,* and the first stanza of *e*
have been introduced. The second stanza of *e* is a continuation of *b.* The last
stanza of *e* and the first two stanzas of *f* also seem to be introductions into the

original text. The thoughts contained in these additional stanzas have their literary connexions with 42 *a–f*, rather than with the sayings which are attached to the Passion Announcements.

(3) In the Vulgate, as contained in Amiatinus, a chapter-division occurs after *b*.

TRANSFIGURATION V
Third Week in Ab.

LECTION 41 (Mark x. 1–16).

Matthew non-*B* 40, 'Concerning those who asked the Lord, Is it Lawful to put away a Wife?'.

Mark non-B 27 continued. Tatian 25. Old Latin 30

(*a*) AND he arose from thence, and cometh into the borders of Judaea and beyond Jordan: and Multitudes come together unto him again; and, as he was wont, he Taught them again.

Mark non-B 28, 'Concerning those who asked the Lord,
Is it Lawful to put away a Wife?'

And there came unto him Pharisees, and asked him, Is it lawful for a man to PUT AWAY his WIFE? TEMPTING him. And he answered and said unto them, What did Moses command you? And they said, Moses suffered

'to write a bill of divorcement,
         and to put her away'.   (Deut. xxiv. 1)

But Jesus said unto them, For your hardness of heart he wrote you this commandment. But from the beginning of the creation,

'male and female made he them'.   (Gen. i. 27)

For this cause

'shall a MAN leave his father and mother,
and shall cleave to his wife;
and the twain shall become one flesh';   (Gen. ii. 24)

so that they are no more twain, but one flesh. What therefore God hath joined together, let not MAN put asunder.

(*b*) AND in the House the Disciples asked him again of this matter. And he saith unto them,

> Whosoever shall put away his WIFE, and marry another,
>   Committeth adultery against her:
> And if she herself shall put away her Husband, and marry
>   another,
> She committeth adultery.

(*c*) AND they brought unto him little CHILDREN, that he should touch them: and the Disciples rebuked them. But when Jesus saw it, he was moved with indignation, and said unto them,

> Suffer the little CHILDREN to come unto me; forbid them
>   not:
> For of such is the Kingdom of God.
> Verily I say unto you,
> Whosoever shall not receive the Kingdom of God as a little
>   CHILD,
> He shall in no wise ENTER therein.

And he took them in his arms, and blessed them, laying his hands upon them.

(Fifth script-division in B)

Triads: wife (including quotation from O.T.), man—man—husband, put away, children.

Major Triads: tempt (of the Pharisees), enter into the kingdom of God.

NOTES

(1) Some texts read in lines 1 and 2 'the regions of Judaea beyond Jordan'.

(2) *The Structure of the 'Diatessaron'.* In Sections 16–24 Tatian is remarkably faithful to the chapter-enumeration of Mark in non-B. In Section 18 he has a reference to the Pascha, taken from John vi. 3; in 24 he includes the Transfiguration; whether 18–24 is a survival of some original heptad, it is hard to say; in any case Tatian has sacrificed any liturgical significance there may be in these readings.

In placing the Transfiguration in 24, he agrees exactly with the non-B enumeration of Mark. From that point, he has to make decisions of a drastic character.

In 25 he places the teachings of Jesus contained in 40 and 41 (non-B 27 and 28).

In 26 and 27 he places teaching material from Matthew and Luke.

In 28 he turns to John. Section 28 of Tatian is the first of eight lections, the setting of which is the Feast of Tabernacles mentioned in John vii. 2, and again in vii. 37; the eight lections correspond to the eight days of the Feast. With great ingenuity Tatian incorporates one Marcan lection into each of these eight longer lections of his own (28–35) and so retains touch with the Marcan chapter-enumeration as we know it in the non-B system. The Marcan lections in question are thus associated with the Feast of Tabernacles, a point which we had been led to anticipate by our liturgical theory.

(3) Eighteen lections have followed one another continuously since the last script-division, which came after Lection 22, though it may be admitted that something rather like a script-division occurred after Lection 30; but it lacked the projecting letter which would catch the eye of the lector, and indicate the point at which he was to begin reading.

This is the first of three script-divisions (if we admit x. 45) with which the Galilean Calendar, as it was revealed by literary criticism, came to an end. We note that it indicates a fairly long lection (perhaps originally two lections) which intervenes between the Second Passion Announcement with its pendent teaching, and the Third Passion Announcement and its pendent teaching. It thus emphasizes the literary structure of this part of Mark.

TRANSFIGURATION VI
Fourth Week in Ab.

LECTION 42 (Mark x. 17–45).
Matthew non-B 41, 'Concerning the Rich Man who Questioned Jesus'; Matthew non-B 43, 'Concerning the Sons of Zebedee'.

Mark non-B 29, 'Concerning the Rich Man who Questioned Jesus'. Tatian 28 (Feast of Tabernacles begins). Old Latin 31 (at b)

(a) AND as he was going forth into the way, there ran one to him, and kneeled to him, and asked him, GOOD Master, what shall I do that I may inherit Eternal Life?

(b) AND Jesus said unto him, Why callest thou me GOOD? None is GOOD save one, even God. Thou knowest the commandments,

> '*Thou shalt not kill, Thou shalt not commit adultery,
> Thou shalt not steal, Thou shalt not bear false witness',
> Thou shalt not defraud,
> 'Honour thy father and mother'.
>   (Exod. xx. 12 ff.; Deut. v. 16 ff.)

* R.V. Do not kill, etc.

(*c*)   And he said unto him, Master, all these things have I observed from my youth.

(*d*)   AND Jesus looking upon him loved him, and said unto him, One thing thou lackest: go, sell whatsoever thou hast, and give to the poor, and thou shalt have treasure in heaven: and come, FOLLOW ME. But his countenance fell at the saying, and he went away sorrowful: for he was one that had Great Possessions. And Jesus looked round about, and saith unto his Disciples, How hardly shall they that have RICHES ENTER INTO THE KINGDOM OF GOD! And the Disciples were amazed at his words.

Tatian 29

But Jesus answereth again, and saith unto them, Children, how hard is it to ENTER INTO THE KINGDOM OF GOD! It is easier for a camel to go through a needle's eye, than for a RICH man to ENTER INTO THE KINGDOM OF GOD. And they were astonished exceedingly, saying unto him, Then who CAN be saved? Jesus looking upon them saith, With men it is IMPOSSIBLE, but not with God:

'for all things are POSSIBLE with God.'   (Gen. xviii. 4, etc.)

New lection, non-B 30, begins in Θ

(*e*)   Peter began to say unto him, Lo, we have left all and have FOLLOWED THEE.

(*f*)   Jesus said, Verily I say unto you, There is no man that hath left house, or brethren, or sisters, or mother, or father, or children, or lands, for my sake, and for the Gospel's sake, but he shall receive a hundredfold now in this time, houses, and brethren, and sisters, and mothers, and children, and lands, with persecutions; and in the world to come Eternal Life. But many that are FIRST shall be LAST; and the LAST FIRST.

(Sixth script-division in B)

Page 1293 of Codex Vaticanus 1209 (Cod. B) from the phototypic edition of Ulricus Hoepli, Milan 1904.

This page is almost entirely taken up with the latter three-quarters of the over-long Lection 42, which comes to an end only nine lines above the bottom of the third column.

At the bottom of the first column, however, we see an undoubted script-division. Nineteen complete lections have passed by since the script-division which occurred after Lection 22. The present Lection (42) is preceded by a script-division which, however, is not illustrated in our text. Here we have a script-division which is not related to the system of lection-enumeration; it divides a numbered lection into two; and once again we ask whether the script-divisions in B do not represent a system independent of the lection-divisions.

It marks a point very near that which we chose by literary analysis as the original end of the Jewish Calendar material. It indicates the Third Passion Announcement, which is the beginning of a lection in many of our authorities. It is one of those very rare instances, however, of a subdivision of a lection which does not begin with the word KAI. The use of the particle ΔE may indicate that in the mind of the author it was not thought of as the beginning of a lection. The sentence indicated by the letter *g* should perhaps form the conclusion of the previous lection (or sub-lection).

The place where we had made our division indicating the end of the Galilean Calendar material was the end of Lection 42, at the foot of the third column. The evidence is interesting. The first line of Lection 43 was omitted by error, and had to be inserted in the margin by the corrector, who was quite probably the original scribe. We can see the distraction which caused the lack of attention which was responsible for the omission. There is a hole in the manuscript, caused perhaps by the arrow which killed the animal whose skin provided the material for this page. It interrupts the word ANTI, and, in consequence, what would have been the short line concluding Lection 42 is extended into a full line. Then came two lines, each of which began with the word KAI, and by one of the commonest of errors in copying, the eye of the scribe fell to the lower of the two lines, and he copied the lower instead of the upper.

TΗΝΨΥΧΗΝΑΥΤΟΥΑΥ
ΤΡΟΝΑΝΤΙΠΟΛΛⲰ͞
ΚΑΙΕΡΧΟΝΤΑΙΕΙCΙΕΡΕΙΧⲰ
ΚΑΙΕΚΠΟΡΕΥΟΜΕΝΟΥΑΥ
ΤΟΥΑΠΟΙΕΡΕΙΧⲰΚΑΙ

The sketch given above is a reconstruction of the original on the basis of this explanation, which is the simplest and most natural. The omitted words formed a whole line in the original, otherwise we cannot explain their omission; therefore the original was written in lines of the length which B uses, and B was copying those lines. If the omitted line was a whole line in the original, so, presumably, was the line above it; therefore that line was a short line as shown in the sketch.

What cannot be proved is that the omitted line (line 3 in the reconstruction) projected into the left-hand margin as shown; we note, however, that it has more letters in it than any of the other lines, and that it is written in the margin of B with its initial letter projecting to the left. It is, therefore, perfectly possible, and may be described as a reasonable conjecture.

I have lengthened the fourth line by taking in the two first letters of B's fifth line, so as to compensate for the shortening caused by the hole in B. This is made up in the fifth line by writing the word KAI at the end of the line in full instead of using an abbreviation as B does.

186

ΠΑΛΙΝΑΠΟΚΡΙΘΕΙϹΛΕΓΙ
ΑΥΤΟΙϹΤΕΚΝΑΠΩϹΔΥ
ΚΟΛΟΝΕϹΤΙΝΕΙϹΤΗΝ
ΒΑϹΙΛΕΙΑΝΤΟΥΘΥΕΙϹ
ϹΕΛΘΕΙΝΕΥΚΟΠΩΤΕΡΟ
ΕϹΤΙΝΚΑΜΗΛΟΝΔΙΑΤ
ΤΡΥΜΑΛΙΑϹΤΗϹΡΑΦΙ
ΔΟϹΙΕΛΘΕΙΝΗΠΛΟΥ
ϹΙΟΝΕΙϹΤΗΝΒΑϹΙΛΕΙ
ΤΟΥΘΥΕΙϹΕΛΘΕΙΝ ΟΙΔ
ΠΕΡΙϹϹΩϹΕΞΕΠΛΗϹϹ
ΤΟΛΕΓΟΝΤΕϹΠΡΟϹΑΥ
ΤΟΝΚΑΙΤΙϹΔΥΝΑΤΑΙ
ϹΩΘΗΝΑΙ ΕΜΒΛΕΨΑϹ
ΑΥΤΟΙϹΟΙϹΛΕΓΕΙΠΑΡΑ
ΑΝΘΡΩΠΟΙϹΑΔΥΝΑΤ
ΑΛΛΟΥΠΑΡΑΘΩΠΑΝΤΑ
ΓΑΡΔΥΝΑΤΑΠΑΡΑΘΩ
ΗΡΞΑΤΟΛΕΓΕΙΝΟΠΕΤ
ΑΥΤΩΙΔΟΥΗΜΕΙϹΑΦΗ
ΚΑΜΕΝΠΑΝΤΑΚΑΙΗΚ
ΛΟΥΘΗΚΑΜΕΝϹΟΙ ΕΦΗ
ΟΙϹΑΜΗΝΛΕΓΩΥΜΙΝ
ΟΥΔΕΙϹΕϹΤΙΝΟϹΑΦΗ
ΚΕΝΟΙΚΙΑΝΗΑΔΕΛΦΟΥ
ΗΑΔΕΛΦΑϹΗΜΗΤΕΡΑ
ΗΠΑΤΕΡΑΗΤΕΚΝΑΗΑ
ΓΡΟΥϹΕΝΕΚΕΝΕΜΟΥΚ
ΤΟΥΕΥΑΓΓΕΛΙΟΥΕΑΝ
ΜΗΛΑΒΗΕΚΑΤΟΝΤΑΠΛΑ
ϹΙΟΝΑΝΥΝΕΝΤΩΚΑΙ
ΤΟΥΤΩΟΙΚΙΑϹΚΑΙΑΔΕΛ
ΦΟΥϹΚΑΙΑΔΕΛΦΑϹΚΑΙ
ΜΗΤΕΡΑϹΚΑΙΤΕΚΝΑΚ
ΑΓΡΟΥϹΜΕΤΑΔΙΩΓ
ΚΑΙΕΝΤΩΑΙΩΝΙΤΩΕΡ
ΧΟΜΕΝΩΖΩΗΝΑΙΩΝΙ
ΑΝΠΟΛΛΟΙΔΕΕϹΟΝΤΑΙ
ΠΡΩΤΟΙΕϹΧΑΤΟΙΚΑΙ
ΟΙΕϹΧΑΤΟΙΠΡΩΤΟΙ
ΗϹΑΝΔΑΕΝΤΗΟΔΩΑΝΑ
ΒΑΙΝΟΝΤΕϹΕΙϹΙΕΡΟϹ

ΛΥΜΑΚΑΙΗΝΠΡΟΑΓΩΝ
ΑΥΤΟΥϹΟΙϹΚΑΙΕΘΑΜ
ΒΟΥΝΤΟΟΙΔΕΑΚΟΛΟΥ
ΘΟΥΝΤΕϹΕΦΟΒΟΥΝΤ
ΚΑΙΠΑΡΑΛΑΒΩΝΠΑΛΙΝ
ΤΟΥϹΔΩΔΕΚΑΗΡΞΑΤΟ
ΑΥΤΟΙϹΛΕΓΕΙΝΤΑΜΕΛ
ΛΟΝΤΑΑΥΤΩϹΥΜΒΑΙ
ΝΕΙΝΟΤΙΙΔΟΥΑΝΑΒΑΙ
ΝΟΜΕΝΕΙϹΙΕΡΟϹΟΛΥΜΑ
ΚΑΙΟΥΙΟϹΤΟΥΑΝΘΡΩ
ΠΟΥΠΑΡΑΔΟΘΗϹΕΤΑΙΤ
ΑΡΧΙΕΡΕΥϹΙΝΚΑΙΤΟΙϹ
ΓΡΑΜΜΑΤΕΥϹΙΝΚΑΙΚΑ
ΤΑΚΡΙΝΟΥϹΙΝΑΥΤΟΝ
ΘΑΝΑΤΩΚΑΙΠΑΡΑΔΩ
ϹΟΥϹΙΝΑΥΤΟΝΤΟΙϹΕ
ΘΝΕϹΙΝΚΑΙΕΜΠΑΙΖΟΥ
ϹΙΝΑΥΤΩΚΑΙΕΜΠΤΥ
ϹΟΥϹΙΝΑΥΤΩΚΑΙΜΑ
ϹΤΙΓΙΩϹΟΥϹΙΝΑΥΤΟ
ΚΑΙΑΠΟΚΤΕΝΟΥϹΙΝ
ΜΕΤΑΤΡΕΙϹΗΜΕΡΑϹΑ
ΝΑϹΤΗϹΕΤΑΙ ΚΑΙΠ
ΠΟΡΕΥΟΝΤΑΙΑΥΤΩΙΑ
ΚΩΒΟϹΚΑΙΙΩΑΝΗϹΟΙΥ
ΙΟΙΖΕΒΕΔΑΙΟΥΛΕΓΟΝ
ΤΕϹΑΥΤΩΔΙΔΑϹΚΑΛΕ
ΟϹΑΟΜΕΝΙΝΑΘΕΛΗΙΤΙ
ϹΩΜΕΝϹΕΠΟΙΗϹΗϹΗΜΙ
ΟΔΕΕΙΠΕΝΑΥΤΟΙϹΤΙ
ΛΕΓΕΜΕΠΟΙΗϹΩΥΜΙΝ
ΟΙΔΑΔΕΙΠΑΝΑΥΤΩΔΟϹ
ΗΜΙΝΙΝΑΕΙϹϹΟΥΕΚΑ
ΞΙΩΝΚΑΙΕΙϹΕΞΑΡΙϹΤ
ΡΩΝΚΑΘΙϹΩΜΕΝΕΝΤΗ
ΔΟΞΗϹΟΥ ΟΔΕΙϹΕΙΠ
ΑΥΤΟΙϹΟΥΚΟΙΔΑΤΕΤΙ
ΑΙΤΕΙϹΘΕΔΥΝΑϹΘΕΠΙ
ΕΙΝΤΟΠΟΤΗΡΙΟΝΟΔΕ
ΓΩΠΕΙΝΩΗΤΟΒΑΠΤΙ
ϹΜΑΟΔΕΓΩΒΑΠΤΙΖΟΜΑΙ

ΒΑΠΤΙϹΘΗΝΑΙΟΙΔΕΕΙ
ΠΑΝΑΥΤΩΔΥΝΑΜΕΘΑ
ΟΔΕΙϹΕΙΠΕΝΑΥΤΟΙϹΤΟ
ΠΟΤΗΡΙΟΝΟΔΕΓΩΠΙΝω
ΠΙΕϹΘΕΚΑΙΤΟΒΑΠΤΙϹΜ
ΟΔΕΓΩΒΑΠΤΙΖΟΜΑΙΒΑ
ΠΤΙϹΘΗϹΕϹΘΕΤΟΔΕΚΑ
ΘΙϹΑΙΕΚΔΕΞΙΩΝΜΟΥΗ
ΕΞΕΥΩΝΥΜΩΝΟΥΚΕϹΤΙ
ΕΜΟΝΔΟΥΝΑΙΑΛΛΟΙϹΗ
ΤΟΙΜΑϹΤΑΙ ΚΑΙΑΚΟΥ
ϹΑΝΤΕϹΟΙΔΕΚΑΗΡΞΑΝ
ΤΟΑΓΑΝΑΚΤΕΙΝΠΕΡΙ
ΑΚΩΒΟΥΚΑΙΙΩΑΝΟΥ
ΚΑΙΠΡΟϹΚΑΛΕϹΑΜΕΝΟ
ΑΥΤΟΥϹΟΙϹΛΕΓΕΙΑΥΤΟΙ
ΟΙΔΑΤΕΟΤΙΟΙΔΟΚΟΥΝ
ΤΕϹΑΡΧΕΙΝΤΩΝΕΘΝΩ
ΚΑΤΑΚΥΡΙΕΥΟΥϹΙΝΑΥ
ΤΩΝΚΑΙΟΙΜΕΓΑΛΟΙΑΥ
ΤΩΝΚΑΤΕΞΟΥϹΙΑΖΟΥ
ϹΙΝΑΥΤΩΝΟΥΧΟΥΤωϹ
ΔΕΕϹΤΙΝΕΝΥΜΙΝΑΛΛ
ΑΝΘΕΛΗΜΕΓΑϹΓΕΝΕ
ϹΘΑΙΕΝΥΜΙΝΕϹΤΑΙΥΜω
ΔΙΑΚΟΝΟϹΚΑΙΟϹΑΝΘΕΛ
ΑΗΕΝΥΜΙΝΕΙΝΑΙΠΡω
ΤΟϹΕϹΤΑΙΠΑΝΤΩΝΔΟΥ
ΛΟϹΚΑΙΓΑΡΟΥΙΟϹΤΟΥ
ΑΝΘΡΩΠΟΥΟΥΚΗΛΘΕ
ΔΙΑΚΟΝΗΘΗΝΑΙΑΛΛΑ
ΔΙΑΚΟΝΗϹΑΙΚΑΙΔΟΥΝΑΙ
ΤΗΝΨΥΧΗΝΑΥΤΟΥΛΥ
ΤΡΟΝΑΝ ΤΙΠΟΛΛΩ
ΚΑΙΕΚΠ ΟΡΕΥΟΜΕΝΟΥ
ΑΥΤΟΥΑΠΟΙΕΡΙΧΩ
ΤΩΝΜΑΘΗΤΩΝΑΥΤΟΥ
ΚΑΙΟΧΛΟΥΙΚΑΝΟΥΟΥΙ
ΟϹΤΙΜΑΙΟΥΒΑΡΤΙ
ΜΑΙΟϹΤΥΦΛΟϹΠΡΟϹ
ΑΙΤΗϹΕΚΑΘΗΤΟΠΑΡΑ
ΤΗΝΟΔΟΝΚΑΙΑΚΟΥϹΑϹ

Mark non-B 30, '*Concerning the Sons of Zebedee*'.
Tatian 30. *Old Latin* 32

(*g*) AND they were in the way, going up to Jerusalem; and Jesus was GOING BEFORE THEM: and they were amazed; and they that FOLLOWED were afraid.

(*h*) AND he took again the Twelve, and began to tell them the things that were to happen unto him, saying,

> Behold, we go up to Jerusalem;
> And the SON OF MAN shall be delivered unto the chief priests and the scribes;
> And they shall condemn him to death, and shall deliver him unto the Gentiles;
> And they shall mock him, and shall spit upon him, and shall scourge him, and shall KILL HIM;
> And AFTER THREE DAYS he shall RISE AGAIN.

(*i*) AND there come near unto him James and JOHN, the sons of Zebedee, saying unto him, Master, we would that thou shouldest do for us whatsoever we shall ask of thee.

(*j*) AND he said unto them, What would ye that I should do for you? And they said unto him, Grant unto us that we may sit, ONE ON THY RIGHT HAND, AND ONE ON THY LEFT HAND, in thy GLORY. But Jesus said unto them, Ye know not what ye ask. Are ye able to DRINK the CUP that I DRINK? or to be BAPTIZED with the BAPTISM that I am BAPTIZED with? And they said unto him, We are able.

(*k*) AND Jesus said unto them, The CUP that I DRINK ye shall DRINK; and with the BAPTISM that I am BAPTIZED withal shall ye be BAPTIZED: but to sit ON MY RIGHT HAND OR ON MY LEFT HAND is not mine to give: but it is for them for whom it hath been prepared.

(*l*) AND when the ten heard it, they began to be moved with indignation concerning James and JOHN.

(*m*) AND Jesus called them to him, and saith unto them, Ye know that they which are accounted to rule over the gentiles lord it over them; and their great ones exercise authority over them. But it is not so among you:

> But whosoever would become Great among you, shall be your MINISTER:
> And whosoever would be FIRST among you, shall be SERVANT of all.
> For verily the Son of Man came not to be MINISTERED unto, but to MINISTER,
> AND to Give his LIFE a ransom for many.

(Isa. xli. 8, xlii. 1, etc., liii. 12)

(*Possible script-division in* B)

Triads: good, God, can and possible (one word in Greek), many possessions and rich (different words in Greek), kingdom of God, follow, drink—cup—drink (twice), baptism (twice), minister, give.

Major Triads: enter into the kingdom of God, drink, cup, right and left hand, first (and last), (James and) John, life (soul), baptize, the announcement of the Passion.

NOTES

(1) This long lection which closes the sixth heptad in the system of B is much too long. In non-B it is divided into two; and this is supported by a script-division in B. Codex Θ divides it into three, for it has marginal notes indicating a 'beginning' opposite *e* as well as *f*. The Vulgate according to Amiatinus supports the non-B division. In Θ, however, the division comes between *g* and *h*, not between *f* and *g*.

(2) Literary analysis led us to place the end of the 'Galilean' material, with its Three Mountains and its Three Passion Announcements, at the end of this lection, after the words 'a ransom for many'. The liturgical theory led us to adopt this point as the end of the lections set for the liturgical year; unquestionably this is not so in the enumeration of B as we now have it; 42 lections are insufficient; we need seven more.

On the other hand, when we go back and examine Lections 37, 40, and 41, as well as 42, we can see that a number of originally independent lections have been compressed into the over-long lections which are now presented to us. If we use our own judgement and divide them naturally, we find we have forty-nine or fifty or even more. We suggest that the last fourteen lections of the Galilean Year were compressed into seven so as to find room for the material at present situated in 43–48 or 49. We think 42*m* is the original conclusion of the liturgical year. If the Day of Atonement was the Jewish form of the ritual of the divine king who dies for his people (and we think it is), nothing could be more suitable than 42*g–m*.

(3) Lection 42*g–m* is the gospel for the Fifth Sunday in Lent in the Greek Calendar, being the Third Passion Announcement. We have pointed out the literary and liturgical relations between the three Passion Announcements with their appended teachings; we have seen reason to connect them with preparation for baptism in the later practice of the church; and we notice in Mark that they lead right into the story of the Last Supper. These literary connexions are obvious in Mark; and in the case of Luke and John the principal material of *g–m* is found in connexion with the Last Supper itself.

Now in the case of the Greek Calendar, we may fairly argue that the same tradition is continued; for the reading of this gospel on the Fifth Sunday in Lent would be succeeded by the reading of the Passion on the Sixth Sunday (Palm Sunday), and the Passion begins with the reference to the Pascha which leads into the Last Supper.

If the three Passion Announcements and pendent teachings in Mark were employed in the ritual which led through baptism to the eucharist, then of course the references to the cup and to baptism in *g–m* would be very easy to understand. And then, too, looking at the liturgical year as a whole, we note that it begins in its first lection with a reference to baptism, and concludes in its last lection with a reference to the eucharist (or to baptism and eucharist).

(4) We conclude that the liturgical year closed at this point.

7. TABERNACLES

When a Jew said 'the feast', he meant Tabernacles. It was the greatest festival of the year. We have already set out the calendar for the month in the introduction to the first lection, to which reference should be made (*see* p. 117).

From the point of view of the old nature religion, it was the ingathering of the last fruits of the earth, including the figs, but particularly the vines. It should be compared with the rites of Dionysus, from which, perhaps, it had borrowed a few ceremonies: the processions with branches of palms and of certain other trees; the ritual songs, and so forth. The branches were carried round the altar seven times, and Psalm cxviii was sung with its refrain of 'Hosanna'. This is the sort of ceremony with which the Lord is welcomed into Jerusalem in Lection 44. Everything in this sequence of lections is suitable to Tabernacles.

At the end of the eight days prayer was offered for rain.

This was the festival at which Solomon had dedicated the original temple. The old ritual of the divine king to which reference has been made revolved around the ideas of the king, the temple, and the city; and these were all represented in the thought and ritual of this feast. The Day of Atonement ritual seems to have been a form of the ritual of the divine king especially suited to the high priest, who had now practically taken over the functions of the king.

In order to preserve a connexion with the preceding festivals, the Rabbis said that the Day of Atonement was the day on which Moses descended a second time from Mount Sinai, with the new Tables of the Law. The reading of the Law was a great feature of this festival.

More interesting, possibly, from our point of view was the connexion with 'apocalyptic' and even 'eschatological' ideas. In the New Year Festival of the ancient world, the king-priest represented the sun-god who was also the creator. This idea could only exist in Israel, of course, with great differences, and by New Testament times it had expressed itself in a new form. The idea of the king-priest who in some way was the representative of the creator was thrown into the future; he became the king-messiah whom God would send to Israel, to overcome Israel's enemies, and to reign in glory on earth. This in its turn was set against ideas of creation and judgement.

The reading of the creation-story, we are told, was a feature of these New Year rituals. Creation, too, had to be renewed; as indeed primitive man could see it did renew itself each year, passing through the death of winter into the new life and new birth of spring; but Jewish imagination made something more magnificent of it. The Almighty God would surely renew his whole creation; old things would pass away; new things would come into being; and men and nations would be judged.

In some sense they believed this really happened in the great festival. 'The world is judged at four periods of the year', we read in the *Tractate Rosh Hashanah*: 'On Passover in respect of the growth of corn; on the feast of Pentecost in respect of fruit trees; on the feast of the New Year, when all human beings pass like lambs before God's throne in order to be judged...and on the feast of Tabernacles concerning the rain'.

We see here the apocalyptic or eschatological, appearing perfectly naturally in the midst of the ritual and the agricultural. We find the same mixture in Lection 49 with which our gospel closes. After going through some of the conventional apocalyptic imagery it remarks abruptly, 'From the fig-tree learn a parable'. In Revelation, which makes a wonderful use of the imagery of Tabernacles, we have a strange mixture of the two kinds of symbolism which are kept separate in Lection 49; what Revelation says is, 'The sun became black as sackcloth of hair and the moon became as blood; and the stars of the heaven fell into the earth even as a fig-tree casteth her untimely figs when it is shaked by a mighty wind' (vi. 12, 13).[1] This is the world-tree, which we also have in Lection 18g; but the whole world, as we see, is subject to agricultural moods and changes; it grows old, it grows young; it has its spring and summer and autumn and winter; it groans and travails in pain; it passes through judgement into renewal; it will have its summer season once again, and so forth.

Here is the secret of the mystical language of Jesus, and now we have got it, it is too clear and bright to see. It is mystical, it is eschatological; it is apocalyptic, it is prophetic; it is liturgical, it is sacramental; and it is never more one than when it is the other. We must hold on to all these brightly coloured beams of light at once, and see them interlacing with one another in a pure and blinding white. That is all we have to do; but how are we to do it? Who is equal to it?

When in doubt, let us keep our feet on the earth, and begin with the agricultural, which is where he began. He planted a seed.

TABERNACLES I

First Week in Elul (August–September): Sixth Month. The seven following Lections (43–9) are so arranged that the seventh will fall on the Feast of Tabernacles, and so form the climax of the liturgical year.

LECTION 43 (Mark x. 46–52).

Matthew non-B 42, 'Concerning the Two Blind Men'.

[1] And Revelation here is merely following the oldest form of the words as they are found in Isa. xiii. 10.

Mark non–B 31, 'Concerning Bartimaeus'. Tatian 31.
Old Latin 33

AND they come to Jericho: and as he went out from Jericho, with his Disciples and a great Multitude, the son of Timaeus, Bartimaeus, a BLIND beggar, was sitting by the way side. And when he heard that it was Jesus OF NAZARETH, he began to cry out, and say, Jesus, thou son of DAVID, have mercy on me. And many rebuked him, that he should hold his peace: but he cried out the more a great deal, Thou son of DAVID, have mercy upon me. And Jesus stood still, and said, CALL ye him. And they CALL the BLIND man, saying unto him, Be of good cheer: rise, he CALLETH thee. And he, casting away his garment, sprang up, and came to Jesus. And Jesus answered him, and said, What wilt thou that I should do unto thee? And the BLIND man said unto him, Rabboni, that I may receive my sight. And Jesus said unto him, Go thy way; thy Faith hath Saved thee. And straightway he received his sight, and Followed him in the way.

> *Triads:* blind, call, son of David (completed in Lection 44).
>
> *Major Triads:* David, Nazarene (translated 'of Nazareth').

NOTES

(1) The title in Θ is 'Concerning Blind Bartimaeus'.

(2) In the *Diatessaron* the blind man says, 'Lord, that I may see thee'; and this may have been the reading in Marcion's gospel.

TABERNACLES II
Second Week in Elul.

LECTION 44 (Mark xi. 1–11).
Matthew non-B 45, 'Concerning the Ass and the Foal'.

Mark non-B 32, 'Concerning the Colt'. Tatian 39. Old Latin 34

(a) AND when they draw nigh unto Jerusalem, unto Bethphage and BETHANY, at the MOUNT OF OLIVES, he sendeth two of his Disciples, and saith unto them, Go your way into the village that is over against you: and straightway as ye enter into it, ye shall find a 'COLT tied' (Gen. xlix. 11), whereon no man ever yet sat; LOOSE him, and bring him. And if any one say unto you, Why do ye this? say ye, The Lord hath need of him; and straightway he will send him back hither. And they went away, and found a 'COLT tied' at the door without in the open street; and they LOOSE him. And certain of them that stood there said unto them, What do ye, Loosing the COLT? And they said unto them even as Jesus had said: and they let them go. And they bring the COLT unto Jesus, and cast on him their garments; and he sat upon him. And many spread their garments upon the way; and others branches, which they had cut from the fields. And they that went before, and they that followed, cried,

Hosanna;
Blessed is he that cometh in the name of the Lord:

(Ps. cxviii. 26)

Blessed is the kingdom that cometh, (the kingdom) of our father DAVID:
Hosanna in the highest.

Old Latin 35

(b) AND he entered into Jerusalem, into the Temple; and when he had looked round about upon all things, it being now eventide, he went out unto BETHANY with the Twelve.

Triads: colt (4), loose, David (completing triad begun in Lection 43).

Major Triads: David, Mount of Olives, Bethany.

NOTES

(1) In B the words 'at the mount' fill half a line, the remainder being left blank. 'Of Olives' comes at the beginning of the next line.

(2) Tatian places this narrative after the anointing at Bethany, at the Pascha, following John.

(3) The 'colt tied' is a quotation from the Blessing of Jacob in Gen. xlix which has obvious references to a vintage festival. The ritual of spreading cloaks and branches and singing Ps. cxviii is from the customs at Tabernacles.

TABERNACLES III
Third Sunday in Elul.

LECTION 45 (Mark xi. 12–19).
Matthew non-B 47, 'Concerning the Withered Fig-Tree'.

Mark non-B 33, 'Concerning the Withered Fig-Tree'. Tatian 32

(*a*) AND on the morrow, when they were come out from BETHANY, he hungered. And seeing a FIG TREE afar off having leaves, he came, if haply he might find anything thereon; and when he came to it, he found nothing but leaves; for it was not the season of Figs.

(*b*) AND he answered and said unto it, No man eat fruit from thee henceforward for ever. And his Disciples heard it. And they come to Jerusalem: and he entered into the TEMPLE, and began to cast out them that sold and them that bought in the TEMPLE, and overthrew the tables of the money-changers, and the seats of them that sold the doves; and he would not suffer that any man should carry a vessel through the TEMPLE. And he Taught, and said unto them, Is it not written,

'My house shall be called a house of PRAYER for all the nations'? (Isa. lvi. 7)
but ye have made it 'a den of robbers'. (Jer. vii. 11)

(*c*) AND the chief priests and the Scribes heard it, and sought how they might destroy him: for they feared him, for all the Multitude was astonished at his Teaching.

(*d*) AND every evening he went forth out of the city.

Triads: fig-tree (with Lection 46), temple, prayer—pray (with 46).

NOTES

(1) The minor triads support the combination of Lections 45 with 46*a* by the non-*B* system. The Vulgate system in Amiatinus includes 46*b* as well; this Vulgate lection is numbered 36.

(2) In Tatian 32 we find (i) the Cleansing of the Temple, (ii) the Poor Widow from 48, (iii) the Pharisee and the Publican, (iv) the first part of the Fig-Tree story, and (v) Nicodemus.

(3) If this incident took place in connexion with the Feast of Tabernacles, the action of Jesus was perfectly natural, and the explanation 'for it was not the season of figs' may be dismissed as a gloss. On the other hand figs have been reported near Jerusalem at Passover (on some unusual species of tree?).

(4) Tatian reads: 'No man shall eat fruit of thee for ever.'

TABERNACLES IV
Fourth Week in Elul.

LECTION 46 (Mark xi. 20–xii. 12).

Matthew non-*B* 47 continued; Matthew non-*B* 48, 'Concerning the Chief Priests and Elders who Questioned the Lord'; Matthew non-*B* 50, 'Concerning the Vineyard'.

Mark non-B 33 continued. Tatian 33

(*a*)   AND as they passed by in the morning, they saw the FIG-TREE withered away from the roots. And Peter calling to remembrance saith unto him, Rabbi, behold, the FIG-TREE which thou cursedst is withered away. And Jesus answering saith unto them, Have FAITH in God. Verily I say unto you, Whosoever shall say unto this Mountain, Be thou taken up and cast into the sea; and shall not doubt in his heart, but shall BELIEVE that what he saith cometh to pass; he shall have it. (Cf. Ps. xlvi. 2; Zech. xiv. 4.)

(*b*)   Therefore I say unto you, All things whatsoever ye PRAY and ask for, BELIEVE that ye have received them, and ye shall have them.

Mark non-B 34, 'Concerning Forgivingness'

And whensoever ye stand PRAYING, forgive, if ye have aught against any one; that your Father also which is in heaven may forgive you your trespasses.

Mark non-B 35, 'Concerning the Chief Priests and Elders
who Questioned the Lord'. Old Latin 36

(*c*)   AND they come again to Jerusalem: and as he was walking in the Temple, there come to him the chief priests, and the scribes, and the elders; and they said unto him, By WHAT AUTHORITY doest thou these things? or who gave thee AUTHORITY to DO THESE THINGS? And Jesus said unto them, I will ask of you one question, and ANSWER me, and I will tell you by WHAT AUTHORITY I DO THESE THINGS. The Baptism of John, was it from heaven, or from men? ANSWER me. And they reasoned with themselves, saying, If we shall say, From heaven; he will say, Why then did ye not believe him?

But should we say, From men—they feared the people: for all held John to be a Prophet indeed. And they ANSWERED Jesus and say, We know not. And Jesus saith unto them, Neither tell I you by WHAT AUTHORITY I DO THESE THINGS.

Mark non-B 36, 'Concerning the Vineyard'. Old Latin 37

(*d*) AND he began to speak unto them in Parables.

A man 'planted a VINEYARD,
    And set a hedge about it,
And digged a pit for the winepress,
    And built a tower',   (Isa. v. 1)
And let it out to HUSBANDMEN,
    And went into another country.

And at the season he SENT to the HUSBANDMEN a SERVANT, that he might receive from the HUSBANDMEN of the fruits of the VINEYARD. And they took him, and beat him, and sent him away empty. And again he SENT unto them another SERVANT; and him they wounded in the head, and handled shamefully. And he SENT another; and him they KILLED: and many others; beating some, and KILLING some. He had yet one,

      'a BELOVED SON':   (Isa. v. 1; Gen. xxii. 2, etc.)

he SENT him last unto them, saying,

      'They will reverence MY SON'.   (Ps. ii. 12)

But those HUSBANDMEN said among themselves, This is the Heir; come, let us KILL him, and the Inheritance shall be ours. And they took him, and KILLED him, and cast him forth out of the VINEYARD. What therefore will the lord of the VINEYARD do? he will come and destroy the HUSBANDMEN, and will give the VINEYARD unto others.

Have ye not read even this scripture;

'The Stone which the Builders rejected,
    The same was made the head of the corner:
This was from the Lord,
    And it is marvellous in our eyes'?   (Ps. cxviii. 23)

196

And they sought to lay hold on him; and they feared the Multitude; for they perceived that he spake the Parable against them; and they left him, and went away.

(This lection ends on a short line in B)

Triads: fig-tree (completing triad begun in Lection 45), faith—believe, pray (completing triad begun in 45), answer, by what authority do these things (4), vineyard (5), husbandmen (5), sent (4), son—son—heir, kill (4).
Major Triads: beloved son.

NOTES

(1) The text of B shows a short line at the end of this lection, which may be a trace of a script-division in the original from which he copied. The liturgical features which have been copious since 44 seem to end here, and a new kind of material begins in 47a–e.

(2) The vintage parable, like its predecessor in Isaiah, is suitable for the Feast of Tabernacles; it may indeed be a folk-song. We note another quotation from Ps. cxviii, which was a feature of the ritual of Tabernacles.

(3) The enumeration of Matthew non-B is now definitely parting company with that of B in Mark; it has reached 50, whereas Mark is still at 46. It does not accept the condensation of these lections which is a feature of B; and it adds more lections.

TABERNACLES V

First Week in Tisri (September–October): Seventh Month. Tisri 1 is the Jewish New Year's Day, the Feast of Trumpets.

LECTION 47 (Mark xii. 13–40).

Matthew non-B 52, 'Concerning those who Questioned the Lord on account of the Tribute'; Matthew non-B 53, 'Concerning the Sadducees'; Matthew non-B 54, 'Concerning the Lawyer who Asked a Question'; Matthew non-B 55, 'Concerning the Question of the Lord'; Matthew non-B 56, 'Concerning the Lamentations for the Scribes and Pharisees'.

*Mark non-*B *37, 'Concerning those who Questioned on Account of the Tribute'. Tatian 34. Old Latin 38*

(*a*) AND they send unto him certain of the Pharisees and of the Herodians, that they might catch him in talk. And when they were come, they say unto him, Master, we know that thou art True, and carest not for any one: for thou regardest not the person of men, but of a Truth Teachest the way of GOD: Is it lawful to GIVE tribute unto CAESAR, or not? Shall we GIVE, or shall we not GIVE?

(*b*) But he, knowing their Hypocrisy, said unto them, Why TEMPT ye me? bring me a penny, that I may see it. And they brought it. And he saith unto them, Whose is this image and superscription? And they said unto him, CAESAR's. And Jesus said unto them, Render unto CAESAR the things that are CAESAR's, and unto GOD the things that are GOD's. And they marvelled greatly at him.

Mark non-B 38, 'Concerning the Sadducees'. Old Latin 39

(*c*) AND there come unto him Sadducees, which say that there is no resurrection; and they asked him, saying, Master, Moses wrote unto us,

'If a man's brother die, and leave a wife behind him, and leave no child, that his brother should take his wife, and raise up seed unto his brother'. (Deut. xxv. 5)

There were SEVEN brethren: and the first took a WIFE, and DYING LEFT NO SEED; and the second took her, and DIED, LEAVING NO SEED behind him; and the third likewise: and the SEVEN LEFT NO SEED. Last of all the WOMAN also DIED. In the resurrection whose WIFE shall she be of them? For the SEVEN had her to WIFE.

(*d*) Jesus said unto them, Is it not for this cause that ye err, that ye know not the scriptures, nor the power of GOD? For when they shall RISE from the DEAD, they neither marry, nor are given in marriage; but are as angels in heaven. But as touching the DEAD, that they are RAISED; have ye not read in the book of Moses, in the place concerning the Bush, how GOD spake unto him, saying,

'I am the GOD of Abraham, and the GOD of Isaac, and the GOD of Jacob'? (Exod. iii. 2 and 6)

He is not the GOD of the DEAD, but of the living: ye do greatly err.

Mark non-B 39, *'Concerning the Scribe'*

(*e*) AND one of the SCRIBES came, and heard them questioning together, and knowing that he had answered them well, asked him, What Commandment is the First of all? Jesus answered, the First is,

'Hear, O Israel; the LORD our GOD, the LORD is One: and thou shalt LOVE the LORD thy GOD with all thy heart, and with all thy soul, and with all thy mind, and with all thy strength'. (Deut. vi. 4)

The second is this,

'Thou shalt LOVE thy neighbour as thyself'. (Lev. xix. 18)

There is none other Commandment greater than these. AND the SCRIBE said unto him, Of a truth, Master, thou hast well said that 'he is One'; and

'there is none other but he': (Deut. iv. 35, vi. 4, etc.)

and to LOVE him with all the heart, and with all the understanding, and with all the strength, and to LOVE his neighbour as himself is much more than all whole burnt offerings and sacrifices. (Cf. I Sam. xv. 22.) And when Jesus saw that he answered discreetly, he said unto him, Thou art not far from the Kingdom of GOD. And no man after that durst ask him any question.

Mark non-B 40, *'Concerning the Question of the Lord'*. Tatian 35. Old Latin 40

(*f*) AND Jesus answered and said, as he Taught in the Temple, How say the SCRIBES that the CHRIST is the Son of DAVID? DAVID himself said in the Holy Spirit,

'The LORD said unto my LORD,
    Sit thou on my RIGHT HAND,
Till I make thine enemies
    The footstool of thy feet'. (Ps. cx. 1)

DAVID himself calleth him LORD; and whence is he his Son? And the great Multitude heard him gladly.

Tatian 40

(g) AND in his Teaching he said, Beware of the SCRIBES,
Which desire to walk in long robes,
    And to have salutations in the marketplaces,
And chief seats in the Synagogues,
    And chief places at feasts:
They which devour WIDOWS' houses,
And for a pretence make long prayers;
These shall receive greater condemnation.

Triads: God (12), Caesar (4), seven, died, left no seed, wife (4), rise, dead, scribe (4), first—first—greatest, Lord (two triads including quotations from O.T.), love (four repetitions, two in the text and two in O.T. quotations), David, widow (see Lection 48).

Major Triads: tempt, David, right hand.

NOTES

(1) The title of non-B37 in Θ is 'Concerning those who Lay in Wait [*enkathetōn*] on account of the Tribute'. The word *enkathetoi* seems to be taken from Luke, and therefore this title does not look original; yet it seems to explain the phrase 'on account of the Tribute' which goes awkwardly with 'Questioned' in the title from Alexandrinus.

(2) This over-long lection is another case of condensation in B. The non-B system divides it into four, and it could easily be made into six; and this, with Lection 48, would make a heptad. It seems likely that Mark has reduced fourteen Jerusalem lections, beginning with 43, down to seven; the reason why Matthew has 55 (56) lections at this point is that he refuses to do this. The difference of seven lections between the count in Matthew non-B and Mark B is not due to the extra material in Matthew, such as the Nativity stories and the Sermon on the Mount. It is taken on board here.

(3) In Matthew non-B, 47ƒ receives the number 55; and this is the first of the final fourteen lections of Matthew (55–68) which we have regarded as equivalent to the fourteen Passion lections of Mark. In actual fact, however, they do not coincide. The fourteen in Mark begin with the Discourse on the Mount of Olives (49) which is numbered 57 in Matthew, and would provide only twelve Passion lections.

We are not concerned of course with Matthew; but if we look closely at Mark, we can see that this is a good treatment of the material he finds there. The last words of 47e are a formula which ends that sequence, which was didactic and controversial; ƒ and g are prophetic. What Matthew does is to give 47*f* a new opening formula and to number it 55; 47*g* is enormously expanded and numbered 56; 48 is omitted altogether; and the enumeration can pass to the Discourse on the Mount of Olives as 57. In this way we get seven prophetic lections in preparation for the Passion Narrative proper: (i) David's son; (ii) the Woes against the Pharisees; (iii) the Mount of Olives, part 1; (iv) the Mount of Olives, part 2; and (v, vi, vii) three Parables of Judgement: see notes on 49 and 50.

(4) In Tatian, who remains loyal to Mark and John, we are still in the Feast of Tabernacles. He places 47*f* in his Section 35, which opens with a reference to the 'great day, the last of the Feast', which means the eighth day of Tabernacles; otherwise it consists entirely of matter taken from John.

Sections 36, 37, 38 of Tatian are entirely Johannine, and the middle one of these (37) is dated at the Feast of the Dedication; but in 38 the 'feast of the Pascha is near' (John xi. 55).

Section 39 of Tatian contains the anointing at Bethany, 'six days before the Pascha' (John xii. 1). Section 40 contains the Woes against the Pharisees; and this is where we find subdivision *g* of our present Lection 47 of Mark. It is remarkable that Tatian has succeeded in getting this second half of non-B40 into his own fortieth Section. See notes at end of Lection 50.

TABERNACLES VI
Second Week in Tisri. Tisri 10 was the Day of Atonement, which was followed on the 15th to the 22nd by the Feast of Tabernacles.

LECTION 48 (Mark xii. 41-4).
Omitted by Matthew. End of last quarter.

Mark non-B 41, 'Concerning the Woman who cast in Two Mites'. Tatian 32. Old Latin 41

(*a*) AND he sat down over against the TREASURY, and beheld how the Multitude CAST money into the TREASURY: and many that were rich CAST in much. And there came a poor WIDOW, and she CAST in two 'mites', which make a farthing.

(*b*) AND he called unto him his Disciples, and said unto them, Verily I say unto you, This poor Widow CAST in more than all they which are CASTING into the TREASURY: for they all did CAST in of their superfluity; but she of her want did CAST in all that she had, even all her living.

(*Seventh script-division in* B)

Triads: widow (completing triad begun in Lection 47), treasury, cast in (7).

NOTE

The number of this lection in the Vulgate according to Amiatinus is identical with non-*B*; it is 41. In Tatian, however, it is moved to an earlier point, and follows the Cleansing of the Temple. Matthew omits it altogether, and so does Marcion.

TABERNACLES VII

Third Week of Tisri. Feast of Tabernacles closes on the eighth day, 'Atzeres', which is the 23rd. This marks the end of the liturgical year, and is the day on which the reading of the Law ends, and begins again.

LECTION 49 (Mark xiii. 1–31).

(For text, see Paschal Lection I, p. 206)

NOTE. This lection would seem to be intended for the first of the fourteen lections which make up the Passion Narrative, and were therefore read at the Pascha. On the other hand we have suggested that it was also read here as the final lection of the year.

ΤΗΑΕΕΚΤΗΣΥΣΤΕΡΗϹϹ
ΨϹΑΥΤΗϹΠΑΝΤΑΟϹΑ
ΕΙΧΕΝΕΒΑΛΕΝΟΛΟΝΤΩ
ΒΙΟΝΑΥΤΗϹ
ΜΘ/ΚΑΙΕΚΠΟΓΕΥΟΜΕΝΟΥΑΥ
ΤΟΥΕΚΤΟΥΪΕΡΟΥΛΕΓΕΙ
ΑΥΤΩΕΙϹΤΩΝΜΑΘΗΤΩ
ΑΥΤΟΥΔΙΑΑϹΚΑΛΕΪΔΕ
ΠΟΤΑΠΟΙΛΙΘΟΙΚΑΙΠΟ
ΤΑΠΑΙΟΙΚΟΔΟΜΑΙ ΚΑΙ
ΟΙϹΕΙΠΕΝΑΥΤΩΒΛΕΠΙϹ
ΤΑΥΤΑΣΤΑϹΜΕΓΑΛΑϹ
ΟΙΚΟΔΟΜΑϹΟΥΜΗΑΦ·
ΘΗΩΔΕΛΙΘΟϹΕΠΙΛΙΘϹ
ΟϹΟΥΜΗΚΑΤΑΛΥΘΗ
ΚΑΙΚΑΘΗΜΕΝΟΥΑΥΤΟΥ
ΕΙϹΤΟΟΡΟϹΤΩΝΕΛΑΙϹ
ΚΑΤΕΝΑΝΤΙΤΟΥΪΕΡϹΥ
ΕΠΗΡΩΤΑΑΥΤΟΝΚΑΘΪ
ΔΙΑΝΠΕΤΡΟϹΚΑΙΪΑΚΩ
ΒΟϹΚΑΙΪΩΑΝΗϹΚΑΙΑΝ
ΑΓΕΑϹΕΙΠΟΝΗΜΙΝΠΟ·
ΤΕΤΑΥΤΑΕϹΤΑΙΚΑΙΤΙ
ΤΟϹΗΜΕΙΟΝΟΤΑΝΜΕΛ

Page 1297 of Codex Vaticanus 1209 (Cod. *B*) from the phototypic edition of Ulricus Hoepli, Milan 1904.

The last of the script-divisions presents no problem. It occurs fairly high in the second column of the page, and is well marked. We see the mu theta in the left-hand margin, which means 49, and the bent bar of the person who inserted our modern chapter-divisions.

This is the exact point where we had decided by an analysis of the chapter-numbers that the Passion Narrative should begin. We are happy to find that the script-division system agrees with us that this is a major divisional point. The script has run on without any break in its continuity through the previous seven lections, and it does so through the following fourteen to the very end of the gospel.

These plates have enabled the reader to have some idea of this important manuscript, and to share with us in the study of it. He can see with his own eyes how the lection-divisions are indicated; he can get some idea of the puzzles that confront the palaeographer; and he can also see that the script-divisions actually do divide the gospel into four main divisions almost exactly as our literary analysis did, the only difficulty arising in chapter 10 where the evidence of the MS. is confused by a textual error.

PART II

THE PASSION NARRATIVE

FOURTEEN LECTIONS FOR THE CHRISTIAN PASCHA

The first of these lections is 49 which also serves as the last lection of Mark i.

The calendar of days and hours for the Jewish Pascha has been given in the liturgical introduction to Lection 25. All that is necessary, in order to avoid complete confusion, is to remember that Christ suffered on the fourteenth of Nisan, and also to remember that what *we* call the evening of Nisan 13, *they* called the evening of Nisan 14★. It all happened on Nisan 14★, Last Supper, Gethsemane, Betrayal, Trials, Crucifixion, Burial and everything; and our Passion Narrative displays it so, from evening to evening.

As it stands it has introductory lections and at least one closing lection; perhaps the original Passion Narrative did not have these. It may have begun with the Last Supper on the first evening, and ended with the burial on the second; or, as some think, with the tribute of the centurion.

Numbers of modern scholars think that it grew up as a ritual for liturgical purposes. It bears all the marks of it. It is even marked out into periods of three hours as if for a day of meditation.

One does not want to reopen questions which have become happily settled, but one rather wonders whether this was not a written document from the first. We all agree that the Jewish teachers made use of the oral method of teaching, and that Jesus and his disciples used it without question as the natural way. But is this the same? It is not like the usual subject-matter which we find in oral teaching; nor has it the same form; it has real continuity from section to section.

Perhaps it might be described as a *megillah*: a roll or scroll. A *megillah* was something shorter and slighter than the great books of the Law and Prophets which were read Sabbath by

★ Or Nisan 15 according to the Synoptists.

Sabbath; and it seems often to have been designed for reading at a special feast-day or fast-day. Thus Esther is the *megillah* for the obscure spring festival of Purim. IV Maccabees may be a *megillah* for Hanukkah (Dedication); and II Esdras for the Fast of Ab. We must not hypnotize ourselves into thinking that the Jews of our period never wrote, or never read aloud. On the contrary there was a place for this. Lection 49 is a tiny prophetic scroll for Sukkoth (Tabernacles); our Passion Narrative (49–62) is perhaps the *megillah* for the Christian Pascha; Hebrews may be a *megillah* for the Day of Atonement, and so forth.

All the evidence will go to show that the Passion was a single lection, as it still is in the Roman ritual. It is a single lection, but it is not read like other gospels, and does not count as the gospel for the day; it is announced and read without the accustomed ceremonies or the accustomed 'tone'; when it is finished, a short gospel is read which is the gospel for the day and has some of the usual ceremonies.

The Passion according to Matthew is read on Palm Sunday; a short gospel from John on the Monday, beginning at xii. 1, 'Six days before the Pascha', and containing the anointing at Bethany; the Passion according to Mark is read on Tuesday; according to Luke on Wednesday; a short gospel from John on Thursday, beginning 'Before the feast of the Pascha', and containing the story of the washing of the feet; and the Passion according to John on Good Friday, beginning at xviii. 1.

In every case except that of John the Passion begins with the reference to the Pascha; in the case of John, the Passion begins with the Lord and his disciples leaving the Upper Room which is natural enough for the lection on the day following Maundy Thursday; but actually, if we take in the Monday and the Thursday, the Johannine lections for the week begin with references to the Pascha.

The four Passions all end at about the same point, as nearly as such a point can be established in their different narratives; Matthew ends with the tribute of the centurion, the request for the body, the burial, and the mention of the women; the short liturgical gospel which follows is the setting of the guard by the chief priests, a story which Matthew alone records. In Mark it ends with the tribute of the centurion, and a mention of the women; the short liturgical gospel contains the burial. In Luke we find the same as Mark. In John it ends with the soldier piercing the side of the Lord; but the short liturgical gospel contains the same material as in the case of Mark and Luke.

Literary analysis, supported by the study of our lection numbers and titles, will convince us that this tradition is sound. The Passion Narrative begins with the reference to the Pascha; it ends with the mention of the women, except in John which has a paragraph of its own here. The following lection begins with the request of Joseph for the body of the Lord and the burial in the tomb. It was intended to be read as a whole and not cut up into smaller lections. We thus come across another confirmation of our liturgical theory. Lections 1–49 were intended to be read as separate gospels, though there may be doubts about some instances. Lections 49–62 enclose a narrative of another order which has never been read piecemeal in the liturgical tradition, at least in the West.

In the oldest gospel, Mark, we find prophetic lections welded to the beginning of the Passion; and this tradition is preserved in Matthew; in Luke the connexion is broken; in John their inward meaning is unfolded by a master of spirituality.

PASCHAL LECTION I, *also read as* TABERNACLES VII

LECTION 49 (Mark xiii. 1–31).

End of Matthew non-B 56; Matthew non-B 57, 'Concerning the Consummation', begins at *c*.

Mark non-B 41 continued. Tatian 41. Old Latin 42

(*a*)   AND as he went forth out of the Temple, one of his Disciples saith unto him, Master, behold, what manner of STONES and what manner of BUILDINGS!

(*b*)   AND Jesus said unto him, Seest thou these great BUILDINGS? There shall not be left here one STONE upon another *STONE, which shall not be thrown down.

* R.V. omit 'stone' the second time: it is in the Greek.

Mark non-B 42, 'Concerning the Consummation'

(c) AND as he sat on the MOUNT OF OLIVES over against the Temple, PETER and JAMES and JOHN and ANDREW asked him privately, Tell us, when shall these things be? and what shall be the Sign when these things are all about to be *consummated?

(d) AND Jesus began to say unto them, TAKE HEED that no man LEAD you ASTRAY. Many shall come in my Name, saying, I AM he; and shall LEAD many ASTRAY.

And when ye shall hear of wars and rumours of wars, be not troubled: 'these things must needs come to pass'; but the END is not yet. (Dan. ii. 29, xii. 4, 8)

For 'nation shall rise against nation,
    And kingdom against kingdom':
                            (Isa. xix. 2; II Chron. xv. 6)
There shall be earthquakes in divers places;
    There shall be famines:
These things are the Beginning of 'Travail'.

(e) But TAKE ye HEED to yourselves:
For they shall deliver you up to councils;
    And in Synagogues shall ye be beaten;
And before governors and kings shall ye stand
    For my sake, for a testimony unto them.
†And unto all the gentiles
    The GOSPEL must first be PREACHED.

And when they lead you (to judgement), and deliver you up,
    Be not anxious beforehand what ye shall SPEAK:
But whatsoever shall be given you in THAT HOUR,
    That SPEAK ye:
For it is not ye that SPEAK,
    But the HOLY ‡SPIRIT.

* R.V. accomplished.
† R.V. And the gospel must first be preached unto all the nations.
‡ R.V. Ghost.

And brother shall deliver up brother to death,
And the father his child;
And 'children shall rise up against parents',   (Mic. vii. 6)
And cause them to be put to death.
And ye shall be hated of all men for my Name's sake:
But he that endureth to the END, the same shall be Saved.
(Dan. xii. 13)

Tatian 42

But when ye see the 'Abomination of Desolation' standing
where he ought not   (Dan. ix. 27, xii. 11)
(Let him that readeth understand),
Then let them that are in Judaea flee unto the mountains:
And let him that is on the housetop not go down,
Nor enter in, to take any thing out of his house:
And let him that is in the field not return back
To take his cloke.
But Woe unto them that are with child
And to them that give suck in THOSE DAYS!
And pray ye that it be not in the winter.

For THOSE DAYS shall be 'Tribulation, such as there hath not
been the like from the beginning of the creation which God
created until now' (Dan. xii. 1; Joel ii. 2), and never shall be.
And except the Lord had shortened the Days, no flesh would have
been Saved: but for the ELECT'S sake, whom he chose, he
shortened the Days. And then if any man shall say unto you,
Lo, here is the Christ; or Lo, there; believe it not: for there shall
arise false Christs and 'false Prophets', and shall shew 'signs and
wonders', that they may LEAD ASTRAY, if possible, the ELECT.
(Deut. iii. 12)
But TAKE ye HEED:
Behold, I have told you all things beforehand.

But in THOSE DAYS, after that 'Tribulation',
'The sun shall be darkened,
And the moon shall not give her light,
And the stars shall be falling from heaven,
And the powers that are in the heavens shall be shaken'.
(Isa. xiii. 10, xxxiv. 4)

And then shall they SEE the SON OF MAN
   COMING in CLOUDS with great POWER and GLORY.
(Dan. vii. 13; Ps. viii. 5)

And then shall he send forth the Angels,
   And shall gather together his ELECT 'from the four winds',
'From the uttermost part of the earth'
   'To the uttermost part of heaven'.
(Zech. ii. 10; Deut. xxx. 4)

Now from the Fig Tree learn her Parable: when her branch
is now become tender, and putteth forth its leaves, ye know that
the summer is nigh; even so ye also, when ye see these things
coming to pass, know ye that it is nigh, even at the doors.

(f)   Verily I say unto you,

     THIS GENERATION shall not PASS AWAY,
      Until all these things be accomplished.
     Heaven and earth shall PASS AWAY:
      But my words shall not PASS AWAY.

(The lection ends on a short line in B)

Triads: stones, lead astray, speak, end (only twice), those days, elect, pass away,
take heed (with Lection 50).

Major Triads: building, destroyed, Mount of Olives, Peter James John Andrew,
gospel preached, that hour, Holy Spirit, I am (it is I), see the *parousia*, cloud,
power, glory, gentiles?

NOTES

(1) There is some variation with regard to the beginning of this lection
in Mark and Matthew, but none with regard to its end except in the Old
Latin system of chapter-enumeration. It ends with the solemn affirmation,
'My words shall never pass away'. The support for this includes the Vulgate
represented by Amiatinus, which divides here, both in Mark and Matthew.
Luke gives important support, though of a negative order; he omits
everything in Mark after these words, though he appends a short exhortation
to watchfulness taken from some other source. In the Roman Missal, the
last gospel of the year (the Twenty-fourth Sunday after Trinity) is taken
from this lection in its Matthaean form; it begins with the 'abomination of
desolation' and ends 'my words shall not pass away'. The gospel for the
First Sunday in Advent is taken from this lection in its Lucan form, and it
ends in the same way. These gospels occur on the last Sunday and first Sunday

of the ritual year, much as our theory of Mark requires. Actually, however, the seventh-century *Comes* shows a form of the Roman rite in which the last Sunday of the year is the Feeding of the Five Thousand; the First Sunday in Advent is the Entry into Jerusalem, but the Second is taken from this lection in its Lucan form; and so they appear to-day in the Anglican rite. Both customs seem to bear witness to the same tradition.

(2) The last line of this lection in *B* is short by about three letters, and while this does not come up to our definition of a script-division, it may be a trace of such a thing; and like the other short lines may serve to indicate such a point.

(3) The amount of evidence in favour of a division at this point is too great to be disregarded; it could hardly have been arrived at by literary analysis, but once it is arrived at, it can be supported by literary analysis; for *f* is a good concluding formula. Besides, it repeats a pattern which we have met before in Mark; Lection 49 is the prophetic gospel in its external aspect; Lection 50 is the prophetic gospel in its internal reality, as it affects the 'house' and its servants.

These points will be dealt with in the Commentary.

(4) The word 'betray' or 'deliver up', used here of Christians, forms a literary link with the Passion Narrative where it is used seven times of Judas (see note on 52), and three times in connexion with Pilate.

(5) The title of this lection, 'The Consummation', is taken from the verb 'consummated' in *c*. It occurs as a noun in Matthew. It should be compared with the title *Atzereth* (completion) used for the last day of the Feast of Tabernacles, on which we have suggested that this lection was to be read. Was it originally the first member of a minor triad, the other two members being 'the end' (*telos*) which occurs twice in the lection?

PASCHAL LECTION II

LECTION 50 (Mark xiii. 32–xiv. 2).

Part in Matthew non-*B* 58, 'Concerning the Day and the Hour', and part in Matthew non-*B* 61, 'Concerning the Coming of Christ'.

Mark non-B 43, 'Concerning the Day and the Hour'.
Tatian 42 and 44

But of THAT DAY or THAT HOUR KNOWETH NO ONE, not even the Angels in heaven, neither the Son, but the Father.

TAKE ye HEED, *be watchful: for ye KNOW NOT when the time is.

* R.V. watch.

It is as when a man, sojourning in another country,
  Having left his House,
And given Authority to his Servants,
  To each one his work,
Commanded also the porter to WATCH.

WATCH, therefore: for ye KNOW NOT when the Lord of the House cometh, whether at EVEN or at Midnight, or at COCK-CROWING, or in the MORNING; lest coming suddenly he find you SLEEPING. And what I say unto you I say unto all, WATCH.

Old Latin 43

Now after two days was the feast of the PASSOVER and the unleavened bread: and the chief priests and the scribes sought how they might take him with subtilty, and kill him: for they said, Not during the Feast, lest haply there shall be a tumult of the people.

Triads: know not, watch ('be watchful' represents a different Greek word).
Major Triads: that day, that hour, evening, cockcrow, morning, sleeping. For Passover, see note on Lection 52.

NOTES

(1) The surprising point about this lection is the inclusion of xiv. 1–2 ('Now the Pascha', etc.) with the last five verses of the apocalyptic discourse. The reference to the Pascha is the obvious point for the opening of the Passion Narrative; the creation of this lection welds the Passion Narrative firmly to the apocalyptic discourse. Tatian, very strangely, inserts xiv. 1–2 in two places: in Section 41 *before* the discourse on the Mount of Olives (i.e. before Lection 49) and in Section 44 before the preparation for the Passover (i.e. before Lection 52).

(2) It almost looks as if a title, 'Concerning That Day and the Hour', had become incorporated into the text.

(3) The lection is singularly constant in all our Biblical authorities, which is interesting, as it would not have been arrived at independently by literary analysis. It is found intact in all the Marcan enumerations, including that of the Vulgate in Amiatinus, though it is not so in the Old Latin. It is still so marked in the English Authorised Version!

(4) Matthew, as we have seen, enlarges this little lection by inserting three parables where he finds only one in Mark. The last of these parables is the Sheep and the Goats, and xiv. 1–2 is combined with it in Lection 61 of Matthew non-B. The outline of Lection 50 of Mark is thus perpetuated in 58–61 of Matthew;

the enumeration is thus ahead of Mark by eleven lections; but this is reduced in the course of the Passion Narrative to seven.

(5) Luke, on the other hand, omits the apocalyptic material in this lection, and begins a new lection with the reference to the Pascha. He thus cuts the connexion which is established in Mark and Matthew. There is, of course, no such connexion in John; and the example of Luke and John has affected the liturgical tradition so strongly that it shows no sign that I can find of the five apocalyptic verses of this lection.

(6) The references to watchfulness and prayer mark this lection as appropriate for a vigil, and the hours of the night, as indicated in the Passion Narrative, are actually mentioned; with the exception of the midnight hour, they form triads with references in the Passion Narrative itself. This relates Lection 50 (perhaps 49 and 50) to the Passion Narrative from a literary point of view, and shows that the composer of Mark had this relation in mind.

(7) This lection is thus the second of the fourteen Passion lections of Mark in B, and of the seven Passion lections in non-B. In the case of Matthew (non-B) we cannot be so sure of our analysis; it is only by the analogy of Mark that we have allotted fourteen lections to the Passion; if this is accepted, the lection which closes with xiv. 1–2 ('Now the Pascha') will be the seventh of seven preparatory lections; seven actual Passion lections indubitably follow.

(8) The reference to the Pascha at the end of Lection 50, repeated in 52, is to be accepted as the true beginning of the Passion Narrative, regardless of the connexions with the apocalyptic discourse in Mark and Matthew, or with the Anointing at Bethany in Mark, Matthew and John.

(9) Tatian has a system of fourteen Passion lections based on the chronology of John, followed by three Resurrection lections. His thirty-ninth section begins 'Jesus therefore six days before the Pascha' (John xii. 1); the six sections of Tatian, 39–44, seem to correspond to these days, and in 44 we find the words 'Ye know that after two days the Pascha' from Matt. xxvi. 2, and also 'On the first day of unleavened bread' from Mark xiv. 12, followed by 'Before the feast of the Pascha' from John xiii. 1; the contents of this section make it clear that these refer to the Wednesday, but the section also includes events of the Thursday morning ('The first day of unleavened bread': Luke xxii. 7) and even of Thursday evening ('When the evening was come': Luke xxii. 14), but only going so far as to include the indication of the traitor. Section 45 of Tatian includes the institution of the Eucharist and the prophecy of Peter's denial. This concludes seven lections (39–45).

The division between Sections 45 and 46 in Tatian is, therefore, nearly the same as the division between Lections 45 and 46 in the non-B arrangement of Mark.

The seven lections from 46 to 52 inclusive cover the remainder of the Passion Narrative as found in Mark, and correspond to 46, 47, 48 in the non-B arrangement. See notes on Lection 62.

PASCHAL LECTION III

LECTION 51 (Mark xiv. 3–9).
Matthew non-B 62, 'Concerning the Woman who Anointed the Lord'.

Mark non-B 44, 'Concerning the Woman who Anointed the Lord'.
Tatian 39

(*a*) AND while he was in BETHANY in the house of Simon the leper, as he sat at meat, there came a woman having an alabaster cruse of OINTMENT of spikenard very costly; and she brake the cruse, and poured it over his head. But there were some that had indignation among themselves, saying, To what purpose hath this waste of OINTMENT been made? For this OINTMENT might have been sold for above three hundred pence, and given to the poor. And they murmured against her.

(*b*) But Jesus said, Let her alone; why trouble ye her? she hath wrought a good work on me. For ye have the poor always with you, and whensoever ye will ye can do them good: but me ye have not always. She hath done what she could: she hath anointed my BODY aforehand for the burying. And verily I say unto you, Wheresoever the GOSPEL shall be PREACHED throughout the whole world, that also which this woman hath done shall be spoken of for a memorial of her.

Triads: ointment.

Major Triads: Bethany, my body, gospel announced in all the world.

NOTES

(1) Even in Mark and Matthew this lection appears to have no necessary relation to its context; the last paragraph of 50 is linked by triads with the first of 52; on the other hand the final affirmation of 51 has a connexion with the first stanza of *e* in 49. These references to the gospel refer in a general way to evangelistic activity, but have they some special reference to the Passion Narrative to which they are attached? Perhaps a third reference to the gospel in the world (or among the nations) was thought of as coming in the resurrection period after the abrupt ending of Mark, as it does in Matthew and in the supplementary lection to Mark.

(2) Luke omits this lection as he has a similar story at a much earlier point, and this enables him to weld the end of 50 into the beginning of 52 as the opening of his Passion Narrative; and this is very likely the oldest model.

(3) In Matthew non-*B* this is the first of the seven lections which comprise the Passion Narrative; and in John, in spite of enormous differences, the same is true for the system of enumeration in *B*.

(4) In the Vulgate as contained in Amiatinus, 51, 52, 53 and possibly even 54 form a single lection preparatory to the Passion Narrative proper; this preparatory lection has the number 44 as in Matthew non-*B* above.

PASCHAL LECTION IV

LECTION 52 (Mark xiv. 10–16).
   Matthew non-*B* 63, 'Concerning the Pascha'.

Mark non-B 44 continued. Tatian 44

(*a*)   AND Judas ISCARIOT, he that was ONE OF THE TWELVE, went away unto the chief priests, that he might DELIVER him unto them. And they, when they heard it, were glad, and promised to give him money. And he sought how he might conveniently DELIVER him unto them.

Mark non-B 45, 'Concerning the Pascha'

(*b*)   AND on the first day of Unleavened Bread, when they sacrificed the PASSOVER, his DISCIPLES say unto him, Where wilt thou that we go and make READY that thou mayest eat the PASSOVER?

(*c*)   AND he sendeth two of his DISCIPLES, and saith unto them, Go into the city, and there shall you meet a man bearing a pitcher of water: follow him; and wheresoever he shall enter in, say to the goodman of the house, The Master saith, Where is my guest-chamber, where I shall eat the PASSOVER with my DISCIPLES? And he will himself shew you a large upper room furnished and ready: and there make READY for us.

(*d*)   AND the DISCIPLES went forth, and came into the city, and found as he had said unto them: and they made READY the PASSOVER.

Mark non-B 45 continued. Tatian 45. Old Latin 44

(*e*)   AND when it was EVENING he cometh with the TWELVE.

Triads: passover (4), disciples (4), make ready.

Major Triads: Iscariot, one of the twelve, deliver (in the sense of 'betray'), evening.

NOTES

(1) The numeral *nu gamma* (53) is not to be found in the margin of *B* so that the point of division between 52 and 53 is a matter of conjecture. Nestle places it after 52*e* and we have followed his example; probably he is relying on the division between non-*B*45 and non-*B*46; in spite of this excellent authority, it might be better to transfer 52*e* into 53 and make it the beginning of that lection; the note of time suggests this, and the word 'twelve' forms a minor triad with the references in that lection. But the division after 52*e* is adopted in Matthew non-*B*.

The omission of the numeral in *B* is probably a mere error, but it is strange that it was never corrected. The lector cannot have known of the existence of a division. Perhaps, therefore, this omission reflects a usage according to which there was no division here. Or were the lection-numbers of *B* a mere survival of an obsolete system which was no longer in use?

(2) The word 'betray' (of Jesus) occurs twice in Lection 52, twice in 53, twice in 54, and once in 55, making seven times for the betrayal by Judas; in 57 it occurs three times of delivering up to Pilate, or to crucifixion.

PASCHAL LECTION V

LECTION 53 (Mark xiv. 17–26).
Matthew non-*B* 63, 'Concerning the Mystic Supper'.

Mark non-B 46, 'Concerning the Betrayal, a Prophecy'

(*a*)   And as they sat and were eating, Jesus said, Verily I say unto you, ONE of you shall BETRAY me, even he 'that eateth with me' (Ps. xli. 9). They began to be sorrowful, and to say unto him ONE by ONE, Is it I? And he said unto them, It is ONE of the TWELVE, he that dippeth with me in the dish.

For the Son of MAN goeth, even as it is written of him:
But woe unto that MAN through whom the Son of MAN is
BETRAYED!
Good were it for that MAN if he had not been born.

And as they were eating, he took BREAD, and when he had BLESSED, he BRAKE it, and gave to them, and said, Take ye: this is MY BODY. And he took a CUP, and when he had given

THANKS, he gave to them, and they all DRANK of it. And he said unto them, This is my 'blood of the covenant' (Exod. xxiv. 8) which is 'shed for many'. (Isa. liii. 12)

(b) Verily I say unto you, I will no more DRINK of the fruit of the vine, until THAT DAY when I DRINK it NEW in the Kingdom of God.

(c) And when they had sung a hymn, they went out unto the MOUNT OF OLIVES.

Triads: twelve (including Lection 52), one (four times), man (four times), drink, betray (including Lection 52 where it is translated 'deliver').

Major Triads: one of the twelve, took—bread—blessed—broke—gave, cup, drink, new, Mount of Olives, that day.

NOTES

(1) The chapter-divisions of B are an attempt to divide the text of the Passion Narrative topically: 53, the Last Supper; 54, Gethsemane; 55, the Arrest; 56, in the Hall of the High Priest; 57, before Pilate; 58, the Soldiers; 59, the Crucifixion. The twenty-four hours are thus divided into seven lections.

(2) In the non-B system of Mark the twenty-four hours are divided into two lections only, the first beginning at evening (see 52e) and the second at cock-crow (see 56d). In the Vulgate system as contained in Amiatinus, the twenty-four hours (less the Last Supper itself) appear as a single lection.

(3) The title of Matthew non-B 64 cannot be accepted as early; it is 'Concerning the Mystic Supper', and occurs before 53a; the next title which comes before 55a is 'Concerning the Betrayal of Jesus', and resembles the non-B title in Mark before 53a. This title seems to be an old one as it uses the personal name. Probably the non-B system in Matthew was originally identical with the non-B system in Mark at this point, and had one long lection beginning at 52e or 53a.

The word 'betray' occurs seven times in Mark 52–5, so that the long lection with this title is one that corresponds well with the literary data. It also occurs three times in 57; but here it must be translated 'delivered up' or 'handed over'; no single English word can be found which will translate it in all its uses.

PASCHAL LECTION VI

LECTION 54 (Mark xiv. 27–42).
Matthew non-B 64 continued.

Mark non-B 46 continued. Tatian 45, 46, 48. Old Latin 45

(*a*) AND Jesus saith unto them, All ye shall be Offended: for it is written,

> 'I will smite the SHEPHERD,
> And the SHEEP shall be scattered abroad'.   (Zech. xiii. 7)
> Howbeit, after I am RAISED UP,
> I will GO BEFORE you into Galilee.

But Peter said unto him, Although all shall be Offended, yet will not I.

(*b*) AND Jesus saith unto him, Verily I say unto thee, that thou to-day, even this night, before the COCK CROW twice, shalt DENY me thrice. But he spake exceeding vehemently, If I must die with thee, I will not DENY thee. And in like manner also said they all. And they come unto a place which was named Gethsemane: and he saith unto his Disciples, Sit ye here, while I PRAY. And he taketh with him PETER and JAMES and JOHN, and began to be greatly amazed and sore troubled. And he said unto them,

> 'My soul is exceeding sorrowful even unto death'.
>   (Ps. xlii. 6 and 11; Ps. xliii. 5)

Abide ye here, and WATCH.

(*c*) AND he went forward a little, and fell on the ground, and PRAYED that, if it were possible, the HOUR might pass away from him. And he said,

> Abba, Father, all things are possible unto thee;
> Remove this CUP from me:
> Howbeit not what I will, but what thou wilt.

And he cometh, and findeth them SLEEPING,

(*d*) AND [he] saith unto Peter, Simon, SLEEPEST thou? couldest thou not WATCH one HOUR? WATCH and PRAY, that ye enter not into Temptation: the spirit indeed is willing, but the flesh is weak. And again he went away, and PRAYED, saying the same words. And again he came, and found them SLEEPING, for their eyes were very heavy; and they wist not what to answer him.

(*e*) AND he cometh the third time, and saith unto them, SLEEP on now, and take your rest: it is enough; the HOUR is come; behold the Son of Man is BETRAYED into the hands of sinners. Arise, let us be going: behold, he that BETRAYETH me is at hand.

Triads: watch, pray, hour, sleep (4), betray (completed in Lection 55).
Major Triads: shepherd and sheep (imperfect triad), go before, deny (*aparneisthai*), hour, cup.

NOTE

The authority for subdivision *d* is an oblique stroke in the margin.

PASCHAL LECTION VII
LECTION 55 (Mark xiv. 43–52).
Matthew non-*B* 65, 'Concerning the Betrayal of Jesus'.

Mark non-B 46 continued. Tatian 48. Old Latin 46

AND straightway, while he yet spake, cometh Judas, ONE OF THE TWELVE, and with him a Multitude with SWORDS and staves, from the chief priests and the scribes and the elders. Now he that BETRAYED him had given them a token, saying, Whomsoever I shall kiss, that is he; TAKE him and lead him away safely. And when he was come, straightway he came to him, and saith, Rabbi; and kissed him. And they laid hands on him, and TOOK him.

But a certain one of them that stood by drew his SWORD, and smote the servant of the high priest, and struck off his ear.

And Jesus answered and said unto them, Are ye come out, as against a Robber, with SWORDS and staves to seize me? I was daily with you in the Temple Teaching, and ye TOOK me not: but (this is done) that the scriptures might be fulfilled. And they all left him, and fled.

And a certain young man followed with him, having a Linen Cloth cast about him, over his naked body: and they Lay Hold on him; but he left the Linen Cloth, and fled naked.

(Lection ends on short line in B)

Triads: swords, take—lay hold (three times of Jesus, once of the young man), betray (a triad begun in Lection 54).

Major Triads: Judas—one of the twelve—betray, linen cloth? (twice here and twice in Lection 61: see also the word 'body').

NOTES

(1) The last line of 55 is short by four or five letters, but as the succeeding line does not project into the margin, we do not classify it as a script-division. It might, however, be a trace of something of the sort. Could it mark the end of a long lection, beginning as early as 52 (or even 50), based on the idea of the betrayal by Judas? The last short line was at the end of 49.

(2) A quotation from the Old Testament seems to have been omitted immediately after the words of Jesus. It seems to be preserved in Luke xxii. 37.

PASCHAL LECTION VIII

LECTION 56 (Mark xiv. 53–72).

Matthew non-B 65 continued; Matthew non-B 66, 'Concerning the Denial of Peter'.

Mark non-B 46 continued. Tatian 49, changing the order of Mark

(*a*) AND they led Jesus away to the HIGH PRIEST: and there come together with him all the chief priests and the elders and the scribes. And Peter had Followed him afar off, even within, into the court of the HIGH PRIEST; and he was sitting with the officers, and warming himself in the light of the fire.

(*b*) Now the chief priests and the whole council sought WITNESS against Jesus to put him to death; and found it not. For many bare FALSE WITNESS against him, and their WITNESS agreed not together.

(*c*) AND there stood up certain, and bare FALSE WITNESS against him, saying, We heard him say, I will DESTROY this SANCTUARY that is 'made with hands' (Ps. cxv. 4, etc.), and in Three Days I will BUILD another 'made without hands' (Dan. ii. 34). And not even so did their WITNESS agree together. And the HIGH PRIEST stood up in the midst, and asked Jesus, saying, Answerest thou nothing? what is it which these WITNESS against thee? But he held his peace, and answered

219

nothing. Again the HIGH PRIEST asked him, and saith unto him,

> ART THOU THE CHRIST,
> THE SON OF THE BLESSED?

and Jesus said,

> I AM:
> AND YE SHALL SEE
> THE SON OF MAN SITTING AT THE RIGHT HAND OF
> POWER,
> AND COMING WITH THE CLOUDS OF HEAVEN.

(Ps. cx. 1; Dan. vii. 13)

And the HIGH PRIEST rent his clothes, and saith, What further need have we of WITNESSES? Ye have heard the blasphemy: what think ye? And they all condemned him to be worthy of death. And some began to spit on him, and to cover his face, and to buffet him, and to say unto him, Prophesy: and the officers received him with blows of their hands.

Mark non-B 47, 'The Denying of Peter'

(d) AND as Peter was beneath in the court, there cometh one of the maids of the HIGH PRIEST; and seeing Peter warming himself, she looked upon him, and saith, Thou also wast with the NAZARENE, even Jesus. But he DENIED, saying, I neither know, nor understand what thou sayest:

(e) AND he went out into the porch; and the COCK CREW. And the maid saw him, and began again to say to them that stood by, This is one of them. But he again DENIED it. And after a little while again they that stood by said to Peter, Of a truth thou art one of them; for thou art a Galilaean.

(f) But he began to curse, and to swear, I know not this man of whom ye speak. And straightway the second time the COCK CREW. And Peter called to mind the word, how that Jesus said unto him, Before the COCK CROW twice, thou shalt DENY me thrice. And when he thought thereon, he wept.

Triads: high priest (6, or 7 if we include Lection 55), witness (6), deny (*arneisthai* twice, and *aparneisthai* once, corresponding to its two occurrences in 54), cock crow.

Major Triads: third *parousia* announcement, destroy, sanctuary, build, Christ and Son of God?, see, right hand, clouds.

NOTES

(1) The non-*B* title 'The Denial of Peter' is unusual in form as it lacks the conventional preposition *peri* (concerning). This omission is not an accident as it is found in Θ as well as in Alexandrinus. The defect in form suggests that the title may be intrusive, in which case the non-*B* system originally resembled that of Amiatinus in having a continuous narrative for the Passion from evening to evening.

(2) The title is a strange one to include the whole narrative of the Crucifixion, and may be compared with another intrusive title. In Matthew non-*B* a title is introduced 'Concerning the Repentance of Judas', and the lection which it introduces includes the whole story of the Crucifixion. This was introduced in order to pick out a passage peculiar to Matthew. In the Passion according to Luke, five of the seven titles are introduced with the same object.

(3) The only titles which have universal support in the synoptists are 'Concerning the Pascha' and 'Concerning the Request for the Body of the Lord'; that is to say, the first and the last. 'The Denying of Peter' in Mark non-*B* 47 receives some support from Matthew non-*B* 67 (at the same point), 'Concerning the Denying of Peter'.

PASCHAL LECTION IX

LECTION 57 (Mark xv. 1–15).

Matthew non-*B* 67, 'Concerning the Repentance of Judas' (beginning after *a*).

Mark non-B 47 continued. Tatian 49 and 50

(*a*) AND straightway in the MORNING the chief priests with the elders and scribes, and the whole council, held a consultation, and bound Jesus, and took him away, and DELIVERED him up to Pilate.

(*b*) AND Pilate asked him, Art thou the KING OF THE JEWS? And he ANSWERING saith unto him, Thou sayest. And the chief priests accused him of many things.

(*c*) And Pilate again asked him, saying, ANSWEREST thou nothing? Behold how many things they accuse thee of.

(*d*) But Jesus no more ANSWERED anything; insomuch that Pilate marvelled. Now at the Feast he used to RELEASE unto them one prisoner, whom they asked of him. And there was one called BARABBAS, lying bound with them that had made insurrection, men who in the insurrection had committed murder. And the MULTITUDE went up and began to ask him to do as he was wont to do unto them.

(*e*) And Pilate answered them, saying, Will ye that I RELEASE unto you the KING OF THE JEWS? For he perceived that for envy the chief priests had DELIVERED him up. But the chief priests stirred up the MULTITUDE, that he should rather RELEASE BARABBAS unto them.

(*f*) And Pilate again answered and said unto them, What then shall I do unto him whom ye call the KING OF THE JEWS? And they cried out again, CRUCIFY him. And Pilate said unto them, Why, what evil hath he done? But they cried out exceedingly, CRUCIFY him. And Pilate, wishing to content the MULTITUDE, RELEASED unto them BARABBAS and DELIVERED Jesus, when he had scourged him, to be CRUCIFIED.

Triads: Pilate (seven times), answered, release, multitude, Barabbas, deliver, crucify.

Major Triads: morning.

NOTES

(1) The words 'in the morning' make a natural opening for a lection; compare 7 and 62.

(2) The word translated 'delivered' is the same as the word translated 'betrayed'. This minor triad seems distinguishable from the heptad in 52–5.

PASCHAL LECTION X

LECTION 58 (Mark xv. 16–23).
Matthew non-*B* 67 continued.

Mark non-B 47 continued. Tatian 50 and 51

And the soldiers led him away within the court, which is the Praetorium; and they call together the whole band. And they clothe him with purple, and plaiting a crown of thorns, they put it on him; and they began to salute him, Hail, KING OF THE JEWS! And they smote his head with a reed, and did spit upon him, and bowing their knees worshipped him. And when they had mocked him, they took off from him the purple, and put on him his garments. And they lead him out to CRUCIFY him. And they compel one passing by, Simon of Cyrene, coming from the country, the father of Alexander and Rufus, to go with them, that he might bear his CROSS. And they bring him unto the place Golgotha, which is, being interpreted, The place of a skull. And they offered him *to DRINK wine mingled with myrrh: but he received it not.

> *Triads:* crucify and cross (in combination with Lection 59).
> *Major Triads:* king of the Jews, drink.

NOTE

There is an annotation in the margin of Θ indicating a 'beginning' at 58*a*. It is, of course, a natural place at which to begin the actual narrative of the Crucifixion.

PASCHAL LECTION XI

LECTION 59 (Mark xv. 24–37).
Matthew non-*B* 67 continued.

Mark non-B 47 continued. Tatian 51 and 52

(*a*) AND they CRUCIFY him, and 'part his garments among them, casting lots upon them', what each should take (Ps. xxii. 18). And it was the THIRD HOUR, and they CRUCIFIED him. And the superscription of his accusation was written over,

THE KING OF THE JEWS.

And with him they Crucify two robbers: ONE ON HIS RIGHT HAND AND ONE ON HIS LEFT. And they that passed by railed on him, 'wagging their heads' (Ps. xxii. 7), and saying, Ha! thou that DESTROYEST the SANCTUARY, and BUILDEST it in Three Days, SAVE thyself, and come down from the CROSS. In like manner also the chief priests mocking him among themselves

---

* R.V. Omits 'to drink': text uncertain.

with the scribes said, He SAVED others; himself he cannot SAVE. Let the CHRIST, the KING OF ISRAEL, now come down from the CROSS, that we may See and Believe. And they that were Crucified with him reproached him.

(b)   AND when the SIXTH HOUR was come, there was darkness over the whole land until the NINTH HOUR. And at the NINTH HOUR Jesus cried with a loud voice,

ELOI, ELOI, LAMA SABACHTHANI?
   which is, being interpreted,
'My God, my God, why hast thou forsaken me?'

(Ps. xxii. 2)

And some of them that stood by, when they heard it, said, Behold, he calleth ELIJAH. And one ran, and filling a sponge full of vinegar, put it on a reed, and gave him to drink (Ps. lxix. 8), saying, Let be; let us see whether ELIJAH cometh to take him down. And Jesus uttered a loud voice, and gave up the ghost.

Triads: crucify (of Jesus) and cross (both including occurrences in Lection 58), save, (third, sixth, ninth) hour, Eloi-Elijah.

Major Triads: cross, destroy, sanctuary, build, King of the Jews, right hand and left, Elijah.

NOTE

A few manuscripts read 'Eli, Eli, lama azaphthani' following the Hebrew of Ps. xxii. 1.

PASCHAL LECTION XII

LECTION 60 (Mark xv. 38–41).
   Matthew non-B 67 continued.

Mark non-B 47 continued. Tatian 52

AND the veil of the SANCTUARY was rent in twain from the top to the bottom.

And when the CENTURION, which stood by over against him, saw that he so gave up the ghost, he said, Truly this man was the Son of God.

And there were also women beholding from afar: among whom were both MARY MAGDALENE, and MARY the mother of James the less and of Joses, and Salome; who, when he was in Galilee, Followed him, and ministered unto him; and many other women which came up with him unto Jerusalem.

Triads: centurion, Mary Magdalene and the other Mary (in combination with Lections 61 and 62).

Major Triads: sanctuary.

Paschal Lection XIII

Lection 61 (Mark xv. 42–7).
Matthew non-*B* 68, 'Concerning the Request for the Body of the Lord'.

Mark non-B 48, *'Concerning the Request for the Body of the Lord'. Tatian 52*

AND when EVEN was now come, because it was the Preparation, that is, the day before the SABBATH, there came Joseph of Arimathaea, a councillor of honourable estate, who also himself was looking for the Kingdom of God; and he boldly went in unto Pilate, and asked for the Body of Jesus. And Pilate marvelled if he were already dead: and calling unto him the CENTURION, he asked him whether he had been any while dead. And when he learned it of the CENTURION, he granted the corpse to Joseph. And he bought a Linen Cloth, and taking him down, wound him in the LINEN CLOTH, and laid him in a TOMB which had been hewn out of a rock; and he ROLLED A STONE against the door of the TOMB. And MARY MAGDALENE and MARY the mother of Joses beheld where he was laid.

Triads (all in combination with 60 and 62): centurion, sabbath, tomb, stone, rolled, Mary Magdalene, Mary.

Major Triads: evening, body (for Linen Cloth see Lection 54).

NOTES

(1) A marginal annotation in Θ indicates a 'beginning' here for the reader, with the letters 'AP' and 'TⲰKP' as in the case of Lection 13.

(2) All four gospels, in all their systems of enumeration, begin a new lection here; so we may conclude that the Passion Narrative proper ended with Lection 60; but the *B* system in Mark is the only one to make a division between 61 and 62; in the others this is the last lection of the gospel and includes the

Resurrection, except for Luke which has an additional lection 'Concerning Cleophas' which contains material peculiar to that gospel.

(3) In the Roman Missal the Passion according to Mark concludes with Lection 60, and then 61 (but not 62) is read formally as the gospel of the day. The other gospels are treated in the same way.

Paschal Lection XIV

Lection 62 (Mark xvi. 1–8).
Matthew non-B 68 continued.

Non-B 48 continued. Tatian 52 and 53. Old Latin 47?

AND when the SABBATH was past, MARY MAGDALENE, and MARY the mother of James, and Salome, bought spices, that they might come and Anoint him. And very early on the first day of the WEEK, they come to the TOMB when the sun was risen. And they were saying among themselves, Who shall ROLL us away the STONE from the door of the TOMB? and looking up, they see that the STONE is ROLLED back: for it was exceeding great. And entering into the TOMB, they saw a Young Man sitting ON THE RIGHT SIDE, arrayed in a white robe; and they were amazed. And he saith unto them, Be not amazed:

> Ye seek *Jesus which hath been Crucified:
> He is RISEN; he is not here:
> Behold, the place where they laid him!

> But go, tell his Disciples and Peter,
> He GOETH BEFORE you into Galilee:
> There shall ye See him, as he said unto you.

And they went out, and fled from the TOMB; for trembling and astonishment had come upon them: and they said nothing to any one; for they were afraid.

Triads (in connexion with Lections 60 and 61): sabbath (the Greek word translated 'week' is *sabbata*), Mary Magdalene, Mary, roll, stone, tomb (6), (anoint, see Lection 51).

Major Triads: very early (translated elsewhere as 'morning'), right hand, risen, go before, see?

* R.V. Jesus the Nazarene: the text is uncertain.

NOTES

(1) In the Roman Missal this Marcan lection still survives as the gospel for Easter Day, the last verse being omitted, thus avoiding using, as its final words, 'they were afraid'. In the *Comes* of the seventh century, three verses are added from the spurious ending, doubtless with the same object. In the same way the Jews avoid reading the last verse of Isaiah.

It is remarkable indeed that after nineteen centuries the original Marcan text should survive in its original liturgical position.

(2) In Tatian, the final Passion lection (52) contains the death of Jesus, the tribute of the centurion, the women, the request for the body, the burial, and all the material of Lection 62 down to 'where they laid him'. The remainder of 62 appears in the early part of Tatian 53, woven into the narrative of Luke; then come sixteen verses of John; and then the first verse of the supplementary lection of Mark, the remainder of which is dispersed through 53 and 55. Tatian 53–5 are resurrection lections supplementary to Mark, only two verses of the genuine Mark extending into 53; 52, it will be remembered, is the last of the fourteen Passion lections beginning with 39.

(3) For the Easter Gospel in the third century, see the Canonical Epistle of St Dionysius of Alexandria.

THE SUPPLEMENTAL RESURRECTION AND ASCENSION LECTION

(being the so-called Spurious Ending of Mark xvi. 9–20)

Mark non-B 48 continued in A C D Θ L W 33, *etc.* *Tatian 53 and 55*

Now when he was risen early on the first day of the week, he appeared first to Mary Magdalene, from whom he had cast out seven devils. She went and told them that had been with him, as they mourned and wept. And they, when they heard that he was alive, and had been seen by her, DISBELIEVED.

And after these things he was manifested in another form unto two of them, as they walked, on their way into the country. And they went away and told it unto the rest: NEITHER BELIEVED they them.

And afterward he was manifested unto the eleven themselves as they sat at meat; and he upbraided them with their UNBELIEF and Hardness of Heart, because they BELIEVED NOT them which had seen him after he was risen. And he said unto them,

> Go ye into ALL THE WORLD,
> And PREACH the GOSPEL to the whole creation.

> He that BELIEVETH and is Baptized shall be Saved;
> But he that DISBELIEVETH shall be condemned.
> And these Signs shall follow them that BELIEVE:

> In my Name shall they cast out devils;
> They shall speak with new tongues;
> They shall take up serpents,
> And if they drink any deadly thing, it shall in no wise hurt them;
> They shall lay hands on the sick, and they shall recover.

So then the Lord Jesus, after he had spoken unto them, was received up into heaven, and sat down at the RIGHT HAND of God. And they went forth and PREACHED EVERYWHERE, the Lord working with them, and confirming the word by the Signs that followed. Amen.

Triads: nil: note seven occurrences of 'believe'—'disbelieve'.

Major Triads: sat at the right hand, preach in all the world (or to the Gentiles).

NOTES

(1) This lection is not a part of Mark, but to call it the spurious ending of Mark is possibly a little misleading. It has become attached to the end of Mark in a great number of manuscripts, and, as it is not an authentic part of the gospel, may be described as spurious, so far as its presence in that position is concerned. In itself it is simply a supplementary lection.

(2) The early date of this lection is proved by its inclusion in Tatian, no doubt as a part of Mark. On the other hand its use of Luke has to be taken into account in considering its composition. It cannot be proved that it shows any knowledge of Matthew or John; with Matthew it has a single point of contact, the command to evangelize the world; with John it also has a single point of contact, the appearance to Mary Magdalene; both of these may have been well enough known in church circles quite apart from any written gospel. It is perfectly possible that this lection came into existence in the 90's, to which decade the composition of Matthew and John may tentatively be assigned.

(3) One's first impression is that it does not continue very smoothly after xvi. 8, as there is a repetition of the reference to the dawn, and another reference

to Mary Magdalene. On second thoughts, however, this is explicable if we translate rather as follows: 'Now he had risen at dawn and appeared.'

(4) The appearances of Jesus to the two and to the eleven should no doubt be regarded as Lucan in origin. There is a difference, however. He reproaches them for not believing those who had seen him risen from the dead; but in Luke he reproaches them for not believing what the scriptures had prophesied. This change of emphasis is very like that which is found in Marcion's Luke; and the rather excessive emphasis on the unbelief of the disciples is also suggestive of Marcion. The 'seven devils' are also Lucan.

(5) Omitting from our consideration the Lucan material, we are left with an appearance to Mary Magdalene, a command to the disciples to evangelize the world, the ascension and session at the right hand of God, and the universal mission of the disciples; the three latter points were almost articles of the creed in some of our authorities which shed light on the period A.D. 100–125. Old Testament texts were selected to prove the ascension, the session at the right hand, and the mission of the twelve, which form a connected group of thoughts. Indeed they sometimes seem to take place on one day; as indeed they do here. The composition of this lection as an epilogue to Mark would dispose of Gnostic theories that the teaching of the disciples by the risen Jesus went on for eighteen months. The two last sentences would seem to be traditional; they do not seem to owe anything to Luke, and their effect is different from that given by the last verses of Matthew.

(6) The command to 'announce the gospel in all the world' is a genuinely Marcan phrase and forms a triad with Lections 49 and 51. While we see no evidence for the theory that the ending of Mark has been lost, nevertheless it is obvious that Mark and his readers had, and were intended to have, clear ideas about the resurrection period, and resurrection appearances, and resurrection sayings. If they were not written down, that is all the more reason for thinking that they were fixed and clear in the oral tradition; our supplementary lection looks like an attempt to write them down with a little help from Luke.

Among these fixed traditions must have been the mission of the apostles to preach the gospel; the four lines in which the command is given in this lection may be regarded as traditional; they certainly do not appear to owe anything to the text of Matthew. Matthew has the same tradition, but in a different form.

(7) The signs which follow the announcement of the gospel (or word) in the case of those who believe are not entirely based on the Marcan gospel; only the first and the last can claim this: 'In my name they shall cast out demons...they shall lay hands on the sick and they shall recover': see Lections 23 and 40. Speaking 'with new tongues' might be based on Acts; but 'new tongues' is rather an original phrase. The references to serpents and to poison are more reminiscent of the anecdotes of Papias or the apocryphal Acts.

In speaking of these signs, our lection says nothing of the Holy Spirit, and this does not encourage us to suppose that it has been influenced by Acts.

Indeed, when we allow for the influence of Luke's gospel, and also possibly for a certain amount of elaboration in the list of the signs, we are left with a rather fresh and original version of what may be the oral tradition:

(i)   Appearance to Mary Magdalene;
(ii) Appearance to the Eleven;
(iii) Mission of the Eleven;
(iv) the Signs: casting out demons and healing;
(v)   Ascension and Session at the Right Hand of God;
(vi) the Eleven go out into the world from Jerusalem.

For the place of these appearances is obviously Jerusalem, and the proof-texts in the *Book of Testimonies* insist on Jerusalem. In this respect the supplementary lection seems not to be in harmony with Mark, which speaks of Galilee.

(8) The Session at the Right Hand is also Marcan and forms a more convincing triad with Lections 47 and 56 than does the occurrence in 62.

(9) The lection was accepted by Tatian, and quoted by Irenaeus, who regards it as a part of Mark's gospel. Nevertheless it was some centuries before it was generally accepted as such by incorporation in copies of the Bible. Its progress in the liturgical system was even slower; a place was found for it, however, in the Roman Missal as the gospel for the Festival of the Ascension, a late addition to the Calendar.

GENERAL INDEX

INDEX OF PASSAGES FROM MARK

For EU product safety concerns, contact us at Calle de José Abascal, 56–1°,
28003 Madrid, Spain or eugpsr@cambridge.org.

www.ingramcontent.com/pod-product-compliance
Ingram Content Group UK Ltd.
Pitfield, Milton Keynes, MK11 3LW, UK
UKHW010341140625
459647UK00010B/746